PRAISE FOR FOOD LOVER'S GUIDE TO PORTLAND

An astoundingly comprehensive guide to Portland food. Crain has unearthed numerous gems in the nooks and crannies of Portland ...

TAMI PARR, author of *Artisan Cheese of the Pacific Northwest*

Indispensable ... Crain's book celebrates the local food scene through hundreds of listings and profiles of Portland producers, purveyors, distillers, bakers, food carts, CSAs, farmers markets and beyond.

ASHLEY GARTLAND, *The Oregonian*

NW Book Lovers is hungry, thanks to Liz Crain. We want her to take us on an eating tour of Portland, hitting all the markets and carts and cafes she writes about in *Food Lover's Guide to Portland* ...

AMIE PASSARO, Pacific Northwest Booksellers Association

More than just a restaurant guide ... contains profiles and interviews with the folks ... producing the high-quality ingredients that are largely responsible for putting this little foodie mecca on the map.

MEGAN ZABEL, Powell's Books

A just-bigger-than-pocket-sized compendium of the PDX eating scene that's sure to resonate with the minds, hearts, and bellies of us all.

MIKE THELIN, *Portland Monthly*

PRAISE FOR TORO BRAVO: STORIES. RECIPES. NO BULL.

These guys make Portland one of the most exciting restaurant cities in the world today.

MARIO BATALI

Toro Bravo is so much more than a cookbook (though it does a damn fine job of being just that). It's a passionate story of how one great chef found his way by following his heart and trusting his gut. It's a practical guide and a culinary *cri de coeur*. This is the real deal. It's the book I'm going to press into everyone's hands. I love it like mad.

CHERYL STRAYED, Author of *Wild*

John Gorham is a chef with a unique personality; he is magic. In his book *Toro Bravo*, he puts all his passion and soul into sharing Spanish cuisine with Americans. I'm certain both professional chefs and home cooks will love it.

FERRAN ADRIÀ, head chef at ElBulli

You're gonna love this cookbook. *Toro Bravo* brought something special to Portland when it opened, and still does: easy-to-love, Spanish-style food in a non-fussy atmosphere.

STEPHEN MALKMUS

So many of my Portland friends have recommended that I eat at Toro Bravo, over the years, that I couldn't ignore their suggestion. I've loved the restaurant's many ferments, amazing food, and entire aesthetic. In the *Toro Bravo* cookbook, chef John Gorham, collaborating with writer Liz Crain, has not only made the flavors of Toro Bravo accessible to home cooks with excellent, easy-to-follow recipes but also shared fascinating stories of his journey to the helm of some of Portland's best restaurants. This book is filled with culinary inspiration.

SANDOR KATZ, author of *Wild Fermentation* and *The Art of Fermentation*

An amazing story of a man's life and the building of a great restaurant. I loved it.

GUS VAN SANT

Here in Portland, Toro Bravo carves an uncommon niche – simultaneously adventurous and comforting. This cookbook, like the restaurant itself, tells the story of one restless spirit's search for home. These are recipes you'll want to both cherish and share.

CARRIE BROWNSTEIN, creator of *Portlandia*

John Gorham seemingly mind-reads what we want to eat: comfort and craft popping with salty, sweet, spicy flavors. No one better translates Portland's raging gustatory desires and DIY spirit. This book captures the joy of Toro Bravo; all heart, no bull.

KAREN BROOKS, author of *The Mighty Gastropolis*

I've known John Gorham for over a decade, since I first got to town and he turned me down for a job. Since that fateful rainy morning, we've cooked together, confided in each other, commiserated (read: partied) together, and grown up significantly. Toro Bravo is the greatest expression of who John really is: nostalgic, spirited, brutally honest, fun as hell, and one of Portland's all-around-greatest chefs. The *Toro Bravo* cookbook captures his vision, ferocity, determination, and hilarity.

JASON FRENCH, chef/owner of Ned Ludd

John Gorham's cookbook is as outrageously delicious as his food, as lively as his restaurant (my second home in Portland), and as personable as he is. It is a shining testament to authentic cooking. Paying homage to the Spanish tradition and expressed in personal terms, John's cooking is entirely unique.

PAUL BERTOLLI, former Executive Chef, Chez Panisse

The *Toro Bravo* cookbook is unique in its storytelling: John's personal story, the stories of the restaurant's evolution, the stories behind the recipes. Toro Bravo's magic lies in its ability to seamlessly merge the art of cooking with the commerce of dining: these are small plates with big ideas.

ANDREW ZIMMERN, co-creator and host of *Bizarre Foods*

Reads like a memoir on a motorcycle ... with plenty of refreshment along the way.

CULINATE

My personal favorite is a Spanish-influenced restaurant called Toro Bravo. I would would walk from Burlington to Portland barefoot for Toro Bravo's brussels sprouts with bacon, sherry, and cream; or their fried anchovies with romesco sauce.

CANDACE PAGE, Vermont Public Radio

In the center of Portland's burgeoning food scene is Toro Bravo, a Spanish-inspired restaurant with a crazy loyal fan base. This book offers a glimpse into what keeps drawing crowds. It's the people, like Gorham, who was born to a drug-adled, teen mom and escaped every summer to his granddad's crab shack, where he learned the joy of food; and it's the recipes (chorizo!), of course. But it's also the oddities – the book dedicates pages to staff tattoos and step-by-step instructions on MacGyvering a fridge – that really bare this place's soul.

TIENLON HO, *BuzzFeed*'s 14 Best Cookbooks of 2013

What you have first is pages and pages of back story, both of chef John Gorham and his Portland tapas restaurant Toro Bravo, as well as food philosophizing and general cooking intel ... When was the last time a cookbook looked so modern and refreshing? The influence of former Lucky Peach publisher McSweeney's is strongly felt on these pages and I hope cookbooks in general veer toward more color, more photos, and more user-friendliness.

PAUL FORBES, *Eater*'s 21 Essential Cookbooks of 2013

Toro Bravo is as much memoir as cookbook, even though it contains 95 recipes from the famed Portland restaurant. This is the story of chef John Gorham, and how his passion for food shaped his life. Gorgeously produced, well-written, and filled with stunning photographs, this is one of the year's finest food books.

DAVID GUTOWSKI, *Largehearted Boy*

Toro Bravo is written in a casual, engaging tone that weaves Gorham's itinerant path into a classic hero's journey narrative that's a search for – and discovery of – home. It's intimate, genuine, risky ... and deeply underscored with a dark thread that makes the victories matter. He's returned from his life's constant travels, rich with the spoils of an international pantry, to the benefit of a city with an endless appetite for the gastronomic novelty of unseen lands.

CHRIS ONSTAD, *Portland Mercury*

John Gorham's story is a good one – just a hard-working dude who loved to cook and made his dream a reality. That and some tempting recipes make it a quick and intriguing read. The tone, as the title implies, is no bull, and the stories of his rise to food stardom are interesting and completely sap-free. It has great photos – it even has a picture of the tattoo on John's ass of a chicken pooping the name of his sous chef (and friend): "Chicken Shit Mills." That should tell you something about what kind of person John Gorham is.

TAYLOR HOUSTON, *LitReactor*'s The Best Books of 2013

Big bold fonts and bright photographs match Gorham's in-your-face style. Anyone wishing to cook some delicious Spanish food, or who enjoys food memoirists like Anthony Bourdain, will enjoy *Toro Bravo*.

JESSICA HOWARD, *Shelf Awareness*

One of the highlights of the book is its consistently authentic tone. The first person narratives and headnotes are actually written in a voice that sounds like a real chef, not a cheerful writer paraphrasing one ... Gorham and Crain manage to braid together their work so it is impossible to distinguish between writers. Their voices meld together seamlessly; it's almost as if their conversations have been directly transcribed from long dinners with plenty of drinks and food flowing between them ... John Gorham and his crew manage to inject soul into every single dish at Toro Bravo, and the book demonstrates how much detail, history and thought go behind every plate you're passed.

KAT VETRANO, *Late Night Library*

Hawthorne Books

Library of Congress
Cataloging-in-Publication Data

Crain, Liz.
The food lover's guide to Portland /
Liz Crain.
pages cm.
Includes index.
ISBN 978-0-9893604-6-3

1. Food – guidebooks.
2. Grocery trade – Oregon – Portland –
    Guidebooks.
3. Cookery, American – Pacific
    Northwest style.
4. Portland (Or.) – Guidebooks.

I. Title.

TX354.5.C73 2014
641.59' 79549 – dc23
2013046589

Hawthorne Books
& Literary Arts

9   2201 Northeast 23rd Avenue
8   3rd Floor
7   Portland, Oregon 97212
6   hawthornebooks.com
5   *Form*:
4   Adam McIsaac/Sibley House
3
2   Printed in China
1   First Hawthorne Edition, 2014

    Set in Sentinel

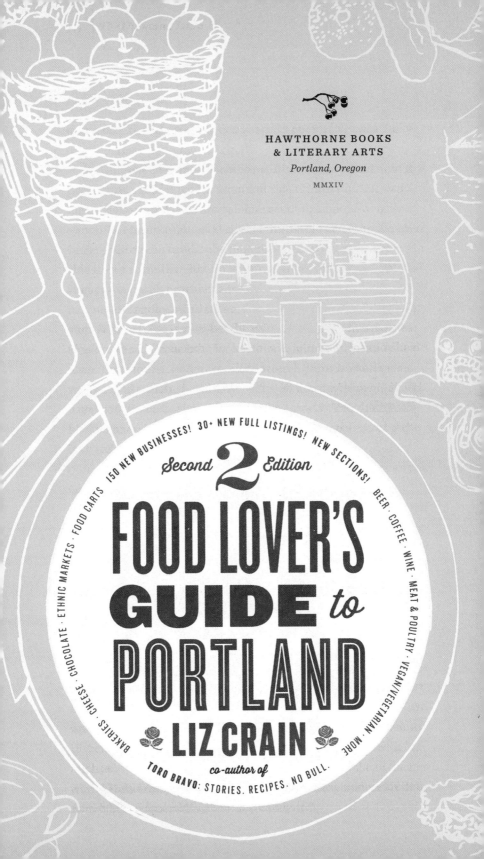

HAWTHORNE BOOKS
& LITERARY ARTS
Portland, Oregon
MMXIV

Second **2** *Edition*
150 NEW BUSINESSES! · 30+ NEW FULL LISTINGS! · NEW SECTIONS!

FOOD CARTS · ETHNIC MARKETS · CHOCOLATE · CHEESE · BAKERIES

BEER · COFFEE · WINE · MEAT & POULTRY · VEGAN/VEGETARIAN · MORE

FOOD LOVER'S GUIDE to PORTLAND

LIZ CRAIN

co-author of
TORO BRAVO: STORIES. RECIPES. NO BULL.

ACKNOWLEDGEMENTS

THANKS TO ALL THE STRONG, STAND-UP WOMEN who helped me on my food writing way when I first moved to Portland, and who continue their mentorship today. Namely: Jo Ostgarden, Audrey Van Buskirk, Angie Jabine, and Kelly Clarke. Thanks to the Hawthorne Books crew of Rhonda Hughes, Adam O'Connor Rodriguez and Adam McIsaac for welcoming me into the wide world of publishing, hiring me when I turned in the first edition's manuscript and publishing the second edition of this book. Thanks to Katy Calcott for her initial encouragement and words of wisdom, to Gary Luke for taking me and the first edition of this book on, to Whitney Ricketts for editing that edition, to Rachel Smith editorial assistant extraordinaire for helping me kick ass with this edition, to Nick Zukin and Brett Burmeister for contributing, to Duc Le for creating a beautiful Web site and blog for me and to Adam McIsaac for brilliantly redesigning this edition.

Thank you to all the producers, purveyors, and other fine Portland food and drink folk who made the research portion of this book so interesting and gratifying. Thanks to my family and friends for putting up with me through the thick and thin of this. Finally, thank you Portland and Portlanders for cooking and serving up my favorite city.

Cheers to many more years of discovering the weird and wonderful culinary culture of Portland.

I MOVED TO PORTLAND IN 2002 with a small amount of money and a big appetite. I didn't go hungry. Quite the opposite.

I first fell in love with Portland food through local farmers markets, food cooperatives, and food carts – all low-dough options stacked with diversity.

Back then most food carts were located in a few different rows in Southwest Portland for the hungry downtown nine-to-fivers and students. These days you can find food cart pods and rows in every corner of town, serving up the standard tacos, hot dogs, and bento, as well as more unusual and delicious fare such as Korean tacos, Bosnian pitas, piston-pulled espresso, homemade ice cream, crêpes, sweet and savory hand pies, and more.

The booming food cart scene speaks to Portland's by-the-bootstraps, do-it-yourself culinary culture. Food business as a labor of love is what Portland is all about.

I've been writing local food stories and restaurant reviews since 2003, and the one thing I've encountered time and time again in Portland is a passion for food made the hard way. Fantastic raw ingredients plus pure and simple passion is what keeps the clock ticking in these parts. Rather than buying flavored spirits, local bartenders infuse their own. Instead of purchasing mixers, bitters, and syrupy sweeteners, they create their own. Portland chefs butcher their own meat, bake their bagels, blend their chocolates, cure their olives, make their cheeses. The list goes on and on. It's all about knowing where your ingredients come from (often local, family-owned farms) and respecting the ingredients enough to take time to see them through every step of the way.

Luckily the fertile Willamette Valley, as well as the diverse growing regions throughout the state, result in incredible, year round food. Looking for meat? You've got local pasture-raised beef, pork, bison, turkey, rabbit, and lamb. Want fish? Choose from salmon, Dungeness crab, albacore, sturgeon, crawfish, oysters, and mussels, all caught nearby. Need fruit? Take your pick of Oregon-grown cranberries, pears, kiwis, quinces, jujube, and pawpaws. And don't forget your veggies. Everything from asparagus, fava beans, and green beans to Brussels sprouts, Jerusalem artichokes, and cardoons are grown on local farms.

Food Lover's Guide to Portland includes local eatery and watering hole recommendations in many chapters, but the focus here is on the producers and purveyors, the folks that make the former possible. I think it's important to give page space to those so often overlooked as the source of our food and beverages. Restaurants and bars are on the public radar, but the farmers, distillers, brewers, roasters, bakers, chocolatiers, and others who make food happen are not always treated with the same fanfare. For the most part I've excluded chains and large corporations for the same reason. Been there, read that.

In the name of full disclosure, during the research and writing of this book I met with no PR or marketing people. It has always been important for me to remove myself from this side of food culture and speak directly to the folks who make food happen. I write about food and drink because I love to cook, eat, drink, and work with food personally and professionally. In other words, these are my people. This is my tribe.

As for this second edition (the first edition was published in 2010), I eliminated all closures, added 150-plus new businesses, 30-plus new full business listings; Nick Zukin wrote a section on **Latino/Mexican Markets** (☞ *p.* 50); Brett Burmeister wrote the **Food Carts** chapter; and many more items were added and expanded. I hope that you make some new, tasty discoveries here. I certainly have. Eat, drink, and be hairy!

FOOD

BEFORE RESEARCHING AND WRITING THIS BOOK, I knew that Portland was blessed by bread – I just didn't know how blessed. Most Portland neighborhoods have a good, sometimes great, retail bakery within walking distance. When I lived in Southeast Portland, I wasn't far from Hawthorne's **Grand Central Bakery**; in North Portland, where I live now, I'm a couple of blocks away from the recently closed Italian bakery **DiPrima Dolci**; and my writing studio in Northwest Portland is a short walk from **Ken's Artisan Bakery**. All three of these bakeries are places to grab a fresh-from-the-oven tasty loaf to go or to stay a while for a cup of coffee or a bite to eat. That's the way it should be – we should all be able to enjoy the yeasty, warm aromas of fresh-baked bread and pastries.

If I had to categorize Portland bakeries, I'd say this: lots of pain au levain, a tilt toward European-style darker roasty-toasty crusts, and almost-always-good coffee. The majority of Portland bakeries use high-quality, often local, ingredients such as organic free-range eggs, small-batch butter, and quality flour such as **Shepherd's Grain**. Shepherd's Grain is a Food Alliance-certified flour produced by thirty-plus no-till Pacific Northwest growers.

This chapter is divided into two sections: savory and sweet. Most bakeries tip the scale to one or the other.

SAVORY

Dave's Killer Bread and NatureBake

www.daveskillerbread.com, www.naturebake.com
5209 SE International Way, Milwaukie   503-335-8077
M–F 7:30am–6pm, Sa 8am–5pm, Su 9am–5pm (call ahead for group tours).

James Dahl started the whole-grain-heavy bakery NatureBake with his wife, Wanene, in 1955, and his grandson, Shobi Dahl, runs the family business today. Every day employees arrive at the Milwaukie bakery at 5am to kick off production. A tour of the 50,000-square-foot facility reveals everything from 2,000-pound sacks of wheat kernels and enormous double-hooked dough mixers to floor scales and 90-degree, 90-percent-humidity walk-in proof boxes.

Wholesale commercial sandwich bread doesn't usually get much gastronomic attention, but Dave's Killer Bread is a Portland icon. Throughout the 1980s and '90s, Glenn Dahl, Shobi's father, ran the show at NatureBake. In 2005, Glenn's brother Dave emerged from nearly fifteen years in prison a reformed man; he wanted to make right by rejoining the family business. He quickly proved himself with the development of Dave's Killer Bread, which has become one of the company's top-selling product lines.

Dave's Killer Bread is studded with high-quality ingredients such as organic flax seeds, honey, molasses, and amaranth. It is never frozen and is bought back from retail operations if it's on the shelf for more than three days. Grab a Dave's Killer Bread loaf – available in markets throughout Oregon, Washington, California, Idaho, and Alaska – and you'll feel the difference. They're arm-curl-heavy, loaded with fresh sprouted grains, buckwheat, and millet. Even with all the wholesome ingredients, the loaves are still soft and, like most commercial loaves, they're barely crusted, making them an easy sell for folks who love mushy white bread.

Stop by The Healthy Bread Store to purchase warm, just-off-the-cooling-rack breads, along with discounted factory seconds, cookies, and more.

Delphina's Bakery

www.delphinasbakerycafe.com

📍 4636 NE 42nd Ave, Portland 📞 503-281-1373 🕐 M–F 6am–4pm, Sa–Su 8am–2pm

When Pix Patisserie's Cheryl Wakerhauser moved to Portland, she worked at Delphina's for a stint. This family-run artisan and sandwich bread bakery has been in the wholesale retail baking business since 1983 (old for Portland standards), when it got its start in the back room of the kitchen of the now-closed Delphina's Restaurant on Northwest 21st Avenue.

These days, Delphina's specializes in bread – everything from baguettes and boules to sandwich breads and rolls – but they also bake standard pastries such as Danishes, scones, and muffins. Since 2000, Delphina's has been in its current facility with a counter service café serving soups, sandwiches, and panini. A good low-dough option is Delphina's Flour Hour – two-for-the-price-of-one artisan loaves Tuesday through Friday from 2:30pm to close.

Fleur de Lis Bakery & Café

www.fleurdelisbakery.com

📍 3930 NE Hancock St, Portland 📞 503-459-4887
🕐 Tu–F 7:30am–6pm, Sa–Su 8am–3pm

The opposite of hip, this Portland bakery has been all about amazing baked goods with no pretense since 2005. Located in the former Hollywood Library building, it's owned by prior **Pearl Bakery** owner Greg Mistell. There are usually several Fleur de Lis breads available at any given time, including a few different ciabattas and multigrains in addition to the pain au levain and house baguette. On the sweet side you'll often find ginger molasses cookies, glazed almond rings, fruit pies, cakes, croissants, palmiers, and fruit crostatas.

Fleur de Lis wholesales baked goods to some of the best cafés and restaurants around town, including **Laurelhurst Market Butcher Shop** (☞ *p.* 66). It also does a killer counter-service breakfast and lunch with breakfast pastries, hot and cold sandwiches, soups, and salads. The café is spacious with a big covered outdoor patio out front that's perfect for dining in. There's a cold drink case near the counter along with hot **Stumptown Coffee** and **Foxfire Tea**.

Grand Central Bakery

⌘ www.grandcentralbakery.com
📍 714 N Fremont St, Portland 📞 503-546-5311
🕐 7am–6pm every day
📍 2230 SE Hawthorne Blvd, Portland
📞 503-445-1600 🕐 M–F 7am–7pm, Sa–Su 7am–6pm
📍 1444 NE Weidler St, Portland
📞 503-288-1614 🕐 7am–6pm every day
📍 2249 NW York St, Portland 📞 503-808-9860
🕐 M–F 6:30am–4pm, Sa–Su 7am–4pm
📍 3425 SW Multnomah Blvd, Portland
📞 503-977-2024 🕐 M–F 7am–7pm, Sa–Su 7am–6pm
📍 7987 SE 13th Ave, Portland 📞 503-546-3036
🕐 7am–6pm every day
📍 4440 NE Fremont St, Portland 📞 503-808-9877
🕐 Sa–Su 7am–4pm

Although Grand Central got its start in Seattle, it has steadily become a predominantly Portland institution specializing in wholesale and retail European-style artisan breads, pastries, sweets, and breakfast and lunch fare, and is well known for its como, ciabatta, peasant loaf, and dark, slightly sweet campagnolo.

Gwenyth Bassetti started Seattle's Grand Central Bakery in 1989, and in 1993 her son and daughter – Ben and Piper Davis – and some close friends carried the successful business down to

Portland. At that point, there were only a couple of bakeries in town proofing and turning out artisan, European-style bread.

Twenty-plus years later, there are seven Grand Central Bakeries in Portland, along with a thriving wholesale business and a cookbook – *The Grand Central Baking Book* by Piper Davis and Ellen Jackson. Grand Central's Portland grain silo, filled with Shepherd's Grain flour – is located at the NW York Street location. Each Grand Central location has the same local/seasonal menu and most of the from-scratch house-made soups, salads, and sandwiches are loaded with local seasonal ingredients.

The focus at Grand Central is home hearth–style baking, so there's not too much going on in house that's fancy or hard to pronounce. It's all about rustic sweets and savories and simple, rich-crusted classic artisan breads. According to co-owner Piper Davis, "What I'm excited about are things like biscuits, pie dough, and excellent, honest cake." Grand Central's summer strawberry-rhubarb Danish is one of the best I've ever had. Flaky, buttery, moist, and perfectly in-season.

Ken's Artisan Bakery

⊘ www.kensartisan.com
♥ 338 NW 21st Ave, Portland ☎ 503-248-2202
🕒 M–Sa 7am–6pm, Su 8am–5pm

Since 2001 Ken Forkish and his bakery crew have been hand-mixing, dividing, and shaping some of Portland's best wholesale and retail French loaves. The space is small, loud, and almost always packed. Standing in line for your country brown, raisin pecan, or multigrain bread, you witness the action in the small exposed back-of-the-house bakery. Forkish's twenty-plus staff work around the clock, doing everything from slow feeding the levain (bread starter) and mixing up to 250 pounds of dough at a time, to slow proofing the bread (letting the dough rest before baking). There aren't any proof boxes – sealed areas that encourage dough to rise more quickly – since Forkish wants a long, slow, and flavorful 78-

to 80-degree proof. That's usually the ambient temperature of the bakery, so the bread is simply left out on racks to proof.

On any given day at Ken's, there's an abundance of loaves, baguettes, and boules to choose from. The four daily doughs – which rotate throughout the week – make ciabatta, twice-a-day-baked baguettes, pain rustique, French rye (Saturdays only), and more. There's also a wide assortment of pastries, tarts, sandwiches, and hot and cold drinks available. Lucky for you, you can read all about Forkish's breads in his James Beard Award-winning cookbook *Flour Water Salt Yeast*.

Forkish also owns the wildly successful **Ken's Artisan Pizza** as well as **Trifecta Tavern & Bakery**, both in Southeast Portland, but he spends more time at the bakery. According to Forkish, "This is a more complex operation. We're open twelve hours a day, seven days a week. Our first baker arrives around 2:30 in the morning, and we start baking bread usually

Sicilian pizza and hippie vibe
Al Forno Ferruzza
♦ 2738 NE Alberta St, Portland
☎ 503-253-6766
🔗 www.503alforno.com

East Coast neo-Neapolitan
Apizza Scholls
♦ 4741 SE Hawthorne Blvd, Portland
☎ 503-233-1286
🔗 www.apizzascholls.com

Farm-fresh cornmeal-crust deep dish
Dove Vivi Pizza
♦ 2727 NE Glisan St, Portland
☎ 503-239-4444
🔗 www.dovevivipizza.com

In an old brick firehouse neighborhood pizza-plus joint
Firehouse
♦ 711 NE Dekum St, Portland
☎ 503-954-1702
🔗 www.firehousepdx.com

Classic pizza parlor with loaded pies
Flying Pie Pizzeria
♦ 7804 SE Stark St, Portland
☎ 503-254-2016
🔗 www.flying-pie.com

Twelve-inch wood-fired Italian pies
Ken's Artisan Pizza
♦ 304 SE 28th Ave, Portland
☎ 503-517-9951
🔗 www.kensartisan.com

Neighborhood hub, by-the-slice, & big pies
The Mississippi Pizza Pub
♦ 3552 N Mississippi Ave, Portland
☎ 503-288-3231
🔗 www.mississippipizza.com

Italian wood-fired pizza oven
Nostrana
♦ 1401 SE Morrison St, Portland
☎ 503-234-2427
🔗 www.nostrana.com

Excellent pizza + housemade ice cream
Lovely's Fifty-Fifty
♦ 4039 N Mississippi Ave, Portland
☎ 503-281-4060
🔗 www.lovelysfiftyfifty.com

NEWER BAKERIES

German breads and pastries
Fressen Artisan Bakery
523 NE 19th Ave, Portland
503-953-3222
www.fressenartisanbakery.com

Gluten-free sweet and savory
New Cascadia Traditional Bakery
1700 SE 6th Ave, Portland
503-546-4901
www.newcascadiatraditional.com

Huge selection in the Pearl
Lovejoy Bakers
939 NW 10th Ave, Portland
503-208-3113
www.lovejoybakers.com

House-milled and wood-fired
Tabor Bread
5051 SE Hawthorne Blvd, Portland
971-279-5530
www.taborbread.com

BAGEL SHOPS

Mom and pop
Bagel Land
4118 NE Fremont St, Portland
503-249-2848

New York style bagels
Bowery Bagels
310 NW Broadway, Portland
503-227-6674
www.bowerybagels.com

Classic boiled
Kenny & Zuke's Delicatessen
1038 Stark St, Portland
503-222-3354
www.kennyandzukes.com

Coffeeshop + tangy bagels
Spielman Coffee Roasters
2128 SE Division St, Portland
503-467-0600
www.spielmanbagels.com

around 4:00." Asked what he considers to be the bakery's strong suits, Forkish quickly answers, "Consistency and a great staff." I'd say it's also crust and crumb; every loaf I've had has been roasty-toasty on the outside and deliciously sweet, sour, salty, and porous on the inside.

Little T American Baker

www.littletbaker.com
2600 SE Division St, Portland   503-238-3458
M–Sa 7am–5pm, Su 8am–2pm

Owner Tim Healea hails from Portland bakery gold-standard **Pearl Bakery** (☞ *p.* 23). "Little T" was his nickname at the 2002 *Coupe du Monde de la Boulangerie* in France (an international artisanal baking competition held every four years in Paris). His team won the silver medal.

Little T's tasty breads are different every day, but there's always an assortment of popular "slabs" – focaccias topped with everything from olives and sea salt to fresh rosemary – as well as more traditional choices such as baguettes and ciabatta. It's not exactly a warm, dusty, rosy-cheeks sort of bakery. In fact, Little T is more like a lot of Portland's newer cafés with its polished concrete floors, minimal industrial design, tall windows, and exposed beams. What the space lacks in warmth it makes up for with its baked goods.

The large deli case showcases the breads and sweet treats (cookies, sweet rolls, scones, biscotti, and tarts) baked in the back. Breakfast and lunch offerings include soup, panini, and a tasty meatloaf sandwich served with a pickled chutney.

There's beer, wine, **Foxfire Tea**, **Stumptown Coffee**, and **Columbia Gorge** juices in this counter service bakery/café. Of note: The hot breakfast pretzel bread topped with ham and cheddar is a thing of beauty.

Marsee Baking

🔗 *www.marseebaking.com*
📍 1625 SE Bybee Blvd, Portland
    📞 503-232-0000 🕐 6am–5pm every day
📍 9100 N Vancouver Ave, Portland
    📞 503-295-4000 🕐 M–F 7am–3pm

I often pick up Marsee Baking's sandwich breads at **New Seasons Market** (located throughout Portland) despite the bakery's acquisition by Tully's in 2000. Marsee Baking opened in 1993 as a small European-style retail bakery, and several Portland locations followed. These days, Marsee Baking has narrowed its retail focus and stepped up the wholesale side with a large product base that includes cheesecakes, muffins, scones, and more distributed through Sysco and Peterson. Only one retail Marsee bakery remains – in Sellwood – with breads, pastries, coffee, espresso, and breakfast and lunch menus.

Pearl Bakery

🔗 *www.pearlbakery.com*
📍 102 NW 9th Ave, Portland 📞 503-827-0910
    🕐 M–F 6:30am–5:30pm, Sa 7am–5pm,
    Su 8am–3pm

Pearl Bakery has been the local gold-standard artisanal bakery since it opened in the Pearl District in 1997. Besides rocking an amazing bread, pastry, and dessert counter, Pearl Bakery's breads and other baked goods can be found in many esteemed Portland restaurants such as **Higgins Restaurant and Bar**, **Castagna**, **Giorgio's Restaurant**, **Tabla Mediterranean Bistro**, **23Hoyt**, **Clyde Common**, and more. Pearl Bakery

Indian Kati rolls
Bollywood Theater
📍 2039 NE Alberta St, Portland
📞 971-200-4711
🔗 *www.bollywoodtheaterpdx.com*

Long line for killer sandwiches
Bunk Sandwiches
📍 621 SE Morrison St, Portland
📞 503-477-9515
🔗 *www.bunksandwiches.com*

Panini and more
Eugenio's
📍 3584 SE Division St, Portland
📞 503-233-3656
🔗 *www.eugenios.net*

Cheesesteak love
Grant's Philly Cheesesteak
📍 15350 NE Sandy Blvd, Portland
📞 503-252-8012

Big-ass New York deli–style sandwiches and house-made pastrami
Kenny & Zuke's Delicatessen
📍 1038 SW Stark St, Portland
📞 503-222-3354
🔗 *www.kennyandzukes.com*

Variety of sandwiches and dogs
Kenny & Zuke's BagelWorks
📍 2376 NW Thurman St, Portland
📞 503-954-1737
🔗 *www.kennyandzukes.com*

Seasonal takes on classics
Meat Cheese Bread
📍 1406 SE Stark St, Portland
📞 503-234-1700
🔗 *www.meatcheesebread.com*

Messy classics with an attitude
Michael's Italian Beef and Sausage Co.
📍 1111 SE Sandy Blvd, Portland
📞 503-230-1899
🔗 *www.michaelsitalianbeef.com*

Refined sandwiches on Fleur de Lis bread
Petisco
📍 1411 NE Broadway, Portland
📞 503-360-1048
🔗 *www.petiscopdx.com*

also wholesales to local markets such as **Foster & Dobbs Authentic Foods, Pasta-works**, and **City Market**.

Pearl Bakery distinguishes itself by making its bread with unbleached wheat flour and sea salt, its pastries with local rBST-free butter, and by never adding dough conditioners or preservatives to its products. Some breads that you'll always find in house include paesano, ciabatta, pugliese, and various pain au levain such as baguettes and walnut levain.

Keep in mind that Pearl Bakery sandwiches are very tasty, making it a nice pit stop after a trip to the downtown **Powell's City of Books** – especially if you love Batdorf & Bronson coffee as much as I do.

Petite Provence Boulangerie & Patisserie

www.provence-portland.com

♀ 4834 SE Division St, Portland ☎ 503-233-1121 ◐ Su–Th 7am–8pm, F–Sa 7am–9pm
♀ 1824 NE Alberta St, Portland ☎ 503-284-6564 ◐ 7am–9pm every day
♀ 16350 SW Boones Ferry Rd, Lake Oswego ☎ 503-635-4533 ◐ 7am–10pm every day
♀ 408 E 2nd St, The Dalles ☎ 541-506-0037 ◐ 7am–3pm every day

Petite Provence Boulangerie & Patisserie's four locations each have slightly different menus, but the gist is American-French renditions such as eggs Benedict, crêpes, and risotto cakes for breakfast, French onion soup and croque-monsieur for lunch, and braised lamb shank for dinner. At each location you'll find artisanal breads and sweet and savory baked goods in the case, including croissants, brioche, pains au chocolat, and more.

SWEET

Baker & Spice

www.bakerandspicebakery.com

♀ 6330 SW Capitol Hwy, Portland ☎ 503-244-7573
◐ Tu–F 6am–6pm, Sa 7am–6pm, Su 7am–3pm

Baker & Spice is a vibrant neighborhood bakery ten minutes from downtown Portland. Husband-and-wife team Julie Richardson and Matt Kappler co-own the bakery, churning out everything from daily hand-rolled hearth breads (including ciabatta, baguettes, whole grain loaves, challah on Fridays, and more), to sweet and savory European butter pastries, tarts, tea cakes, and custom cakes.

After graduating from New York's Culinary Institute of America, Richardson moved to Ketchum, Idaho, and opened Good Earth Bakery when she was only twenty-three years old. Four years later, after closing that bakery, Richardson moved to Portland.

Baker & Spice launched in 1998 as a booth at the downtown **PSU Portland Farmers Market**. The business built up a following for several years before it went brick-and-mortar in Hillsdale in 2005. Customers lined up at the farmers markets for Baker & Spice breads and pastries, and others special ordered the rustic pies and cakes enrobed in butter cream, mascarpone cream, or ganache. Richardson's hands are full these days running Baker & Spice as well as her second business, the baking supply store **The Cakery** (☞ *p.* 167), eight doors down from the bakery.

In recent years Richardson has scaled down the wholesale side of her business in order to focus on her retail space and on a select number of neighborhood restaurants. Grab a cup of **ZBEANZ** coffee or **Tao of Tea** tea at Baker & Spice and stay a while in the big window or the abundant seating space.

Bakeshop

⊘ www.bakeshoppdx.com
♀ 5351 NE Sandy Blvd, Portland *☎* 503-946-8884
◔ W–Su 7am–2pm

When Kim Boyce moved to Portland in 2010, food folks wondered where the former Spago and Campanile pastry chef would land. About a year later, Boyce opened her Northeast wholesale and retail bakery Bakeshop, which specializes in pastries and whole grain goodness apropos for the author of the 2011 James Beard Award-winning cookbook *Good to the Grain*. Some tasty treats you might choose from when visiting: rhubarb hand pies, raspberry crumble bars, iced oatmeal cookies and strawberry barley scones. You can also find Bakeshop goods at **Ristretto Roasters**, **Heart Coffee Roasters**, **Sterling Coffee Roasters**, and other local businesses.

Crema Bakery & Cafe

⊘ www.cremabakery.com
♀ 2728 SE Ankeny St, Portland *☎* 503-234-0206
◔ 7am–6pm every day

Although this coffee shop/pastry shop/bakery is one of many Portland spots to offer house-baked sweets and savories, from-scratch soups, and delicious coffee, Crema has built a solid following. Crema is usually very busy, but you can always grab a bite and go for a walk around the neighborhood – Laurelhurst Park is close, along with other sights and shops. I recommend the turkey and Swiss roll with

BOB'S RED MILL WHOLE GRAIN STORE

Although Milwaukie is seven miles south of Portland, a trip to Bob's Red Mill Whole Grain Store and its 300-plus bulk foods is worth the journey. At Bob's there's an entire aisle of standard and unusual flours, including rice, soy, teff, fava bean, almond, and hazelnut.

Morgan Grundstein-Helvey, former owner of Dovetail Bakery, is a big fan: "I love the bulk aisle. I mean, it's like, 'Here's some green pea flour, what do I do with this?' Or coconut flour? I think, 'Well, I better try it.'"

Not only can you load up on a variety of hot cereals, grains, and legumes, you'll also find elusive items, such as date sugar, cranberry beans, barley grits, and kamut berries.

Check out the small in-shop library of DIY books on everything from sprouting and bread-making to gluten-free cooking. If you want to head home with your very own grain mill, there are several to choose from. And if you're lucky, you just might brush shoulders with rosy-cheeked Bob Moore himself, who founded the business in 1978.

♥ 5000 SE Int'l Way, Milwaukie
☎ 503-607-6455
🔗 www.bobsredmill.com
🕐 M–F 6am–6pm, Sa 7am–5pm. Take a tour of the mill M–F at 10am or 11am.

honey mustard glaze as a yummy one-handed lunch – and don't miss the earthquake cookies for dessert. Please keep in mind that there have been plenty of staff changes at Crema in recent years, and consistency of food, drink, and service waxes and wanes. But when it's good, it's really good.

Helen Bernhard Bakery

🔗 www.helenbernhardbakery.com
♥ 1717 Broadway, Portland ☎ 503-287-1251
🕐 M–Sa 6am–6pm, Su 8am–3pm

This old-school, eighty-plus-year-old, always bustling bakery is the kind of bakery I grew up with in the Midwest. Brightly lit, with female bakers in white pullovers and hairnets helping customers to cookies, pastries, doughnuts, coffee cake, tarts, and birthday cakes, it's sugared with nostalgia.

On one end of the bakery are bagged sweet and savory baked goods – tiny parcels of macaroons, bagged sandwich breads, and buns to grab-and-go – and on the other end, there's a small coffee station next to a table mostly used for wedding consults.

Kids love the icing-topped sugar cookies, and adults love the diverse coffee and tea cakes that are hard to come by in a town more focused on European pain au levain and rustic desserts. A recent Helen Bernhard Bakery addition: bring in a photo or image and, for $6, the bakers will put it on top of a cake for you.

JaCiva's Bakery and Chocolatier

See page 41

Nuvrei Pastries

🔗 *www.nuvrei.com*

📍 404 NW 10th Ave, Portland 📞 503-546-3032 🕐 M–Sa 7am–5pm, Su 8am–5pm

Then-twenty-five-year-old French-trained Marius Pop opened Nuvrei Pastries in 2004; since then he's commandeered an unrivaled wholesale and retail pastry business to the tune of ten thousand pastries a week. According to Pop, the secret to Nuvrei's success has been minimal movement – in other words: baby steps.

He's proud to admit that he works an average of 120 hours a week, gets paid the same as his lowest-paid employees, and doesn't have time for much besides work.

Before Nuvrei came on the scene, Portland's coffee shop cuisine was defined for the most part by cold bagels, stale mystery bars, and dry muffins. Nuvrei's twenty-plus coffee shop clients – including **The Fresh Pot**, **Stumptown Coffee**, and **Coffeehouse Northwest** – now proudly serve buttery orange-cinnamon Danishes, delicious turkey and cream cheese croissants, ginger molasses cookies, and cherry walnut scones with rum glaze, all freshly baked in the wee hours and delivered before the cock crows.

With only pastries and sandwiches on rotation, and a tiny cafe above the bakery, Pop is able to focus on consistency one croissant at a time.

Pix Patisserie and Bar Vivant

🔗 *www.pixpatisserie.com*

📍 2225 E Burnside St, Portland 📞 971-271-7166 🕐 2pm–2am every day

What started off as a small, cubby-sized dessert and confection house in Southeast Portland is now solely an East Burnside sweet tooth and Spanish tapas institution. The original Southeast Pix was home to one of my favorite Portland food events, Dim Sum Yum Yum (tiny desserts with bubbly and dessert wine pairings),

and the North Portland Pix was Portland's answer to French café seating. I'm happy to report that the new location incorporates both.

These days, owner Cheryl Wakerhauser keeps it all under one roof with equal sweet and savory action. When the weather is decent,

CHERYL WAKERHAUSER

OF **PIX PATISSERIE** AND **BAR VIVANT**

Grew up in: Wisconsin.

Grew up on: Frozen pot pie, tater tots, and pizza.

Earliest business ventures: Selling candy at school and making/selling Cabbage Patch Kids' clothing.

"Discovered" food: In the Philippines during a college exchange program.

Moved to Portland in: 2003.

Pix Patisserie got its start at: PSU Farmers Market.

Top seller at the farmers market: Sticky mouse bars – her mom's version of Rice Krispy treats made with Cheerios and dipped in chocolate.

Kept her farmers market desserts and sweet treats cool with: Ice packs in an old aquarium.

Pix's biggest day of the year: Bastille Day.

Pix's most popular frozen treat: Beer float with Rogue Chocolate Stout and house mocha ice cream.

Favorite oyster: Chelsea gem.

Her favorite frozen Pix treat: Chocolate coconut sorbet.

She's most excited about: Her new commercial kitchen, converted from her old garage.

Her first commercial kitchen: The basement of a Portland sorority house; it had a commercial stove and eight burners.

the wicker chairs on the front deck face out toward the street and sun, and the small tables get topped with wine, espresso, Belgian beer, French macarons, ganache-covered cakelets, housemade chocolates, ice creams, sorbets, and more. In recent years, Wakerhauser has figured out ways to spend more time experimenting with ingredients she's passionate about – she's been pulling, blowing, and ribboning sugar into towering art pieces, for one. Pix Patisserie hosts more regular events than just about any other place in town: its Annual Bastille Day Bash, Gastronomical Trivia Night, Dim Sum Yum Yum, and much more.

My favorite Pix treats in no particular order: the wide array of constantly changing buttercream-filled French macarons (port, fleur de sel, pistachio, passion fruit, raspberry, blueberry), the truffles (the Pistache and Drunken Cherries are especially delicious), The Royale (a chocolate mousse, hazelnut praline, and dacquoise orb coated in ganache), the Basque cider and txakoli, and all of the savory tapas. I especially love all of the tasty Pix drinks, including the Lindemans Framboise float with vanilla ice cream and the house beer float, which is a wizardly froth of Rogue Chocolate Stout and house-made mocha ice cream. The mocha ice cream may not be magic when eaten solo (made with cocoa powder and no eggs), but that's because Wakerhauser had the float in mind when crafting it (it melts and melds well).

St. Honoré Boulangerie

www.sainthonorebakery.com

- 2335 NW Thurman St, Portland · 503-445-4342 · 7am–8pm every day
- 3333 SE Division St, Portland · 503-279-4433 · 7am–10pm every day
- 315 1st St, Lake Oswego · 503-445-1379 · M–F 7am–7pm, Sa–Su 7am–8pm

There's so much to choose from at Dominique Geulin's St. Honoré Boulangeries – artisan European-style breads; baguette sandwiches; all sorts of meaty and cheesy quiches; sweet and savory French pastries such as pain au chocolat, brioche, and canelet; all sorts of desserts; and big, brimming salads. The large, open-air kitchens are where the action is – white-aproned staff pump out golden, chewy baked goods from large custom-built firebrick ovens. The small indoor and outdoor marble tables with wicker chairs are perfect for losing track of time.

Lunch is most popular at St. Honoré, but every meal is worth the trip. All three locations are perfect for dessert or nibbles ranging from fruit tarts and éclairs to opera cream cake and hazelnut dacquoise cake. The beauty of St. Honoré is that no matter how busy it is, food and drink funnel out fast from the kitchen.

Tonalli's Doughnuts & Cream

- 2805 NE Alberta St, Portland · 503-284-4510 · 7am–midnight every day

This Alberta street-corner shop offers fifty-plus **Cascade Glacier** ice creams, some of which deserve a black light, they're so electric-bright (neon flavors such as funfetti, bubble gum, cotton candy, and birthday cake); thirty-plus types of doughnuts, running the gamut from glazed and holes to maple bars and fritters; and **Portland Roasting Company** coffee and **Stash Tea**.

The best part of Tonalli's is its massive selection, which usually trumps quality. You can get your ice cream in a waffle, cake, or sugar cone, or in a cup, banana split, shake, or malt. Tonalli's is good for groups (there's plenty of seating) or a quick, cheap stop.

Two Tarts Bakery

www.twotartsbakery.com

- 2309 NW Kearney St, Portland · 503-312-9522 · Tu–Sa 10:30am–6pm, Su noon–5pm

I had my first Two Tarts cookie – a tasty cappuccino cream – downtown at **World Cup Coffee & Tea** (☛ *p.* 124) in **Powell's City of Books**. Founded in 2007, this small (in more ways than one) cookie company began with a handful of wholesale accounts, but now retails cookies and caters tiered cookie towers.

II

KENNETH "CAT DADDY" POGSON & TRES SHANNON

OF **VOODOO DOUGHNUT**

Shannon owned this short-lived Portland institution with Ben Ellis: X-Ray Cafe.

Pogson's first business: Started a movie theater in the sixth grade.

Another pre-Voodoo Shannon/Pogson business idea: Portland tourist chauffeur service with 1950s cars and a mother-in-law special. Pogson: "Get rid of your mother-in-law for an entire day and we will take her around town for all her favorite things and make her the happiest woman in the world."

How Voodoo Doughnuts came to be according to Pogson: "We begged, we borrowed, we stole. We hung around apartments that were being remodeled, hanging around the dumpsters waiting for cabinets and two-by-fours."

Number of doughnuts they can crank out of the downtown location every day: 20,000 to 30,000.

Doughnut 101: The larger the doughnut, the worse it tastes – it soaks up grease and doesn't release it.

Best Voodoo April Fool's joke: Going-out-of-business sale.

Owner Elizabeth Beekley, who trained at the Culinary Institute of America, turns out the tiny tasties – most measure in at about one inch in diameter – including pecan tessies, not-so-thin-mint bars, pistachio shortbreads, peanut butter creams, and double chocolate chews. In addition to the retail shop and local farmers markets, you can find Two Tarts cookies at **Foster & Dobbs Authentic Foods**, **Zupan's Markets**, **City Market**, **Pastaworks**, **Coffeehouse Northwest**, and other spots around town.

Voodoo Doughnut

🔗 *www.voodoodoughnut.com*
📍 22 SW 3rd Ave, Portland 📞 503-241-4704
   🕐 open all day, every day
📍 1501 NE Davis St, Portland 📞 503-235-2666
   🕐 open all day, every day
📍 20 E Broadway, Eugene 📞 541-868-8666
   🕐 M–W 6am–midnight, Th–Su open all day

"I now channel the Voodoo spirit through pre-Scientology Isaac Hayes, through the Cruller Chandelier of Life, down upon these two souls," says Kenneth "Cat Daddy" Pogson. Pogson is wearing a gold-and-white Mexican wrestling outfit and is in the process of marrying a couple standing in front of a four-foot-wide wall-mounted doughnut at the original downtown Voodoo Doughnut on April Fool's Day. It gets weirder.

Although Voodoo Doughnut has only been around since 2003, it's a *Keep Portland Weird* institution. The tiny original doughnut shop, opened by longtime friends Tres Shannon and Kenneth Pogson, is famous for around-the-clock hours and oddball doughnuts like the Cock-n-Balls (which looks the part), the bacon maple bar (which Anthony Bourdain made famous on his Food Network show *No Reservations*), an oyster-topped doughnut, and even medicine-topped doughnuts (Pepto-Bismol frosting and crushed Tums) before the county health department stepped in. The best time to visit Voodoo is in the wee hours after a night on the town. There's usually lots of slurring among the late-night crowd, which fried dough seems to pair well with, and a long line out the door.

With three shops and a thriving wholesale business, Voodoo goes through more than two tons of doughnut ingredients a week. Additional shops are in the works. Although Voodoo is all about strange flavor combinations and wacky-looking doughnuts, Pogson says that half of Voodoo's sales are true-blue classics such as fritters and plain glazed doughnuts.

OREGON IS HOME to over twenty fine dairies and cheesemakers – from big, well-known dairies like **Tillamook** and **Rogue Creamery** to smaller farmstead cheesemakers like **Juniper Grove Farm** and **Rivers Edge Chèvre**. The region's good grass and therefore good milk lead to good cheese. Oregon's cheese has gotten a lot of positive press in recent years, including a nod by Jeffrey Roberts, author of *The Atlas of American Artisan Cheese*, who acknowledged that cheesemakers in the Willamette Valley "take full advantage of what the valley provides for dairy, wine, and now cheese."

Although our state is producing some fine cheeses, Portland's markets and restaurants haven't quite caught up in terms of the wide variety of stinky, sticky, soft, and hard cheeses available. If you're able, be sure to visit **Cheese Bar** (*see below*) in Southeast Portland; it is hands down the best cheese shop in the city and the only Portland shop/bar solely devoted to cheese. Owner Steve Jones has done a top-notch job of introducing Portlanders to the wide world of cheese.

Portland farmers markets are also fantastic outlets for locally produced farmstead and artisanal cheese. Many local cheesemakers set up at area farmers markets, and you can usually try before you buy.

According to local cheese expert and author Tami Parr, in recent years "there's a new generation of cheesemakers emerging in the state. Some recently opened businesses include **Portland Creamery**, **Briar Rose Creamery** (in Dundee), and **Full Circle Creamery** (Scio) – all run by younger people entering the cheese business not as farmstead cheesemakers seeking to keep their farms operational, but as entrepreneurs interested in artisan cheese and healthful local food."

And local is clearly where it's at. In 2013 Oregon won many awards at the annual American Cheese Society competition in Madison, Wisconsin, including top honors for cheeses from **Ancient Heritage Dairy**, **Rogue Creamery**, **Quail Run Creamery**, and others. Here's to Oregon cheese getting more of the attention it deserves.

Cheese Bar

🔗 *www.cheese-bar.com*

📍 6031 SE Belmont St, Portland 📞 503-222-6014 🕐 T–Su 11am–11pm

When I ask Steve Jones of Cheese Bar what his favorite types of cheese are, he answers: "I'm wild about washed-rind cheeses – stinky, creamy, ooey-gooey ones. When I bring cheeses like this to parties, I hover over them and my wife eventually walks over and says, 'Please step away from the cheese, Steve.'" It's not really fair to ask Jones to pick one favorite, since his dine-in or grab-and-go Cheese Bar usually has at least two hundred different types of cheese in stock.

TAMI PARR
OF **PACIFIC NORTHWEST CHEESE PROJECT**

Started her blog, Pacific Northwest Cheese Project, in: 2004

The blog features: Interviews with Pacific Northwest cheesemakers, cheese reviews, cheese industry news, and more.

Professionally: Parr worked as an attorney at Portland General Electric during the Enron debacle.

She left the legal field altogether in: 2006.

She's now: A full-time freelance food writer.

In 2009: Her book *Artisan Cheese of the Pacific Northwest* was published.

In the book: Profiles of Pacific Northwest cheesemakers, cheese recipes, tasting notes, and suggestions.

In 2013: Her book *Pacific Northwest Cheese: A History* was published.

In the book: The history of cheesemaking in the region to the present.

Where she likes to go for good cheese service: Cyril's at Clay Pigeon Winery, Paley's Place, and Cheese Bar.

Dairy that Parr likes to make at home: Paneer, dulce de leche, yogurt, and butter.

On Parr's horizon: More cheese writing for local and national publications and hosting a lot more cheese classes around town.

Jones opened Cheese Bar – the only specialty cheese shop/bar in Portland – in early 2010, shortly after closing his first, very successful Northwest Portland cheese business, Steve's Cheese. Cheese Bar is the Portland go-to for regional and international wrapped-to-order cheese. From soft-ripened Italian robiola to semifirm, salty tuada, Jones carries only the best. He's visited all of the U.S. dairies and cheesemakers that are regularly represented in his case, and many of the European dairies and creameries as well.

Cheese Bar's dine-in, order-at-the-bar menu is small, affordable (most food is $2 to $10), and delicious with sandwiches, salads, snacks, and usually a hot plate or two. There's wine and beer to drink, with foods such as sardines on toast, garbanzo tuna salad, and of course lots of cheese.

It's try-before-you-buy retail at Cheese Bar, so you'll never plunk down $20 a pound for something that doesn't make your mouth happy. Jones and his employees are all about dialogue, so a typical purchase involves a discussion – as long or short as you want – about what type of cheese you're seeking, when you want to eat it, and what you're planning to serve it with.

Cheese Bar also carries various non-perishable specialty foods such as **Arbequina olive oil**, locally produced **Nonna's Noodles**, **Boat Street Pickles**, and **Claudio Carollo** chocolates. Basically, most specialty ingredients on the short menu are for sale. You can also purchase cheese cutters, boards, and various other cheese paraphernalia, or you can borrow the house raclette machine if you purchase a quarter wheel or more of raclette.

Jones offers occasional after-hours dinners and classes at Cheese Bar. Stop by or check the website for more information.

Elephants Delicatessen

See page 91

Foster & Dobbs Authentic Foods

See page 92

Kookoolan Farms Cheese Classes

www.kookoolanfarms.com
♀ 15713 Highway 47, Yamhill ☎ 503-730-7535

Since 2008, Chrissie and Koorosh Zaerpoor of Kookoolan Farms have been hosting open-to-the-public cheesemaking classes in their farm kitchen in Yamhill (an hour's drive southwest of Portland). Kookoolan is an amazingly diverse small farm with orchards, vegetable gardens, chickens, and a few Jersey milking

Bar Avignon
♀ 2138 SE Division St, Portland
☎ 503-517-0808
www.baravignon.com

Beast
♀ 5425 NE 30th Ave, Portland
☎ 503-841-6968
www.beastpdx.com

Belmont Station and Biercafe
♀ 4500 SE Stark St, Portland
☎ 503-232-8538
www.belmont-station.com

Cheese Bar
♀ 6031 SE Belmont St, Portland
☎ 503-222-6014
www.cheese-bar.com

Clyde Common
♀ 1014 SW Stark St, Portland
☎ 503-228-3333
www.clydecommon.com

DOC
♀ 5519 NE 30th Ave, Portland
☎ 503-946-8592
www.docpdx.com

Leisure Public House
♀ 8002 N Lombard St, Portland
☎ 503-289-7606
www.leisurepublichouse.com

Le Pigeon
♀ 738 E Burnside St, Portland
☎ 503-546-8796
www.lepigeon.com

Paley's Place
♀ 1204 NW 21st Ave, Portland
☎ 503-243-2403
www.paleysplace.net

Saraveza
♀ 1004 N Killingsworth St, Portland
☎ 503-206-4252
www.saraveza.com

The Victory Bar
♀ 3652 SE Division St, Portland
☎ 503-236-8755
www.thevictorybar.com

European-style goat cheese

Alsea Acre Goat Cheeses

♀ PO Box 142, Alsea

☎ 888-316-4628

Fresh & aged sheep's and cow's milk cheese

Ancient Heritage Dairy

♀ 2595 NW Elm Lane, Madras

☎ 541-460-5032

🔗 www.ancientheritagedairy.com.

Raw aged goat cheese

Fairview Farm Dairy

♀ 2340 SW Fairview, Dallas

☎ 503-623-4744

🔗 www.fairviewfarmdairy.com

Fresh & aged certified organic goat cheese

Fraga Farm

♀ 28580 Pleasant Val. Rd, Sweet Home

☎ 541-367-3891

🔗 www.fragafarm.com

French-style goat cheese

Goldin Artisan Goat Cheese

♀ 32880 S Sawtell Rd, Molalla

☎ 503-810-1954

🔗 www.goldinartisangoatcheese.com

Very popular, visitors welcome, large cow's milk cheese factory

Tillamook County Creamery Assoc.

♀ 4175 Hwy 101 N, Tillamook

☎ 503-815-1300

🔗 www.tillamook.com

Wide variety of cow's and sheep's milk cheese

Willamette Valley Cheese Co.

♀ 8105 Wallace Rd NW, Salem

☎ 503-399-9806

🔗 www.wvcheeseco.com

cows. Kookoolan delivers meat, produce, and eggs regularly to Portland restaurants such as **Bijou Café**, **Bar Avignon**, **Biwa**, **Beast**, and **Al-Amir**.

The farm's cheese classes, taught by various local cheesemakers, are generally three hours long and cover everything from the history and culture of the particular cheese or cheeses being taught to step-by-step DIY cheesemaking techniques. Classes cost $50 per person and include a $10 coupon good toward anything in the Kookoolan Farms store. The store stocks cheesemaking books, cheese cultures, and cheesemaking supplies, along with chicken, chicken eggs, and kombucha.

The cheese classes cover topics such as home dairying and how to make fresh mozzarella, cheddar, Gouda, and basic soft cheese. In the class I took, we made a few types of fresh goat cheese (including chèvre and ricotta), then we tasted more than twenty goat cheeses from around the world. Visit Kookoolan's website to sign up for classes and do so well in advance – many of their classes sell out early.

New Seasons Market

See page 79

Pastaworks

See page 93

Sheridan Fruit Company

See page 95

Urban Cheesecraft

🔗 www.urbancheesecraft.com

Since 2008 Claudia Lucero's Portland company, Urban Cheesecraft, has offered beginning cheesemaker kits for $30 and less. Lucero's kits give you the tools and ingredients you need to make everything from ricotta and mozzarella to paneer and queso fresco.

Lucero is committed to making cheesemaking accessible to others. She stresses that you don't have to have access to farmstead raw milk or a huge kitchen and cellar in order to make cheese – you can make it in an apartment kitchen with plain old store-bought milk.

Each Urban Cheesecraft kit makes up to ten batches of cheese and includes supplies such as instructional booklets, cheesecloth, dairy thermometers, and vegetable rennet. You can find Urban Cheesecraft cheese kits in town at the **Urban Farm Store** (☞ *p.* 187), **Alberta Cooperative Grocery** (☞ *p.* 62), **Food Front Cooperative Grocery** (☞ *p.* 62), **New Seasons Market** (☞ *p.* 79), **Foster & Dobbs Authentic Foods** (☞ *p.* 92), **Mirador Community Store** (☞ *p.* 166), **Montavilla Farmers Market** (☞ *p.* 172), and other locations. Check out the Urban Cheesecraft website for other cheesemaking supplies and kit refills, as well as information about Lucero's Portland cheese demonstrations and fresh cheese classes.

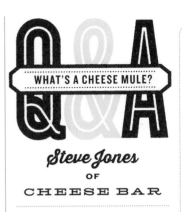

WHAT'S A CHEESE MULE?

Steve Jones
OF
CHEESE BAR

How would you describe Cheese Bar?
Cheese Bar is a cross between an old-world delicatessen and a *tabac*.

What's a *tabac*?
In France and Italy there are these places called *tabacs*, and they're on almost every corner. It's where old men come in the morning to buy their tobacco, and then they'll stand and have a glass of espresso and maybe a croissant. And then in the evening they'll come back and have a glass of grappa and a piece of cheese or something.

I've always really liked the social aspect of them. People coming in and out – and quite often they're in and out in twenty minutes. It's really the only fast option you have in Europe – everything else takes forever. So it's kind of cool you can get a little bite or boost and keep on moving. That's kind of been my intention with this. If people want to linger, they can, but Cheese Bar is more for when you're on your way home and you stop and have a glass of beer and a piece of cheese, or a glass of wine and a small bite.

CONTINUES ➧

38

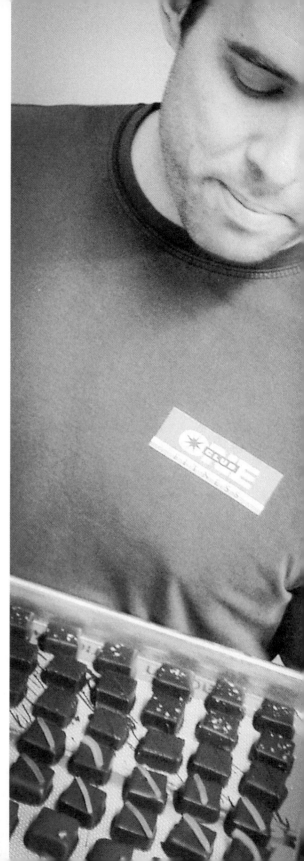

How do you store your cheese?

We store everything in paper, which makes a huge difference. I did an internship at Neal's Yard Dairy in London and my internship was in their cheese caves. That gave me a lot of tricks to keep cheese better longer. The good or bad news is we don't keep cheese around long enough here for it to be an issue anymore because we do so much wholesale now.

What's a cheese mule?

Shipping is a huge hurdle, so when someone is visiting a farm or someone from a farm is coming to Portland we bribe them into carrying cheese for us. We do a lot of that, actually. All of my producers know that if someone's coming to town they should give me a call; it's a guaranteed deal and we take care of the person who brings the cheese. We either give them cheese or bribe them with some other foodstuffs.

Which Portland restaurants purchase the most volume from Cheese Bar?

Beast, **DOC**, Le Pigeon, and Victory are the top four. But **Clyde Common** also buys quite a bit. **Belmont Station** also sells our cheese, which I love because it's one of my favorite places in town. **Leisure Public House** up in St. Johns also sells our cheese. That's what really makes me happy: all the small places, like **Victory** – the volume of cheese they go through in their bar just blows my mind.

PORTLAND IS OBSESSED WITH CHOCOLATE – all kinds of dipped, rolled, and formed deep, dark, single-origin, handcrafted goodness. There are the stalwarts such as **Moonstruck Chocolatier** (☞ *p.* 42), **JaCiva's Bakery and Chocolatier** (☞ *p.* 41), and **Van Duyn Chocolates** (☞ *p.* 44), but there's young cacao blood flowing through town as well. Several Portland chocolatiers and chocolate retailers have come into their own in the past several years, crafting such noteworthy chocolate creations as gold-gilded chocolate icons, caramelized honey–cacao bean brittle, single-origin drinking chocolate, 77% Costa Rican chocolate sorbet, and single-variety chocolate bars. Portland is also home to a few notable vegan chocolatiers who primarily through other vendors. Set forth boldly and embrace Portland's other bean: cacao.

Alma Chocolate

⊘ www.almachocolate.com
♥ 140 NE 28th Ave, Portland **✆** 503-517-0262
◷ M–Th 11am–6pm, F–Sa 11am–7pm, Su Noon–5pm

When Alma Chocolate owner Sarah Hart started making chocolates, she knew little more than what she'd read in a few books and learned from a class on tempering chocolate. Her daughter was set to graduate from high school, Hart was about to turn forty, and Alma Chocolate was kicking its dark chocolate baby feet. Hart began experimenting with chocolate molds and that's when her iconographic chocolates came to fruition – the organic dark chocolate icons of the Virgin Mary, Buddha, and Celtic crosses, all gilded in twenty-three-karat gold leaf, are what Hart's known for.

Early on Hart enlisted the help of former Western Culinary Institute teacher Ian Titteron, who privately taught her how to work with chocolate every Sunday for a year. At the end of the year Hart invited her friends to sample and order chocolates. She thought she might sell $500-worth, but instead she sold $5,000. For three weeks Hart worked around the clock filling orders. After two years of selling chocolates through friends' shops and at the downtown farmers market, Hart opened Alma Chocolate in 2006.

The shop is tiny, with only a small window bar and limited seating, but Hart uses every square inch to display handcrafted bonbons, barks, salted

chocolate caramels, and beautiful gilded chocolate icons. Hart's personal favorites include the Thai peanut butter cups and the Sabrina – a chocolate bonbon with marzipan and fig gelée. She also prefers South American chocolate to most African chocolate; she primarily uses chocolate from Venezuela and Ecuador. Alma serves **Spella Caffé's** (☞ *p.* 122) ristretto-style coffee and espresso, and in addition to chocolates, there are usually chocolaty cakes and cookies available.

Cacao

⌘ www.cacaodrinkchocolate.com
♥ 414 SW 13th Ave, Portland ☎ 503-241-0656
　🕐 M–Th 10am–8pm, F–Sa 10am–10pm, Su 11am–6pm
♥ 712 SW Salmon St, Portland ☎ 503-274-9510
　🕐 M–W 9am–6pm, Th–Sa 9am–8pm, Su 10am–6pm

Since 2006 Cacao has served Portland's chocolate needs by specializing in two things: hundreds of amazing bars sourced from around the world and very special drinking chocolates. The chilly original downtown shop (they keep the shop at about 66 degrees so the chocolate isn't compromised) is stocked with everything from truffles and chocolate confections to hot chocolate mixes and chocolaty sauces and syrups. It's most known, though, for its wide range of bars that include single-origin and rare-species cocoa bean bars from top local and international chocolate makers. Chocolatiers often featured at Cacao include Bonnat Chocolatier, Claudio Corallo Chocolates, Patric Chocolate, and Francois Pralus.

Yes, there are $22 chocolate bars on the shelves, but there are plenty of more affordable options as well. Owners Jesse Manis and Aubrey Lindley definitely favor small-batch artisan chocolates, and for these specialty chocolates you'll pay a price, but they also carry many big-name European chocolates, some of which are more reasonably priced. You can learn heaps about chocolate, as I have, at Cacao – regions, chocolate-making techniques, chocolate origins – or you can just order a drinking chocolate and flip through a magazine at the window bar.

Cacao's drinking chocolates incorporate excellent, high-cacao-content chocolate into cream and milk for a thick but creamy drink. Cacao also serves a highbrow version of American-style hot chocolate that is thinner and more mild. Both are made with solid chocolate as opposed to powder or syrup.

In 2008 the Cacao Annex location opened in the Heathman Hotel just a few blocks away. It's about a quarter of the size of the original shop and carries a smaller selection of bars and more packaged truffles and chocolates. Cacao also furnishes chocolates for the Heathman Hotel's turn-down service and VIP baskets.

DePaula Confections

⊘ www.depaulaconfections.com
♀ 6140 SW 41st Ave, Portland ☎ 503-892-2462

Although DePaula Confections doesn't have a storefront (you can visit the facility by appointment only), you can find its chocolates at various locations around Portland, including **Cacao** (☞ *opposite page*) and **The Meadow** (☞ *p.* 98), or you can purchase them online. DePaula's bite-size chocolates and confections include a Grand Marnier-infused dark chocolate, a chipotle chile dark chocolate, a raspberry eau-de-vie chocolate, and a lavender vanilla chocolate.

JaCiva's Bakery and Chocolatier

⊘ www.jacivas.com
♀ 4733 SE Hawthorne Ave, Portland ☎ 503-234-8115
    🕑 M–Th 7:30am–6pm, F–Sa 7:30am–10pm
♀ After Dark at same location 🕑 F–Sa 6pm–10pm

Since 1986 JaCiva's Bakery and Chocolatier has been crafting classic chocolates and baked goods. With all the new chocolate shops and bakeries in Portland, it's good to know that the old guard is still going strong.

JaCiva's space is threefold: the chocolate shop/bakery is in the center, flanked by a small, private "Wedding Room" for private events on one side and the twenty-seat dessert house **After Dark** on the other, which specializes in house chocolates, cakes, and tortes. In the shop, you'll find everything from a rotating cake case filled with colorfully decorated birthday cakes, cheesecakes, and cakes shaped like flower bouquets, to a large case of tortes, pastries, and coffee cakes.

Interestingly shaped chocolates are JaCiva's specialty – large white and milk chocolate chess sets, chocolate saws, wrenches, squirrels, cats, and more. JaCiva's obviously has many molds to work with, but if they don't have what you're after, they'll use any mold that you provide.

Lulu's Raw Chocolate Alchemy

⊘ www.luluschocolate.com

These all-organic, raw, four-ounce jarred vegan chocolate spreads made by Louise "Lulu" Sharpe blend fair trade Ecuadorian chocolate with ingredients such as agave nectar, rose oil, Celtic sea salt, and extra-virgin coconut oil. Some spots around town that retail Lulu chocolates include **Alberta Cooperative Grocery** (☞ *p.* 62), **Food Front Cooperative Grocery** (☞ *p.* 62), **People's Food Co-op** (☞ *p.* 63),

Alma Chocolate (☞ *p.* 33), **Proper Eats Market & Cafe** (☞ *p.* 106), **Simply Nourishing**, and **The Meadow** (☞ *p.* 98).

Missionary Chocolates

⌘ www.missionarychocolates.com
⚐ 2712 NE Glisan St, Portland ☎ 503.890.9721 🕐 Tu–F 11am–4pm, Su 12-5

Melissa Berry's gluten-free, vegan truffles incorporate local and often organic ingredients and can be found at many locations, including **Food Front Cooperative Grocery** (☞ *p.* 62), **Food Fight! Vegan Grocery** (☞ *p.* 100), and **Sheridan Fruit Company** (☞ *p.* 95). For a full listing of locations, or to order truffles online, visit the website.

Moonstruck Chocolate

⌘ www.moonstruckchocolate.com
⚐ 6600 N Baltimore Ave, Portland ☎ 503-247-3448
 🕐 Su–Th 8am–5pm
⚐ 608 SW Alder St, Portland ☎ 503-241-0955
 🕐 Su–Th 8am–6pm, Sa 10am–6pm, Su 10am–5pm
⚐ 700 SW Fifth Ave, Portland ☎ 503-219-9118
 🕐 M–Sa 10am–8pm, Su 11am–6pm
⚐ 526 NW 23rd Ave, Portland ☎ 503-542-3400
 🕐 M–Th 8am–10pm, F–Sa 8am–11pm, Su 9am–9pm
⚐ 45 S State St, Lake Oswego ☎ 503-697-7097
 🕐 Su–Th 9am–7pm, F–Sa 9am–8pm
⚐ 11705 SW Beaverton–Hillsdale Hwy, Beaverton ☎ 503-352-0835
 🕐 M–Sa 8am–10pm, Su 9am–9pm

I knew I needed to try Moonstruck Chocolate when writer Steve Almond (author of *Candy Freak* and several short story and essay collections) concluded a reading with a few choice words about a box of Moonstruck truffles. I thought that if

he was singing Moonstruck's praises, I should probably try it. I wasn't disappointed.

Since 1993 Moonstruck Chocolate has been crafting high-end, custom chocolates the old-school way. All Moonstruck truffles are made from specially blended chocolates, shaped, dipped, decorated, and wrapped by hand. In the summer of 2008, master chocolatier and chef Julian Rose transitioned Moonstruck's chocolates to be 100% natural, switching to natural food coloring and eliminating trans fats.

In Moonstruck's "chocolate lab," you might find a tray of tea-infused truffles (the bergamot-rich Earl Grey is perfect). In the winter, the lab might hold a few lace hearts made from finely spun, spaghetti-like chocolate, perfect for a Valentine's Day gift. Seasonal chocolates can be found in Moonstruck's five Portland chocolate cafés, along with the occasional towering chocolate sculpture that Chef Rose crafts and delivers himself. Unfortunately, those aren't for sale.

Sahagun Chocolate Shop

www.sahagunchocolates.com

Elizabeth Montes was a doll and puppet painter in New York City before she caravanned across the country to Portland nearly a decade ago and gave herself to chocolate. Truffle-making had been a hobby for years, and in 2001 Montes began handcrafting chocolates out of her apartment kitchen and vending them at the PSU Farmers Market. Several years later, she opened Sahagun Chocolate Shop. Although the retail shop is now closed, Sahagun continues to sell her tasty chocolates online.

Montes crafts beautiful handmade dark chocolate truffles, barks, and clusters, including pistachio-Meyer lemon bark, cardamom-infused dark truffles, and Calimyrna fig and Marcona almond chocolates. Although Montes does make milk chocolates she favors dark chocolate sourced from some of the world's top chocolate makers such as Michel Cluizel, Valhrona, and Chocovic.

Make sure to try Sahagun's luscious caramels. They're salty, buttery, and sweet all at once. And I do mean "all at once" – there's no nibbling or pulling apart with these. Pop the whole thing in your mouth and bite down so that the caramelized sugar, blended with cream but not thickened by corn syrup, washes over every last one of your taste buds in a rush of roasty, salty sweetness.

Stirs the Soul Chocolate

www.stirsthesoul.com

Daren Hayes's raw, organic chocolate bars and confections made with agave nectar are handcrafted in Southeast Portland from fair trade chocolate. Some Stirs the Soul Chocolate bars include goji berries in dark chocolate, orange ginger, cayenne cinnamon, and maca mesquite. Local purveyors of Stirs the Soul Chocolates include **New Seasons Market** (☞ *p.* 79), **Proper Eats Market & Cafe** (☞ *p.* 94), **People's Food Co-op** (☞ *p.* 63), and **Food Front Cooperative Grocery** (☞ *p.* 62).

Bees & Beans

⌗ *www.beesandbeans.com*
♥ No physical location, available directly online or in markets and cafes around Portland
☎ 503-869-4105.

After ten years in the culinary world of high-end restaurants and hotels, pastry chef Faith Dionne took four years off to build a family. During that time she tinkered with small caramel candies, gave them to friends and family, and ultimately launched Bees & Beans, founded in 2010.

Dionne's chocolate bars are inspired by place and season. There's the summery Mint Bar, with peppermint cream fondant, and the Berry Bar, inspired by berry picking on Sauvie Island. Look for limited releases such as the Sitka, Alaska bar with Alaskan sea salt and spruce tip caramel. You can purchase Bees & Beans bars at businesses such as **Pastaworks**, **Cheese Bar**, **Ruby Jewel**, **Food Front NW**, and **Whole Foods Market Fremont**. A full listing of retail locations can be found at the website.

Van Duyn Chocolates

⌗ *www.vanduyns.com*
♥ 3111 NW Industrial Ave, Portland ☎ 503-227-1927
🕘 M–F 9:30am–5:30pm, Sa 10am–4:30pm

This local chocolate company has been around since 1927, crafting all sorts of chocolate treats and truffles.

There are truffles, cordials, barks, brittles, and more to choose from in the shop or online. Van Duyn Chocolates often has bags and boxes of preselected and wrapped treats, making it a good place to grab a quick gift. The chocolates are generally straightforward with basic fillings. Van Duyn also makes sugar-free chocolates.

Woodblock

www.woodblockchocolate.com
No physical location, available directly online or in markets and cafes around Portland.

Woodblock owners Jessica and Charley Wheelock are not chocolatiers; they're bean-to-bar chocolate makers who travel to chocolate farms, roast with a machine made in 1905, and hand wrap their products. Burlap sacks of raw cacao beans fill their Southeast facility (not open to the public), where they temper, tinker and test. With limited ingredients Woodblock Chocolates are mind-bogglingly good. The focus is on the chocolate's natural flavor. Every bar is 70% chocolate with cane sugar and occasionally a dusting of salt or cacao nibs. The milk chocolate goat milk and cocoa butter bar is really good. You can find Woodblock Chocolates at **Cacao**, **Cheese Bar**, **Foster & Dobbs**, **The Meadow**, **Zupan's Markets**, and other markets, cafés, and bars around town.

Xocolatl de Davíd

www.xocolatldedavid.com
1406 SE Stark St, Portland

While working as a sous chef at Park Kitchen, David Briggs spent much of his free time teaching himself to make chocolates in his small apartment kitchen. When **Park Kitchen** owner Scott Dolich tasted his homemade truffles, he quickly made them the restaurant's check treat. Briggs launched Xocolatl de Davíd in 2006, and it is now his full-time gig. Briggs crafts handmade, rolled and dipped savory truffles and confections, chocolate bars and more. Two of his favorite ingredients are exotic sea salts (most of which he sources from **The Meadow** [☞ *p.* 98]) and the Basque pepper piment d'espelette. His chocolate caramel made with a Japanese sea salt that has been crystallized on seaweed is fantastic, as is the chocolate caramel made with a Welsh sea salt that has been smoked with wood from a seven-hundred-year-old oak tree.

Although Briggs switches up his chocolates from time to time, he's generally most fond of a 74% organic chocolate from the Dominican Republic, a 68% Bolivian chocolate, and a 72% Ecuadorian chocolate. Xocolatl de Davíd truffles, confections, and more can be found at various locations around town, such as **Meat Cheese Bread**, **The Meadow** (☞ *p.* 98), **Park Kitchen**, **Foster & Dobbs Authentic Foods** (☞ *p.* 92), **Cheese Bar** (☞ *p.* 33), **Cacao** (☞ *p.* 40), and **Townshend's Alberta Street Teahouse** (☞ *p.* 136).

AN ENTIRE BOOK could be devoted to Portland's many ethnic markets. I love discovering produce, spices, meats, and seafood at the wide array of ethnic markets that can be found in every Portland neighborhood. As a general rule, these markets are small, family-run establishments with diverse products. All of the markets included here specialize in food and drink, but that doesn't mean you won't find international calling cards, children's toys, herbs and herbal tonics, magazines, and movies from overseas as well. That's the joy of ethnic markets – you never know what you'll discover.

Willamette Week – Portland's local alternative weekly newspaper – prints **Market Guide**, an annual spring guide to Portland food and drink markets, and it typically features many ethnic markets. Grab a copy when it comes out; they do a great job covering every quadrant and getting out to some of the tasty and trek-worthy city limit spots. You can also access the guide online.

AFRICAN

Merkato

📍 2605 NE Martin Luther King Jr Blvd, Portland 📞 503-331-9283 🕐 M–Sa 9am–9pm

There are a lot of Ethiopian markets in Portland, but this one – just up the street from one of my favorite Portland Ethiopian restaurants, **Queen of Sheba** – has a really nice staff and a good selection of spices. For the most part, Merkato is a typical corner shop loaded with sodas and snacks, but next to the Pringles you'll also find black cumin, ajwain seeds, various flours, and legumes. You can purchase green Ethiopian coffee beans to roast at home as well as traditional clay Ethiopian coffee vessels. Merkato also sells injera, the spongy, slightly sour Ethiopian skillet bread, fresh by the bagful.

ASIAN

Anzen

📍 736 NE Martin Luther King Jr Blvd, Portland 📞 503-233-5111 🕐 M–Sa 9am–6:30pm, Su noon–5pm

One hundred–plus-year-old Anzen is an eclectic one-stop shop with everything from Asian movie rentals, kitchenwares, and medicinal herbs to books, home décor, and food and drink all packed in a small space across from the Oregon

JORINJI MISO

I first tried Earnest and the late Sumiko Migaki's Jorinji Miso after I discovered it in **Anzen's** (☞ *p. 46*) refrigerated section. I picked up a package and was sold the moment I saw the Portland, Oregon, address.

Earnest, who was born and raised in Portland, met Sumiko in Japan when he was teaching English there in the late 1980s. At their wedding a few years later, they gave their guests small containers of local red and white (fortunate colors in Japan) miso as gifts. After the wedding they visited the small factory in Sumiko's hometown that had produced the miso – and that visit changed everything. Two years later, after moving to Portland, Earnest and Sumiko decided to start making miso themselves.

Jorinji Miso is crafted in small batches with non-GMO soybeans (expensive and rare for commercial miso) and no added MSG. On average, Jorinji produces 100-plus pounds of miso a week – including white, red, dark red, and low-sodium varieties. Jorinji Miso takes anywhere from three months to three years to craft and can be found in many local Asian markets in addition to **New Seasons Market**, **City Market**, and local restaurants such as **Biwa** and **Saucebox**.

Although traditional miso is Jorinji's main product, they also make miso dressings, miso cookies, chickpea miso, and a delicious amaranth juice extract.

Convention Center. In the front of the shop you'll even find good-quality vegetable and herb seeds. Bonus: You can park in the adjacent lot on the north side of the building.

Diversity is key at Anzen. At the seafood counter toward the back of the store you'll find several types of wakame salads and pickled daikon mixed in with the sushi-grade seafood. There's also a great selection of miso – including local **Jorinji Miso** (*look to your left*) – fresh and frozen noodles, tofu, natto, matcha, and all sorts of spicy, salty, and sour condiments.

Unfortunately, Anzen's produce selection is on the light side, but you'll find fresh burdock root, lotus, radish sprouts, and more. For quick grab-and-go food, there's hom bao and shumai in the hot case in the back.

Fubonn Shopping Center

See page 83

H Mart

 www.hmart.com
📍 13600 SW Pacific Hwy, Tigard 📞 503-620-6120
🕐 9am–10pm every day

Ten miles south of Portland in Tigard is the enormous Korean H Mart with its fluorescent-lit, clean, well-stocked aisles of Asian food, drink, and more. The first thing you encounter at H Mart is the food court, with everything from frozen yogurt and smoothies to rice puffs, noodles, and sweet red bean waffles. In the deli you'll find huge dishes filled with loads of pickled and salted vegetables and seafood, including small salted clams and salted calamari. Go to the meat department for a large selection of thinly sliced beef and pork, and peruse the

*House-made ramen and other
Japanese noodles*

Biwa
- 215 SE 9th Ave, Portland
- 503-239-8830
- www.biwarestaurant.com

Ramen goodness

Boke Bowl
- 1028 SE Water Ave, Portland
- 503-719-5698
- www.bokebowl.com

Housemade spicy Asian noodles

Frank's Noodle House
- 822 NE Broadway, Portland
- 503-288-1007
- www.franksnoodlehouse.com

Addictive from-scratch daily soups

Ha & VI
- 2738 SE 82nd Ave, Portland
- 503-772-0103

Vietnamese classic

Pho Oregon
- 2518 NE 82nd Ave, Portland
- 503-262-8816

Classic Italian

Piazza Italia
- 1129 NW Johnson St, Portland
- 503-478-0619
- www.piazzaportland.com

All kinds of Asian noodles

Tanuki
- 8029 SE Stark St, Portland
- 503-477-6030
- www.tanukipdx.com

Traditional Italian

Taste Unique
- 2134 SE Division St, Portland
- 503-206-7059
- www.tasteunique.com

non-perishable aisles for Asian beer, condiments, dried noodles, and teas.

The produce department takes up the bulk of H Mart and includes interesting greens like dandelion greens and dropwort, along with a huge cooler stocked with unusual fresh herbs. If you need a five-pound bag of peeled garlic, you can get it here. H Mart's seafood department has lots of big and small dried fish, as well as live abalone, tilapia, lobster, and clams. There's also plenty of fresh and frozen whole and filleted fish, and a big sushi-grade section stocked with a rainbow of roe. All of H Mart's fresh fish is on ice and labeled as wild or farm-raised.

Uwajimaya

See page 86

Vieng Lao Oriental Market

- 1032 N Killingsworth St, Portland ☎ 503-285-7833
- M–Sa 10am–7pm, Su 10am–5pm

This is a good place to get your kimchi makings: napa cabbage, bok choy, daikon, ginger, and lotus root are all good here. The Vietnamese shop is small but packs in a lot. The entryway room is stocked with a nice variety of refrigerated and binned produce, big sacks of rice, and other shelved foods. The adjacent room is where you'll find bamboo and stainless Asian cookware and a few aisles of non-perishables like coconut milk, rice wine vinegar, and canned seafood and vegetables. There are also all kinds of frozen and refrigerated goods, mainly seafood, including boiled and shelled surf clams, live crab, and a variety of fish sauces and uncooked cassava.

The family that owns Vieng Lao is very friendly, the prices are fair, and the care taken with the produce is notable. Everything in the case, including the greens and herbs, is always good looking and fresh.

EUROPEAN & EASTERN EUROPEAN

Good Neighbor European Deli Market

📍 4107 SE 82nd Ave, Portland 📞 503-771-5171 🕐 M–Sa 10am–9pm, Su 11am–7pm

This mostly Russian market across the street from Century 16 Eastport Plaza movie theater and near Domino's Pizza doesn't share much in common with its big-chain neighbors. Step inside and you'll hear very little English in this beacon of Eastern European food and culture.

The bread section, which skirts the entrance, is filled with all sorts of unusual international breads such as Tabrizi Barbari, Riga, and dark Borodinsky rye. You can also get Good Neighbor house-baked bread behind the counter.

There are usually samples by the deli counter, which holds everything from cured meats, sausages, and cheese (lots of cultured milk products such as kefir and soft farmers cheeses) to whole dried fish, loads of different caviars, and a wide array of pickled fruits, vegetables, and nuts.

Other items to choose from at Good Neighbor include imported cookies and sweets; canned meat and fish (there are usually a couple of canned mystery meats and fishes in Kerr jars on the shelves); sweet and sour spreads such as young walnut jam, sour cherry jam, and plum butter.

Toward the back of Good Neighbor, there's an entire case devoted to pelmenis – Siberian meat-filled dumplings that are popular throughout Russia. Scoop up Good Neighbor's mild and tasty house-made pickles – they're sold by the pound from large buckets.

INDIAN

Fiji Emporium

🔗 *www.fijiemporium.com*
📍 7814 N Interstate Ave, Portland 📞 503-240-2768 🕐 Tu–Sa 11am–7pm

Since 1994 this small North Portland Indian shop has been a source for everything from halal goat and lamb, jarred ghee, coconut oil, and chutneys to fresh taro, coconut, and long beans. Although there are some Indian movies, music, incense, henna design books, and housewares, most of Fiji Emporium's shelf space is dedicated to food and drink.

In the back are two chest freezers packed with halal goat and lamb chops, steaks, and sausages, as well as big bags of peeled garlic, curry leaves, and frozen palm nuts. There's also a stand-up freezer filled with muscovy duck, pigeons, green shell mussels, and more.

Fiji Emporium carries loads of spices (green cardamom, ajwain, and mace) as well as big sacks of pulses and grains (black lentils, split pigeon, moth bean, and split mung bean), but you can also stock up on frozen naan and samosas, bag-and-boil curries, and ready-to-cook pappadam. And if you're looking for those colorful candied fennel seeds often used as an after-dinner treat at Indian restaurants, look no further: they've got them by the bagful here.

LATINO/MEXICAN by **NICK ZUKIN**, *owner of Mi Mero Molé*

"Where can I buy fresh tortillas?" "Who makes good tres leches?" As the owner of a taqueria and a food blogger, I hear questions like these every day. People are shocked when I start listing off Mexican markets within walking distance from their homes or when I name a dozen or more places making carnitas daily and selling the pork confit by the pound. But people shouldn't be surprised. Portland has a flourishing Latino community with a long history in Oregon.

Mexicans have been coming to the Pacific Northwest since the time of the Spanish explorers, but it was the bracero program during World War II that started a steady migration of Hispanics looking for work in the state. Woodburn, where the *Fiesta Mexicana* has been celebrated every summer for over fifty years, is only thirty miles from Portland and has a population nearing 60% Latino. Closer to Portland, Hillsboro and Gresham each are about 20% Hispanic compared to Portland, which is 10%. Portland may be the whitest major city in the U.S., but Latinos make up Portland's largest minority and with only a little effort, there is great Mexican, Salvadoran, Peruvian, Cuban, and other Latin American foods to be enjoyed.

For those looking to make Hispanic foods at home, here is a list of the best Latino markets in the Portland area.

El Campesino Fruteria

📍 17871 SW Tualatin Valley Hwy, Beaverton 📞 503-601-6006 🕐 7am–10pm every day

At last count, this tienda focusing on fruits, spices, and chiles, had at least six different kinds of bananas of all shapes and sizes and five different roasted squash seeds. El Campesino would be a destination just for the fact that it's one of the only places in PDX to find costeños, the dried Oaxaca chile integral to mole amarillo. The owner's brother has opened a Campesino on SE Powell Boulevard that makes fresh tortillas and has a respectable butcher's counter. *What they're best for*: large produce selection, fresh squash blossoms in season, young coconuts, maguey leaves, red and green pickly pear fruits, large dried chile selection, costeños, chia, mango with chamoy, salted plum, housepickled pig ears, tepache soda.

Don Pancho

📍 2000 NE Alberta St, Portland
📞 503-282-1892 🕐 8:30am–9pm every day

Most of the tiendas not on the outskirts or suburbs of Portland are small with little food that doesn't come in a can. Don Pancho is an exception. While most supermarkets in Portland carry a solid selection of Hispanic basics, Don Pancho is a close-in destination for specialty items and meats. *What they're best for*: small selection but good quality produce, good quality dried chiles, nice carniceria, carnitas, housemade lard, marinated meats, canned squash blossoms and huitlacoche, black and red Yucatecan recados, taqueria.

Lents International Farmers Market

🔗 *www.lentsfarmersmarket.org*
📍 Crossroads Plaza, SE 92nd Ave and Foster Rd, Portland 🕐 Mid–June–mid–Oct Su 9am–2pm

One of Portland's several great smaller farmers markets with a more international focus. One of their best vendors, N&N Amaro Produce, is also the supplier of rare herbs like papalo, hoja santa, and pipiche for many of the other markets listed here. Of course they sell more typical Mexican produce like chiles, cal-

---

NICK ZUKIN

OF **MI MERO MOLE**,
CO-AUTHOR OF
**THE ARTISAN JEWISH
DELI AT HOME**

Known for: Being the first person with a dedicated food blog in Portland (Extramsg.com) and later PortlandFood.org, writing about Portland's restaurants and markets, including exhaustive surveys of ethnic and humble dishes.

Previous job: Web developer.

Most in-depth food reporting: He rated more than 50 taco trucks in the Portland area and ate more than 70 burgers in less than three months to count down the top 10 for alt-weekly *Willamette Week*.

First food love and why: Mexican food. He grew up in Oregon with a father from California and a mother from Arizona, so enchiladas, chile rellenos, shredded beef tacos, fajitas, chili con carne, and more were his local, family foods.

His Southeast Portland restaurant that specializes in Mexico City street food: Mi Mero Mole.

First restaurant that he opened and still co-owns: Kenny & Zuke's, a Jewish Delicatessen.

Kenny & Zuke's led to his first co-authored cookbook: *The Artisan Jewish Deli at Home.*

His current top five local taco trucks are: Los Alambres, Antojitos Yucatecos, La Flor de Guelaguetza, Ely's, and El Nutri.

abaza, and tomatillos. They can be found at the Forest Grove Farmers Market on Wednesdays, as well. Several other vendors, including the community table, offer Hispanic produce. Sisters Tamales offers excellent tamales and aguas frescas.

San Francisco Tienda Mexicana
📍 17112 SE Powell Blvd, Portland ☎ 503-512-7738 🕐 8am–10pm every day

For a long time, San Francisco Tienda was one of Salem's best markets with an excellent taqueria in the back. When they moved to Portland, they became one of only two markets soaking and grinding corn to make tortillas. They also have locations in Wilsonville and Beaverton. *What they're best for*: fresh masa, blue and white corn tortillas made with natural masa, blue and white corn tlayudas, large tortilla presses, pan dulce baked in house, good carniceria, marinated quail and game hens, barbacoa, pickled pig ears, ceviches, jarred squash blossoms.

Super Mercado Mexico
📍 970 SE Oak St, Hillsboro ☎ 503-352-4200 🕐 7am–9:30pm every day

When Grande Foods closed in Cornelius, Super Mercado Mexico became the best Hispanic market in Washington County. If they made their own masa, they might be the best in PDX. As it is, they'll just have to settle for having a fantastic meat counter and produce aisle. *What they're best for*: excellent produce selection, papalo in season, hoja santa in season, pipiche in season, fresh garbanzos, pan dulce baked in house, excellent carniceria with huge selection of meats, marinated steaks, rotisserie chickens, ribs, mojarra fritas, offal carnitas, housemade lard, salsas, bulk cremas, quince paste, guava paste, one of few places to find quality canned squash blossoms and jarred huitlacoche, taqueria.

La Tapatia Supermercado
📍 18330 SE Stark St, Portland ☎ 503-491-1848 🕐 8am–10pm every day

Easily the best Hispanic supermarket east of the West Hills, with a huge selection of fresh and dry goods – and prices often below WinCo or Walmart for better quality. One of only two markets to soak and grind their own corn for tortillas. Bonus: Thursdays through Sundays the Mexican bazaar called the "Oregon Flea Market" opens up next door. *What they're best for*: fresh masa, corn tortillas made with in house masa, very good and inexpensive produce selection, pan dulce baked in house, very good carniceria, marinated steaks, excellent chorizo, moronga, carne seca, carnitas, pollos asados grilled over coals out front, housemade lard, taqueria specializing in guisados.

||||||||||||||||||||||||||||||||||||||||||||||||||||||||||||||||||||||||||||||||||||||||||||||||||||||

MIDDLE EASTERN

Barbur World Foods

www.barburworldfoods.com
9845 SW Barbur Blvd, Portland · 503-244-0670 · 7am–10pm every day

Any time I'm out on Barbur Boulevard, I make a pit stop at this family-owned-and-run European and Middle Eastern grocery store that's about fifteen minutes from downtown Portland. It's a great place for staple shopping as well as for food gifts and hard to find imports. The pickle, olive, and condiment aisle is one of my favorite parts of Barbur World; other standouts include the halva, feta, olive oil, and imported beer selections. You can get your staple shopping done – produce, meat, dairy etc. – while ordering food to go at the deli (shawarma, falafel, house-baked pita, kabobs, Lebanese pizzas) and picking up supplies for stuffed grape leaves and Turkish coffee.

Halal Meat and Mediterranean Food

11535 SW Pacific Hwy, Tigard · 503-293-3020 · 10:30am–8pm every day

Right after the "Welcome to Tigard" sign on Southwest Pacific Highway, and just before the big Fred Meyer, is Halal Meat and Mediterranean Food. Although the specialty is, of course, halal meat – meats butchered according to Muslim customs, in many ways the Islamic counterpart to kosher – there are also kitchen and home supplies, spices, bread, coffee, tea, and even some clothing. Most of the meat at Halal Meat is cut to order, and there's an abundance of goat and lamb. This is a good place to find offal, such as heart and tongue. Because it's a halal market, you won't find pork, the meat of any carnivorous animals, or alcohol.

International Food Supply

www.internationalfoodsupply.com
8015 SE Stark St, Portland · 503-256-9576 · M–Sa 10am–8pm

I love walking through International Food Supply while waiting for a table at the nearby Lebanese restaurant **Ya Hala** (owned by the same family that owns International Food Supply). There's a small produce section and dairy section, but most of the shop is filled with non-perishables such as olive oils, preserves, canned beans, olives, and grains. I like to get my cured grape leaves here along with all the fillings.

FOOD CARTS ARE BIG IN PORTLAND. Unlike in Manhattan, where you'll find carts peppered around the city on the wide sidewalks, Portland's five hundred–plus are mostly concentrated in several areas around town. These dense food cart areas are generally referred to as "pods" or "rows." The biggest are downtown, but you'll find plenty of food carts on the Eastside as well. In recent years, the food cart scene has exploded. Production companies pass through town to film the vibrant carts, and major national and international publications cover the low-cost-of-entry cart culture.

There are so many food carts in Portland that it would be impossible to chronicle them all here, which is why I've enlisted the help of food cart expert **Brett Burmeister** of the popular website *Food Carts Portland*. In this chapter Brett reviews Portland's major pods and rows and recommends some of his favorites.

Portland has defined itself as a street food capital in the U.S. The city's unique food cart culture got its start the mid-'80s when carts started parking downtown in lots and now there are six large lots (a.k.a. pods) downtown boasting two hundred-plus vendors. On the eastside, there are twenty more lots with an additional two hundred-plus vendors. Thai, BBQ, Portuguese, Swedish, Guamanian – you name it, Portland food carts have it. Portland is so food cart crazy it hosts two annual food cart festivals, including *Willamette Week*'s **Eat Mobile**, which always attracts a huge crowd. It would be impossible to list and review all of Portland's food carts, but I've highlighted some of my favorite pods, carts, and vendors here.

Things to know about Portland food carts:

- Downtown carts are normally open Monday through Saturday, 11am–3pm; Sundays in the Summer.
- Eastside carts are normally open Tuesday through Sunday, 12pm–6pm, so there are more dinner options.
- Portland food carts usually take both cash and credit cards, but be prepared with cash just in case.
- Winter is challenging for food cart vendors, so be sure to call ahead or check their websites for current hours.

SW 9th Ave/10th Ave and Alder St Pod (Downtown Library)

With sixty vendors, this pod, located right on the downtown streetcar line, has the largest single concentration of food carts in the U.S. The food carts here surround an entire city block and then some. Notable vendors and foods here include

The People's Pig, Korean from **#1 Bento, Savor Soup House**, Thai street food from **Nong's Khao Man Gai**, fish and chips from **The Frying Scotsman**, veggie rice and bean bowls from **The Whole Bowl**, and Carolina barbecue from **A Little Bit of Smoke**.

Food Innovation Center

– *fic.oregonstate.edu*
– 1207 NW Naito Pkwy, Suite 154, Portland – 503-872-6680

A lot of Portland food entrepreneurs, including plenty of food cart vendors, have the Food Innovation Center (FIC) to thank. FIC is a joint venture between Oregon State University and the Oregon Department of Agriculture that employs professional chefs, food scientists, food processors, a marketing team, and other specialists to work toward the mission of "advancing Northwest foods."

SW 5th Ave and Stark St/Oak St Row (Business District)

This is the lot that started it all. Vendors here such as **Tabor** (Czech food) and **Real Taste of India** have been feeding Portland office workers a mix of Mexican, Thai, Vietnamese, pizza, Mediterranean, and more for more than ten years. On a cool rainy day, walk to the 2nd floor of the U.S. Bank Tower on SW 5th and Oak for seating.

SW 3rd Ave and Washington St/Stark St Row (Business District)

An oldie but goodie, this lot has been anchored by **Tito's Burritos** on the south end and **Francisco Taqueria** on the north end for years. Want to try some Egyptian? **El Masry** is open twenty-four hours a day serving up light and fluffy falafel. All dishes at **Salmon Fusion** come with smoked salmon. Many vendors in this lot re-open late on the weekends to serve the bar crowd.

SW Corner of N Mississippi Ave and Skidmore St Pod (Mississippi Marketplace)

This lot – one of Portland's prettiest and most comfortable – hosts twelve vendors with plenty of tented seating for patrons. Onsite pub **Prost!** serves up steins of your favorite German beer and you can even bring the cart food inside. Notable vendors include southern cooking from **Miss Kate's Southern Kitchen**, vegan bowls from **Native Bowl**, Korean fusion from **Koi Fusion**.

SE 82nd Ave and Harney St Pod (Cartlandia)

Cartlandia is the largest pod on the Eastside, located right along the Springwater Corridor, with nearly twenty vendors selling everything from traditional Amer-

OTHER NOTABLE **FOOD CARTS** AROUND TOWN

Handmade breakfast sandwiches & wraps
The Big Egg
♦ 4233 N Mississippi Ave, Portland
✐ www.thebigegg.com

Grilled cheese in an old school bus
The Grilled Cheese Grill
♦ 1027 NE Alberta Ave, Portland
♦ 113 SE 28th Ave, Portland
♦ SW 10th & Alder/Washington,
   Portland
☎ 503-206-8959
✐ www.grilledcheesegrill.com

Deep fried anchovies or foie gras on chips
EuroTrash
♦ 998 SW Washington St, Portland
☎ 253-861-6733
✐ www.eurotrashcart.com

Handcrafted pies and baked goods
The Honey Pot
♦ 4290 SE Belmont St, Portland
♦ 4220 N Mississippi Ave, Portland
☎ 503-729-4099
✐ www.thehoneypotbakery.com

To be told what you will eat for breakfast
Yolk
♦ SE 4804 SE Woodstock Blvd,
   Portland
☎ 503-568-0787
✐ www.facebook.com/yolkpdx

Grilled pizza with your favorite toppings
Pulehu Pizza
♦ 432 SW 3rd Ave, Portland
☎ 503-915-6869
✐ www.pulehupizza.com

Guamian cuisine
PDX671
♦ 5221 NE Sandy Blvd, Portland
☎ 971-570-0945
✐ www.pdx671.com

Panuchos, aka Yucatan-style tacos
El Taco Yucateco
♦ 1930 NE Everett St, Portland
☎ 503-544-0659
✐ www.facebook.com/pages/
   El-Taco-Yucateco

ican and Thai to Hawaiian shaved ice. It's also the first food cart lot to have a beer garden. Notable vendors and foods here include pasties from **London Pasty Company**, **Traditional Russian Cuisine**, **Kesone Asian Fusion**, Salvadoran pupusas from **Pupuseria la Miguelena**, and Philly cheesesteaks from **Cheesesteak Nirvana**.

SE 2nd Ave and Oak St Pod (The Row)

The Row was designed and is managed by food cart owners and it's often referred to as "The Superpod" due to the quality of vendors who call it home. Wood-fired pizza from **Pyro Pizza**, Belgian fries and poutine from **Potato Champion**, handcrafted gourmet burgers from **Burgatroyd**, roast beef and french fry sandwiches from **Big-Ass Sandwiches**, Greek food from **Nikki & Lefty's**. The Row regularly hosts open-to-the-public themed family dinners where all the cart vendors create dishes.

SE 12th Ave and Hawthorne Blvd Pod (Cartopia/Late Night)

Imagine a hot summer night around midnight, a ton of bikes stacked and leaned against each other, a small boombox playing some tunes, people eating fried pies and poutine. Cartopia is Portland's only late-night pod open till 4am with wood-fired pizza, fried pies from **Whiffies**, crêpes from **Perierra Crêperie**, Belgian fries from **Potato Champion**, and more. Bonus if you ride your bike, because there is very little parking in the area.

WOULD LARRY DAVID of *Curb Your Enthusiasm* dub you a "sample abuser" – the person at an ice cream shop who samples a little of this, that, and the other before ordering a simple scoop of vanilla? If so, this chapter should help you zero in on and start spooning up some of Portland's best cold stuff. From gelato and sorbetto to ice cream and frozen yogurt, this town's packed with all kinds of mouth-numbing, brain-freezing sweets, and most of it is made in house in small batches, often from local fruits, nuts, and dairy.

FROZEN YOGURT

Fifty Licks

www.fifty-licks.com

♀ *Truck*: 4262 SE Belmont St, Portland

♀ *Shop*: 2021 SE Clinton St, Portland ☎ 954-294-8868 🕐 Su–Th 3–10pm; F–Sa Noon–11pm

Chad Draizian began selling ice cream out of his pool-blue, red-lettered food truck made with a Carpigiani Italian ice cream machine. Owner and ice cream maker Draizian's passion for the science behind ice cream might is part of what make his flavors, such as pineapple jalapeño and single malt scotch, so good. In addition to scoops, the shop has a vintage waffle maker, and fancy-pants waffle toppings include candied rosemary and orange peel, along with jimmies.

Ruby Jewel

www.rubyjewel.net

♀ 3713 N Mississippi Ave, Portland ☎ 503-505-9314 🕐 Noon-10pm every day

♀ 428 SW 12th Ave, Portland ☎ 971-271-8895 🕐 Noon-10pm every day

Lisa Herlinger debuted her delicious, all natural ice cream treats at the downtown **PSU Farmers Market** in 2004. After garnering a loyal customer base she's since opened two stores – one in North Portland and one downtown. Herlinger's mostly locally sourced ingredients come together in tasty flavors such as Oregon strawberry and honey lavender. The ice cream is good, but the cookie + ice cream sandwiches are where it's at. When you walk by either of the Ruby Jewel shops, the smell of fresh waffles, cookies, and ice cream is overwhelming. Ruby Jewel also offers vegan options, signature sundaes, and special flavors for each store and season, including brown sugar sour cream and ginger cookie with pumpkin.

Skinnidip

♀ 2230 W Burnside St, Portland ☎ 503-222-5230
  🕘 Su–Th noon-10pm, F–Sa noon-11pm
♀ 433 NW 10th Ave, Portland ☎ 503-224-0704
  🕘 M–Th 11am–9pm, F–S 11am–10pm, Su noon–8pm

Skinnidip has a little something for everyone. Topping options for the four flavors of frozen yogurt are honey, lychee, and granola, as well as Cap'n Crunch, tiny marshmallows, and chocolate chips. Get a cup of the fruity fro-yo – the strawberry's great – topped with tiny marshmallows, and you can channel Saturday morning cartoons through your tiny plastic shovel spoon. The fun, colorful space with big paper hanging lamps and loud pop music is next door to a gas station and convenience store. Don't park in their lot or you'll get towed.

What's the Scoop?

🔗 www.whatsthescoopdx.com
♀ 3540 N Williams Ave, Portland ☎ 971-266-1787 🕘 Su–Th noon-10pm, F–Sa noon-11pm

This little North Portland scoop shop uses liquid nitrogen to freeze their ice cream, which results in fewer ice crystals and a smooth consistency. The Ostrovskys make just about everything from scratch and source ingredients as locally as possible. They're also thoughtful enough to put a chocolate chip in the bottom of your waffle cone to prevent leaking. When it comes to flavors you'll find everything from spiced chocolate tequila and peanut butter curry to straight-up mint and vanilla. If you like booze in your ice cream, try the yummy Tennessee Honey made with Jack Daniels and homemade honeycomb candy. And if you have a hard time deciding you can always go for the sampler – four flavors and four toppings for six bucks.

GELATO

Alotto Gelato

🔗 www.alottogelato.biz
♀ 931 NW 23rd Ave, Portland ☎ 503-228-1709 🕘 Su–Th noon-10pm, F–Sa noon-11pm

Although I'm frightened by the large, severe-looking metal pig sculptures out front (don't let sugar-high children near those dagger-sharp ears), Alotto Gelato is harmless. This small, family-run gelato/sorbetto shop does cold stuff right, with lots of super-fresh local ingredients, including its whole milk and cream. On any given day you might find peanut butter chocolate chip, cinnamon, strawberry, rose petal, and Madagascar vanilla among the fourteen flavors in the case. The yellow cake with chocolate icing gelato is better than most real cakes. There's also **Tazo Tea** and **Stumptown Coffee** and espresso.

Staccato Gelato

⚭ www.staccatogelato.com
♥ 232 NE 28th Ave, Portland ☎ 503-231-7100
🕐 M–Th noon-10, Sa 8am–11pm, Su 8am–9pm

This fun and colorful gelateria serves up house-made gelato, Ristretto Roasters coffee, and house-made doughnuts Friday through Sunday. The eighteen rotating flavors of gelato are made with hormone-free milk and cream. On any given day, you'll find flavors that include passion fruit, strawberry rhubarb, cantaloupe, prickly pear, Girl Scout Thin Mint, and more. There's also a kids' area and outdoor seating.

Via Delizia

⚭ www.viadelizia.com
♥ 1105 NW Marshall St, Portland ☎ 503-225-9300
🕐 M–Th 7:30am–9pm, F–Sa 7:30am–10pm,
   Su 8am–8pm

This Pearl District Italian dessert house and café is open for breakfast, lunch, dinner, and dessert seven days a week. The menu is loaded with all sorts of sweet and savory Italian treats, but the real reason to come here is for the dessert and gelato. The twenty-four rotating house gelato flavors include vanilla bean, coconut, lychee banana, coffee, lavender, and caramel. Other Via Delizia desserts to choose from include tiramisu, chocolate fondue, mixed berry crêpes, roasted peaches with mascarpone and rum chantilly cream, and all sorts of cakes, pies, and cupcakes.

Nostalgic candy, globetrotting treats and freshly spun vegan cotton candy
Candy Babel
♥ 1237 NE Alberta St, Portland
☎ 503-867-0591
⚭ www.candybabel.com

School bus with classic American candies
Chalk-let Candy
♥ 3267 SE Hawthorne Blvd, Portland
☎ 503-539-2253
⚭ www.chalk-letbus.com

Milkshakes, soda fountain, and loads of bottled pop
Cosmic Soda Pop and Candy Shop
♥ 817 SE 34th Ave, Portland
☎ 503-894-8980
⚭ www.cosmicsodacandy.com

Cute, classic neighborhood candy shop
Hattie's Sweet Shop
♥ 4185 NE Fremont St, Portland
☎ 503-477-0497
⚭ www.hattiessweets.com

Housemade sweets and retro candies
Northwest Sweets
♥ 740 NW 23rd Ave, Portland
☎ 503-360-1350

Fun downtown candy/soda shop for all ages
Rocket Fizz
♥ 535 SW 6th Ave, Portland
☎ 503-222-0711
⚭ www.rocketfizz.com

Wall of licorice, fudge, and local Umpqua ice cream
Sweets Etc.
♥ 7828 SW Capitol Hwy, Portland
☎ 503-293-0088
⚭ www.sweetsetc.com

High quality homemade candies in a pint-sized shop
Quin Candy
♥ 1022 W Burnside St, Portland
☎ 971-300-8395
⚭ www.quincandy.com

‖‖‖

ICE CREAM

Blueplate Lunch Counter and Soda Fountain

🔗 *www.eatatblueplate.com*
📍 308 SW Washington St, Portland ☎ 503-295-2583
🕐 M–Th 11am–5pm, F 11am–9pm, Sa 5pm–9pm

If you're after ice cream sodas, egg cream sodas, floats, three-scoop shakes, and sundaes, Blueplate has all of these soda fountain classics and more, all made with Cascade Glacier ice cream. This small lunch counter located in the heart of downtown does American classics right. Sit at the counter or at a table for frozen treats like the Purple Haze – a float or soda made with hibiscus, allspice, and star anise. If you want more than ice cream, there's also classic savory fare such as a roast beef dip, grilled cheese, tomato soup, and a meatloaf sandwich.

Cool Moon Ice Cream

🔗 *www.coolmoonicecream.com*
📍 1105 NW Johnson St, Portland ☎ 503-224-2021 🕐 Su–Th noon-10pm, F–Sa noon-10:30pm

Located just across the street from Jamison Square park, this ice cream shop is every kid's dream: shakes, floats, sundaes, house-made chocolate-dipped frozen bananas, and sweet and golden Belgian waffles. Cool Moon Ice Cream doesn't whip much air into its ice cream, so its cherry almond chip, peaches and cream, lavender honey, and marionberry are all rich and creamy.

If you feel like splurging, order the Real McCall: a ten-scoop ice cream bomb covered in five different sauces, perfect for a pack of kids. Post-brain freeze, lead the pack across the street to run off their sugar highs in the Jamison Square fountain.

You can also buy any Cool Moon Ice Cream in pints to go. Stop by for the daily happy hour from 4–6pm and buy discounted pints. Some other cool Cool Moon stuff: waffle bowls, chocolate-dipped ice cream cones, and orchids and carnivorous plants in the windows.

Salt & Straw

🔗 *www.saltandstraw.com*
📍 2035 NE Alberta St, Portland ☎ 503-208-3867 🕐 11am–11pm every day
📍 838 NW 23rd Ave, Portland ☎ 971-271-8168 🕐 7am–11pm every day

When this gourmet scoop shop opened its first NE Alberta location in 2011 it hit Portland hard (and garnered loads of national media attention from the likes of

Oprah and The *Wall Street Journal*) with immediate lines around the block. In the summer of 2012 I got to hide behind a sound guy and crouch between storage racks at the second-to-open Northwest scoop shop and bakery as Andrew Zimmern of the Travel Channel show *Bizarre Foods* made bone marrow with smoked bing cherries ice cream with Salt & Straw co-owner Tyler Malek for the Portland Bizarre Foods episode. This is the kind of flavor profile that Salt & Straw specializes in – bizarre. Other ice creams regularly available at both shops include arbequina olive oil, honey balsamic strawberry with cracked pepper, coffee and bourbon and pear with blue cheese.

Pix Patisserie

See page 27

Roses Homemade Ice Cream

www.rosesicecream.com
5011 NE 42nd Ave, Portland 503-256-3333 Su noon–9pm, Tu–Sa 11am–9pm

It doesn't get more old-school than Roses Homemade Ice Cream. The thirty-plus house-made ice creams are 14% butterfat, meaning that they're creamier than most commercial ice creams, which usually ring in at 10 to 12% butterfat.

The extra-rich chocolate peanut malted milkshake is so thick and tasty, you'll hardly be able to breathe as you suck it down. Other ice cream flavors include lemon custard, cherry cheesecake, Butterfinger, and birthday cake, and you can order any of the ice creams blended into a milkshake or malted milkshake. You'll most likely hear the sound of one of the several milkshake mixers whirring the moment you step through the door.

Roses also offers ice cream sandwiches, sodas, floats, sundaes, and splits. There are coloring sheets for kids on the counter, booths and tables often filled with older folks who knew Roses way back when, and a big menu filled with classic sandwiches, burgers, and fried baskets loaded with chicken strips, popcorn shrimp, and more.

Tonalli's Doughnuts & Cream

See page 29

PORTLAND COOPERATIVES are an excellent resource for local, farm-fresh foods, culinary education, and community building – plus they're a great place to discover new and often unusual food and drink.

Grocery cooperatives are member-owned and/or democratically run stores that often carry a good selection of natural and local foods. Although most grocery cooperatives require either a membership fee, a certain volunteering commitment, or both from owners and members (who, as a result, have a stake in the business and get in-store discounts), it's not necessary to be a member to shop at them. I've never been a grocery cooperative member, but I still frequent all three of Portland's excellent grocery co-ops because I love the selection.

Alberta Cooperative Grocery

www.albertagrocery.coop
📍 1500 NE Alberta St, Portland 📞 503-287-4333 🕐 9am–10pm every day

Portland's pint-size Alberta Cooperative Grocery packs a lot in. The entryway community board is a great place to tune in to local, sustainable goings-on. I always find out about an intriguing screening, lecture, potluck, or class when I scan it. There are also always suggestion cards push-pinned to the board with responses from co-op owners and managers to requests such as, "I want plantains," or "Please order Soy Vay marinades."

Alberta's bulk section is impressive, with local honeys, raw and light agave syrups, teas, herbs, spices, grains, solar-dried salt, Celtic sea salt, dried persimmons, and more. There's bulk miso and unpackaged tofu in a big tray of water in the fridge near the produce. The produce rinse station is on the floor out front (rather than behind closed doors) and vegetables and fruit are displayed in terracotta dishes and woven baskets. The wine section near the registers is detailed, with typed cards and information about vegan, sulfite-free, organic, and local wines.

Food Front Cooperative Grocery

www.foodfront.coop
📍 2375 NW Thurman St, Portland 📞 503-222-5658 🕐 8am–9pm every day
📍 6344 SW Capitol Hwy, Portland 📞 503-546-6559 🕐 8am–9pm every day

Founded in the early 1970s, Food Front Cooperative Grocery is the largest food co-op in Portland. Since 2008 the co-op has been two-fold with its newest outpost in Hillsdale. Both locations are member-owned and successful, with plenty of charitable community action.

In addition to a wonderful produce department, Food Front has a large deli, a diverse wine and beer selection, a nice meat and seafood selection, bread from several local bakeries, home and body products, and a large snack aisle. To give you an idea of the variety available at Food Front, there are more than ten brands of soy, rice, and nut milks to choose from. Food Front also carries garden supplies such as seed packets, potting soil, and compost.

People's Food Co-op

⊗ *www.peoples.coop*

♥ 3029 SE 21st Ave, Portland ☎ 503-674-2642 ● 8am–10pm every day

People's Food Co-op favors local, farm-direct foods and promises that if it's not local, it's at least organic. It's usually both at People's year round farmers market, which is set up out front every Wednesday from 2 to 7pm, where you can purchase food directly from local farmers.

In the fall and winter, People's carries hard-to-find squashes like kabocha, fruits such as cherimoya, and plenty of microgreens such as sprouted wheatgrass and sprouted sunflower seeds. Year round, the dry bulk section at People's is stocked with dried seaweeds, nuts, teas, spices, and dehydrated fruits. In liquid bulk, you'll find raw, unpasteurized local cider, raspberry honey, and Arbequina olive oil. People's also has a decent selection of mostly local, organic beer, wine, cider, and mead.

Look up, down, and around and you'll find all kinds of member-written tasting notes and information on sprouting grains, grinding your own nut butters (People's has a peanut and almond grinder in house), and more. If a question isn't answered, head over to the reference area stocked with culinary, herbal, and food preservation books. People's is a true green machine, incorporating everything from member-mixed and -built cob (a sustainable building material composed of sand, clay, and straw), a green roof, and a solar chimney, to rain gardens that reduce stormwater runoff.

PORTLANDERS ARE PRIVY TO ALL SORTS of interesting meats: house-made sausage and cured meats of old-school delis; **hazelnut-finished pork** (☞ p. 72) and **foie gras au torchon** (☞ p. 66) of new-to-the-scene butchers; goat meat, oxtails, and whole pigs of ethnic markets; and a jaw-dropping selection of **wild game meats** (☞ p. 69). Portland is carnivorous.

In the winter of 2009, I attended an event where I interviewed all sorts of Portland chefs before and after they got **food-themed tattoos** (☞ *p*. 74). When I talked with Matt Reed, owner of TigerLily Tattoo, he told me a funny story. When his daughter was three she asked him, "Do you know why I like pigs?" He said no and she responded, "Because they're pink *and* they make pork." She's definitely Portland born and raised. Bring on the bacon.

Beyond salty cured pork products, Portland has kick-ass sausage, with **Zenner's Quality Sausage & Smoked Meats** (☞ *p*. 76), **Edelweiss Sausage & Delicatessen** (☞ *p*. 65), **Gartner's Country Meat Market** (☞ *p*. 66), **Altengartz** (☞ *p*. 64), and others producing all sorts of traditional and newfangled dogs and sausages. Portland is home to a wide array of new-school and old-school butcher shops, meat markets, and curing facilities, so stoke up the grill and put some meat on it.

Altengartz

⊗ *www.altengartz.com*
♥ SW 10th Ave and Alder St, Portland ☏ 503-975-2549
🕐 M–Sa 11am–4pm. Late night: Th–Sa 11pm–3am

In 2000 father and son George and Jameson Wittkopp began selling George's bratwurst recipe out of a mobile restaurant at SW 10th and Alder. These days, Altengartz sausage is also available in local markets, although the only place to get Altengartz from scratch vegan sausage is at the mobile restaurant.

Altengartz offers two choices for retail: the quarter-pound authentic German bratwurst or the two-ounce pork breakfast links, both made with local, hormone-free pork from Carlton Farms. Based on old German family recipes, these classic sausages can be found at **Sheridan Fruit Company**, various **Bales Thriftways** and **Lamb's Markets** around the city, **Stroheckers Market**, and other retail locations. Restaurants serving Altengartz sausage include **BridgePort Brewpub, The Mash Tun Brewpub**, and **Oaks Bottom Public House**.

Chop Butchery and Charcuterie

www.chopbutchery.com
📍 735 NW 21st Ave, Portland ☎ 503-221-3012 🕐 M–Sa 9:30am–7pm, Su 10pm–7pm
📍 Portland Farmers Market at PSU; SW Hall & SW Montgomery, Portland

This butcher shop/charcuterie business in Northwest's **City Market**, founded in 1990 by Portland sausage and charcuterie king Fred Carlo, hasn't changed much since it swapped hands (and changed its name) in early 2009. Chop owners Paula Markus and Eric Finley continue to stock house-made pâté and confit, and there's still a great selection of house-made bulk and stuffed sausages ranging from boudin blanc to lamb merguez. The old-world rillettes are a house specialty, including wild boar and fig, and rabbit with guanciale and guinea hen. Chop deals exclusively with beef, lamb, pork, and poultry – most of which is raised on local farms and ranches.

Along with big-ticket items such as smoked duck breast and foie gras, there's also house-smoked tasso and Canadian bacon. In early 2009, Chop built a sizeable new curing room to properly produce meats such as pancetta, guanciale, lonza stagionata, and salume. In addition to the City Market shop, Chop's downtown **PSU Portland Farmers Market** booth is very popular and usually sells about fifty pounds of salume every Saturday.

Steak and lamb chops are cut to order at Chop, and you can also find wild boar meat and rabbit hindquarters. If you don't feel like cooking, choose from numerous heat-and-serve items, including bacon-topped cajun meatloaf, baked pastas, and marinated meats and skewers. Beyond meat, Chop carries farm-fresh chicken eggs.

Hidden Chop gems include a freezer in the back stocked with everything from salt pork, veal liver, and sweetbreads to schmaltz and veal osso buco. There's a parking lot behind City Market just off of NW Johnson Street.

Edelweiss Sausage & Delicatessen

www.edelweissdeli.com
📍 3119 SE 12th Ave, Portland ☎ 503-238-4411 🕐 M–Sa 9am–6pm

I come from German heritage. My family hails from Zinzinnati, and I was lucky enough to live down the street from Edelweiss Sausage & Delicatessen when I first moved to Portland. I allot myself plenty of time when I visit Edelweiss, especially on weekends. I love being surrounded by house-made German foods such as sauerbraten, schinkenwurst, märgen speck, German potato salad, and Rouladen.

One of my fondest Edelweiss finds is the chili-cheese sausage (chopped-up ends of their delicious deli cheeses blended with pork and spices and stuffed in a natural casing), mandatory for most of my local camping trips. Edelweiss crafts all sorts of house sausages, meatloafs, salames, and more. Some of the most popular sausages include the marjoram-coated Nuremberger, Weisswurst, beer brats, Hungarian sausage, and weiners. The house-cured salames (I like the red wine–cured one) are great here, and so are the specialty imports – Emmentaler cheese, pickled herring, berry syrups, spaetzle, and dumpling mixes.

There's seating at the adjoining deli where you can drink beer (great German bottled selection) and sup on any of the house sausages, hot German potato salad, Reubens, and more.

Gartner's Country Meat Market

www.gartnersmeats.com
♦ 7450 NE Killingsworth St, Portland ♪ 503-252-7801 ◑ Tu–Sa 9am–6pm, Su 10am–4pm

Gartner's Country Meat Market has been the real deal since 1959 when the late Jack Gartner founded this family-run Northeast Portland business. Sure, there are fancy chop shops in Portland with pretty-penny pâté, foie gras, and exotic meats, but this is the place for thick, fat-ribboned steaks, German sausages and dogs, and all the standard cuts you expect from an old-school, all-American butcher shop.

My typical Gartner's booty includes steaks and German hot dogs, blended with or without cheese and onions. Other items in the Gartner's case include house-smoked ham, barbecue meat packs, half- or quarter-hogs and beef, stuffed pork chops, sausages, braunschweiger, olive loaf, and more. Gartner's will also clean, butcher, cure, and custom-cut customer-hunted game. If you can't wait until you get home, Gartner's always has cooked dogs and sausages available at the end of the meat counter.

I've never been to Gartner's and pulled a number closer than ten turns from being called. That said, Gartner's is always worth the wait. If you're nice, you might even get a pepperoni stick on the house.

Laurelhurst Market Butcher Shop

www.laurelhurstmarket.com
♦ 3155 E Burnside St, Portland ♪ 503-206-3099 ◑ 10am–10pm every day

Housed in the shell of a convenience store across the street from Music Millennium, Laurelhurst Market is one part butcher shop, one part modern steakhouse. The market is all about fresh and cured meat, and it turns around its products extremely quickly – according to co-owner Ben Dyer, the cases never hold anything more than two days old.

Rotisserie chicken and Peruvian fare

El Inka

📍 48 NE Division St, Gresham

📞 503-491-0323

🔗 www.elinkarestaurant.com

Affordable quality steak

Laurelhurst Market

📍 3155 E Burnside St, Portland

📞 503-206-3099

🔗 www.laurelhurstmarket.com

Offal and foie gras profiteroles

Le Pigeon

📍 738 E Burnside St, Portland

📞 503-546-8796

🔗 www.lepigeon.com

Lamb and Lebanese

Nicholas Restaurant

📍 318 SE Grand Ave, Portland

📞 503-235-5123

🔗 www.nicholasrestaurant.com

Alpine meats and housemade sausage

Gruner

📍 1215 SW Alder St, Portland

📞 503-241-7163

🔗 www.grunerpdx.com

Argentinian grilled meats

Ox

📍 2225 NE Martin Luther King Jr Blvd, Portland

📞 503-284-3366

🔗 www.oxpdx.com

Barbecue

Podnah's Pit Barbecue

📍 1625 NE Killingsworth St, Portland

📞 503-281-3700

🔗 www.podnahspit.com

Spendy steak

RingSide

📍 2165 W Burnside St, Portland

📞 503-223-1513

📍 14021 NE Glisan St, Portland

📞 503-255-0750

🔗 www.ringsidesteakhouse.com

Highbrow burger

Slow Bar

📍 533 SE Grand Ave, Portland

📞 503-230-7767

🔗 www.slowbar.net

Lowbrow burger

Stanich's

📍 4915 NE Fremont St, Portland

📞 503-281-2322

🔗 www.stanichs.com

Burmese stew, cheesesteak and more

Tasty n Sons

📍 3808 N Williams Ave, Suite C, Portland

📞 503-621-1400

🔗 www.tastyntasty.com/sons

Middle Eastern treats

Levant

📍 2448 E Burnside St, Portland

📞 503-954-2322

🔗 www.levantpdx.com

Polish sausage, pierogies and then some

Bar Dobre

📍 3962 SE Hawthorne Blvd, Portland

📞 503-477-5266

🔗 www.bardobre.com

Butcher shop/deli/bar/ restaurant with lots of meaty goodness

Old Salt Marketplace

📍 5027 NE 42nd Ave, Portland

📞 971-255-0167

🔗 www.oldsaltpdx.com

Spanish-inspired tapas

Toro Bravo

📍 120 NE Russell St, Portland

📞 503-281-4464

🔗 www.torobravopdx.com

Restaurant, tavern and bakery

Trifecta

📍 726 SE 6th Ave, Portland

📞 503-841-6675

🔗 www.trifectapdx.com

Creative Frenchy bistro

Little Bird

📍 219 SW 6th Ave, Portland

📞 503-688-5952

🔗 www.littlebirdbistro.com

Tube meat

Zach's Shack

📍 4611 SE Hawthorne Blvd, Portland

📞 503-233-4616

🔗 www.myspace.com/dogswithasnap

||||||||||||||||||||||||||||||||||||||||||||||||||||||||||||||||||||||

RABBIT

In the winter, when local seafood options are slim and produce is often of the starchy and tuberous ilk, farm-raised game gets more attention. And although many people are squeamish or downright opposed to eating rabbit, winter is when you'll find it braised, roasted, and stewed in many of Portland's best restaurants.

Now often considered a gourmet meat, rabbit wasn't always held in such high esteem. Rabbit meat was easy to source and affordable during World War II and into the 1960s, but when the cost of commercial feed increased substantially, several major meat processing plants in the Northwest shut their doors.

Since 1990 Geoff Latham, owner and president of Nicky USA (see next page), has been doing his best to bring rabbit back into local kitchens. One local rabbit farm he works with is Dutcher's Christmas Tree Farm in Boring, Oregon. The forty-plus-year-old, fifteen-acre family farm specializes in Christmas trees but also raises animals and grows organic vegetables.

Rollo Dutcher raised rabbit for the local meat market for several

With four full-time employees, Laurelhurst Market sells house-made pâtés and rillettes, pancettas, foie gras au torchon, bacon, andouille, tasso, deli meats, and sausages. To give you an idea of the caliber of sausage: a recent feature was a Provence-style lamb sausage made with Cattail Creek lamb, fresh mint, house preserved lemon, and oil-cured black olives.

Whole meats in the Laurelhurst Market case usually include air-cured beef and local pork (two of the biggest sellers), chicken, rabbit, buffalo, and lamb. There are also usually a few imported treats like hot or sweet sopressata from Claudio Specialty Foods in Philadelphia. Keep an eye out for the chalkboard that lists available items not in the case – beef marrow bones; beef, veal, and chicken stock; pork shoulder; pork belly; and duck fat.

Laurelhurst Market's specialty is beef – specifically, air-cured, grass-fed Piemontese beef from Montana, which Dyer first tried four years ago when a distributor introduced him to it. He prefers this lean and tender beef's less common, more affordable cuts, such as the flat iron, hanger, and bavette (also known as "culotte"), which are sold in the butcher shop by day ($8–$19 per pound) and served in the Laurelhurst Market dining room by night ($17–$33 per steak).

"For me, tenderloin is one of the most boring steaks in the case, and it's also by far the most expensive," Dyer says. "Twice already this week I've down-sold less expensive cuts to people asking for tenderloin." This may not seem like a stellar business move, but in terms of customer loyalty, this kind of full disclosure is priceless. Even though Dyer sources most of

years in the 1960s, before the cost of feed became prohibitive. His daughter, Michele, returned to those roots several years ago and began raising rabbits with the help of her father. Dutcher currently has 160 rabbits, which include plenty of common breeds, such as California and New Zealand white, as well as several heritage species, such as the rare American chinchilla rabbit.

Farm-raised rabbit is a tender, slightly sweet white meat often prepared the same way as chicken. Rabbit fryers, which are usually nine to twelve weeks old and weigh about two pounds, are generally roasted or grilled while older rabbit is often braised.

what's in the case from within a couple hundred miles, he's willing to make exceptions for outstanding meat.

During the day Laurelhurst Market sells sandwiches – your choice of fillings on **Fleur de Lis** breads (☞ *p.* 18). Most of the sandwich ingredients are prepared in house, including from-scratch deli meats, pickled vegetables, freshly grated horseradish, and house-made cheeses. Although you can't eat them in the dining room (dinner service only), there are a few covered tables in front of the building.

Nicky USA

⚭ *www.nickyusa.com*

📍 223 SE 3rd Ave, Portland 📞 503-234-4263, 800-469-4162 (call for an appointment)

Nicky USA owner Geoff Latham is a friend to many Portland chefs because of his wide array of unusual meats and fowl. Although Nicky USA doesn't have a storefront, there are appointment-only dock sales, as well as delivery, with a $125 minimum purchase. Latham got his start in the wild game business selling rabbit out of the trunk of his car to Portland chefs and restaurateurs. In 1994 he founded Nicky USA, a highly successful business that delivers as far north as Seattle and as far south as Eugene.

If you have a hankering for an antelope leg, suckling pig, or whole goat, look no further. Where else in Portland can you find quail, squab, buffalo, venison, elk, antelope, wild boar, goat, veal, Wagyu and Kobe beef, alligator, rattlesnake, turtle, kangaroo, emu, and ostrich in one location?

The majority of Nicky USA products are farm-raised and less than thirty months of age. Farm-raised game generally has a milder, less "gamey" taste, due to the controlled environment and consistent diet. Latham, who hunts ducks, pheasants, and venison, says, "Think of all the hormones that an elk will release if it runs half a mile in distress before it dies. That affects the meat. Very few hunted animals are put down in a stress-free way."

Nicky Farms is Nicky USA's line of house-processed meats and fowl from Northwest farms and ranches: rabbit and quail from Oregon, Washington, Idaho, and Alberta; buffalo from Enterprise, Burns, and Alberta; venison from the Oregon Coast, Molalla, and Alberta; and elk from Alberta.

In 2001 Nicky USA hosted its first annual (and quite popular) Wild About Game celebration. Today chefs, ranchers, farmers, vintners, and the general public attend the event held at different locations throughout the state. Chefs participate in a cook-off where they are randomly assigned a different game animal (such as rabbit, squab, or venison) and expected to prepare a dish in full view of the attending public before presenting the dishes to a panel of judges.

Olympic Provisions

www.olympicprovisions.com
107 SE Washington St, Suite 132, Portland 503-954-3663
   M 11am–3pm, Tu–F 11am–10pm, Sa 10am–10pm, Su 10am–3pm
1632 NW Thurman St, Portland 503-894-8136
   M 11am–3pm, Tu–F 11am–10pm, Sa 10am–10pm, Su 10am–9pm

Clyde Common restaurant owner Nate Tilden and partners opened their thirty-seat Olympic Provisions restaurant and USDA-certified meat-curing operation in late 2009 in the Olympic Mills Commerce Center. Castagna's former executive chef, Elias Cairo, heads up the now nationally recognized and booming wholesale and retail charcuterie side of the business as co-owner.

Tilden is all about Cairo's emulsified cured meats, such as mortadellas, bologna hot dogs, and lyoners. The German lyoner blends garlic, mustard seed, and salted pork in an eighteen-inch tube the width of a child's wrist. Tilden says Cairo recently served him "a thick slice of lyoner – egg-washed, breaded, and sautéed with a small frisée-and-herb salad." A very special bologna sandwich? "Exactly," Tilden says. "Usually you serve mustard with a dish like that, but you don't have to because the mustard's on the *inside.*"

Says Tilden, "I had this dream with the building. OK, so what if we get in our products – we make our salame, we hang it and it's done. We bring it out, we Cryovac it up, label it. There's a shipping company in this building and we take it there on a cart down through the hallway. They slap a stamp on it, ship it right before a train pulls up. The train's loaded up and heads out to Twin Falls. What a romantic, cool, small-factory feeling."

Olympic Provisions serves tapas-style counter service by day, with plenty of to-go options and table service by night, with Spanish, Portuguese, and North African-inspired small plates. When asked prior to opening in 2009 if there would be any windows into the meat room, Tilden smiled but shook his head. "You'd literally look in and see a guy in shorts and a white jacket cutting apart a cow," he said. Thank you for sparing us.

Otto's Sausage Kitchen

⚲ *www.ottossausagekitchen.com*
📍 4138 SE Woodstock Blvd, Portland ☎ 503-771-6714
🕐 M–Sa 9:30am–6pm, Su 11am–5pm

My favorite thing about Otto's Sausage Kitchen, founded in Portland in 1922, is the fact that year round you can buy house-smoked and -cured sausages and hot dogs straight off the barrel grill out front. Grab a soda and hang out at a sidewalk picnic table, or carry your dog with you into old Woodstock.

With fifty-plus fresh and smoked house sausages ranging from kielbasa and bockwurst to linguica and chorizo, along with head cheese, smoked meats and fish, and sandwich meats, there isn't much more you could ask for.

Before Portland's sandwich and deli revival of 2008, Otto's was one of the few good sandwich delis in town. Otto's is still a great place to get a made-to-order hot or cold sammy meatloaf, BLT, Reuben, French dip, and more. There's also a good beer and wine selection available in the deli or to go.

IS SALAMI RAW?

Elias Cairo
SALUMIST, CO-OWNER
OLYMPIC
PROVISIONS

Salami is indeed raw. The good ones, anyway, are. It is a fermented product. A high quality salami that is nice and slowly made should never reach an internal temperature exceeding 80° F. As raw as a pickle that is fermented is raw. Or as raw as a Wu-Tang song.

You recently moved into a new production facility. What's it like?
The new space opened in January 2014. It's my dream space, weighing in at 35,000 square feet – all of it used entirely for production. I got a bunch of new toys for it – a 300-pound bowl cutter and a lot of room to dry meat; a four-cart smokehouse so I can do a bunch of new products. We also have a welding shop now so that we can weld on site. No more having to go to Nate's dad's house, which I miss in a way. But it's nice to be able to weld all the stuff right there that breaks in shop.

And you're working on a book – give us a teaser?
I am. We're working with author Meredith Erickson. She wrote the

CONTINUES ➤

→ **Q&A**: ELIAS CAIRO, *continued*

Le Pigeon cookbook as well as one of my favorite cookbooks, *The Art of Living According to Joe Beef.* I am so excited about it. We intend on doing a lot of fun stuff, including going back to Switzerland. We're going to visit some of the spots where I did my apprenticeship.

When did you start curing meat?
Well, that is kind of a trick question. As a kid, we made a lot of sausage at home. We slaughtered all the animals that we raised, and hunted quite a bit. So we preserved a mess of meat. But my formal training started when I was eighteen years old in Switzerland.

How many staff do you have now at both restaurants and in production?
With the farmers markets and sales, etc., we have around eighty hopefully happy OPiates.

What's something that most people don't know about Olympic Provisions that's interesting?
I have only lost one employee in the meat department in four years.

Pastaworks

See page 93

Phil's Uptown Meat Market

🔗 *www.philsuptownmeatmarket.com*
📍 17 NW 23rd Pl, Portland 📞 503-224-9541
🕐 M 10am–2:30pm (order pickup and BBQ),
   Tu–F 9am–6pm, Sa 9am–5:30pm

Phil's Uptown Meat Market is in the Nob Hill strip mall that's home to **Uptown Liquor** and several other businesses. The meat and seafood case is stocked with Kobe beef hot dogs, legs of lamb, lamb loin chops, various **Carlton Pork** products, Kobe beef kabobs, and teriyaki flank steak, along with fresh fish. It's a small shop, but there's a lot to choose from, including a shrine of hot sauces and a year round bento grill out front with $5 lunches.

In the back of Phil's, you'll find a deli case with prepared foods such as whole roasted chickens, pasta and fruit salads, sandwiches, and bento boxes, and up front is a barista pulling espresso drinks.

Tails & Trotters

🔗 *www.tailsandtrotters.com*
📍 525 NE 24th Ave, Portland 📞 503.477.8682
🕐 M–F 10am–6pm (Sandwich Counter closes at 5pm), Sa 10am–4pm

Aaron Silverman, former owner of **Greener Pastures Poultry** and **Creative Growers Farm**, and Mark Cockcroft's hazelnut-finished pork business Tails & Trotters specializes in various pork cuts and products ribboned and capped with meltingly rich, nutty fat – all the better to sear, grill, and roast with.

The pigs are raised at Food Alliance-certi-

INK FOR EATS

PDX CHEFS TALK FOOD + TATTOOS

FOR MOST CHEFS, cuts and burns are common – mere flesh wounds that come with their chosen trade. But the bodies of many Portland chefs also carry a more permanent adornment: tattoos. Even Anthony Bourdain, host of the Travel Channel's *No Reservations*, noted the large number of arms inked with knives and whisks in Portland in his 2007 segment on the Pacific Northwest.

In the fall of 2008, Amanda Myers and Paul Zenk, – the owners of Infinity Tattoo in North Portland, – hosted a first-of-its-kind food and ink event. Seven local chefs (and one bartender) paired off with tattoo artists for food-inspired tattoos. That night, tattoos still bandaged, each chef prepared a dish for the tattoo artists, inspired by their tattoo at Acadia Restaurant.

Here are some snippets from my interviews that day with the participating chefs at Infinity Tattoo along with descriptions of the food and drink that they prepared that evening.

John Gorham
Toro Bravo, Tasty n Sons, Tasty n Alder

Tattoo Butcher knife on his side by Rich Cuellar of Grizzly Tattoo.

Dish Sambuca and fennel pork sausages with sautéed bell peppers and onions topped with Parmigiano-Reggiano.

What's your favorite meal to prepare at home? At home I like to pick a cuisine and cook it. A couple weeks ago I cooked a Tuscan dinner, then a Moroccan dinner. I pick a cuisine I don't cook at work and go with it.

What's your favorite tattoo? Definitely the one Tyler [Adams] did of the pin-up girl that's broken into pieces of butchered meat. Chicken shit Mills is another of my favorites.

Where did you get that one? On my butt. My sous-chef chickened out of getting a tattoo, so I got a chicken shitting out his name – "Mills."

What are you getting tattooed today? My butcher knife. I've used it for years now, anyone who's cooked with me knows it. I brought it in today and I used it yesterday. I've had it six years – it's a gift from a friend. She got it in Europe. It's carbon steel – a really soft steel that's easy to sharpen. It's ugly and rusty and I love it.

Why do you think so many chefs have tattoos? For me it's a really big stress release. Also, our craft is really artistic. I think a lot of chefs really appreciate art. And a tattoo is this raw art that you get to carry with you wherever you are. We're not at home a lot, so it's not like we're at home enjoying our art. You get to carry a tattoo around with you.

Karl Zenk
formerly Heathman Restaurant & Bar

Tattoo An image of French Toast (a Kidrobot-brand plush toy) on his leg by Saad Sweilem of Pussycat Tattoo.

Dish Elk heart pasties.

When did you start cooking? 1984.

Favorite meal/food to prepare? Anything with the swine is always good.

What's your favorite tattoo? The dragon that Paul's [Zenk] doing and my pepper shaker. My wife has a salt shaker.

Sarah Higgs
formerly Acadia

Tattoo Silverware on her forearm by Tyler Adams of Grizzly Tattoo.

Dish Chocolate chip cookie sandwiches with bacon ice cream.

What's your favorite food to prepare for someone? I like to cook French-style food, so sausages, pâtés, and more complex dishes.

What's your favorite tattoo? The peacock on my right leg that Alice Kendall did. The tail took three, three-hour appointments.

Why do you think so many chefs have tattoos? Tattoo artists and chefs are cut from the same cloth. They're the same type of person: art-oriented, but practical and they want to make money. So they use their gift to propel them in life. Similar paths, just different textiles.

Gabriel Rucker
Le Pigeon

Tattoo Tin of sardines and can of deviled ham by Amanda Myers of Infinity Tattoo.

Dish Pickled and grilled sardine salad with grilled bread, frisée, radicchio, and pork vinaigrette.

When did you start cooking? When I was eighteen.

When did you get your first tattoo? When I was twenty-four.

What's your favorite tattoo? The tattoo that says "mom" on my ribs. I got it in 2007 on Mother's Day.

Dusty York
formerly of Bluehour

Tattoo "Wine is my death" in Italian on his chest by Matt Reed of TigerLily Tattoo.

Drinks Spiced brandy Alexander and Bluehour gimlet with lavender-infused gin.

Why do you think so many food and drink professionals have tattoos? I have no idea, but one idea is that restaurant work is so stressful; doing that leads to tattoos, putting that same thing into your body. It's pretty masochistic.

How did you decide on this tattoo? It's incredibly ironic because I'm a bartender and I don't drink.

Tommy Habetz
Bunk Sandwiches

Tattoo Brook trout swimming through a heart on his upper arm by Alice Kendall of Infinity Tattoo.

Dish Smoked trout salad with Marcona almonds and fried onions.

When did you get your first tattoo? In 2005, I got a deadly nightshade – (Atropa belladonna) right after Gotham Tavern opened. I guess it was foreshadowing.

What's the most painful tattoo you have? A scorpion on my forearm. The tail's on my wrist.

Why do you think so many chefs have tattoos? Because we're cool and chicks dig tattoos.

John Eisenhart
Pazzo Ristorante

Tattoo A barramundi (a large-scaled Australian river fish) on his upper arm by Tim Jordan of Optic Nerve Arts.

Dish Panfried barramundi with shaved heritage carrots and carrot vinaigrette.

How many tattoos do you have? Six.

What's your favorite one? The parodies of stickers/labels from the 1970s on the back of my arm. Cap'n Crud, Tricks Practical Joker Cereal ...

Why do you think so many chefs have tattoos? We dig pain.

Adam Higgs
Acadia

Tattoo Old French salami advertisement by Paul Zenk of Infinity Tattoo.

Dish Smoked bone-in pork belly and spareribs with mustard.

Why do you think so many chefs have tattoos? It's rock star to be a chef and rock star to have tattoos, so they go hand in hand.

When did you get your first tattoo? In about five minutes.

BISON

Not so long ago, bison, also known as American buffalo, roamed the continent from northern Canada to Mexico. The woolly and wild herd animal provided food, shelter, clothing, and fuel for American Indians until the late 1800s when unregulated hunting and westward expansion brought the population, once estimated at 60 million, down to less than 1,000.

Today most bison in America, with the exception of those in wildlife reserves and reservations across the country, are commercially raised. Oregon is home to several bison ranches, including Joe and Karen Schueller's 120-acre **Rain Shadow El Rancho** in Scio, an hour north of Eugene. Depending on the season, the Schuellers usually have anywhere from twenty to fifty bison on their ranch.

Bison is touted for its rich, sweet flavor, although the meat is leaner than skinned chicken. The Schuellers sell their bison meat to restaurants and markets throughout the state, and Karen Schueller has three words of advice for cooking it: low and slow.

"When you cook bison you have

fied **Pure Country Pork** in Ephrata, Washington, and fed hazelnuts for the last six to eight weeks before slaughter. Most pigs eat eight pounds of feed a day and gain about two to three pounds a day. On a hazelnut diet, pigs eat less but gain more – from five to six pounds of feed a day they gain about four pounds daily. Once the animals are slaughtered, the meat is then trucked to Portland and processed at **Nicky USA** (☞ p. 69).

Silverman and Cockcroft produce a full line of cured meats and sausages as well as butcher, package, and distribute a wide array of pork cuts to restaurants and markets in Portland, Eugene, and Seattle. In town, their pork is often available at farmers markets, **Laurelhurst Market** (in the butcher shop and in the restaurant – ☞ p. 66), **Chop Butchery and Charcuterie** (☞ p. 65), **Pastaworks** (☞ p. 93), **Nicky USA** (☞ p. 69), and regularly at restaurants such as **Nostrana**, **Beast**, **clarklewis**, and **Park Kitchen**. For a complete list of up-to-date Tails & Trotters locations, visit the website. Various cuts are priced from $5 a pound retail.

Zenner's Quality Sausage & Smoked Meats

✆ www.zenners.com
♥ 2131 NW Kearney St, Portland ☎ 503-241-4113

Zenner's Quality Sausage & Smoked Meats has been around since the mid-1920s and has been run by only two men: first George Zenner, Sr., and now George Zenner, Jr. The company crafts small-batch sausages and other cured and smoked meats for local restaurants and markets in its 3,500-square-foot production facility. Most links, dogs, and sausages at Zenner's are made with real cow and sheep

to be careful not to overcook it ... it doesn't have the fat marbling that beef does, so it cooks faster," she says. "Typically we tell people with bison steaks to raise the grill up a bit. And when broiling it, lower the rack a notch to keep it farther away from the heat. The meat can really dry out if it's overcooked."

If you'd like to check out the largest land mammal in North America since the end of the Ice Age, call and schedule a visit to the ranch. You can purchase bison meat on site and, if you're lucky, catch a glimpse of the standoffish herd. The Schuellers make weekly bison deliveries to Portland restaurants and markets such as **Park Kitchen**, **Clyde Common**, **The Farm Café**, **clarklewis**, **¿Por Qué No?**, **Pastaworks**, and **Food Front Cooperative Grocery**.

casings, lending them a distinctive snap, as well as a less-than-uniform look.

The Original Pancake House – a Portland institution – has been serving up pork maple sausage links from Zenner's since day one. In fact, in 2008 when Zenner's made a short-lived switch from corn syrup to turbinado sugar in those links without notifying Original Pancake House, customers weren't too happy. Zenner's apologized and hightailed it back to the 1960s recipe. **Rheinlander German Restaurant** and **Gustav's Pub & Grill** use several sausages from Zenner's as well, including the German and the ground bulk bratwurst.

Zenner's sausages are available in other local restaurants such as **Helser's** (one of my favorite Portland breakfasts is the Helser's two-sausage breakfast with potato cakes), **Besaw's**, and **Sanborn's Restaurant**, and markets such as **Phil's Uptown Meat Market** (☞ *p. 72*), **Haggen Food & Pharmacy**, **Market of Choice**, **QFC**, and **Cash & Carry**. Zenner's also provides the official hot dog and sausage of Portland's **Moda Center**.

You can purchase a case of sausage, smoked bacon, ham, or Canadian bacon directly from the Zenner's facility in Northwest Portland. And if you have a hankering for a big batch (130–240 pounds) of your grandma's homemade sausage, Zenner's will craft it for you as long as you provide the recipe and agree to buy the entire batch. They'll even store it for you if your fridge and freezer are full.

PORTLANDERS ARE ADAMANT about local, seasonal produce, and we're lucky that our temperate climate and humus-rich soil support a wide variety of fruits and veggies. I've been introduced to all kinds of produce since I moved to Portland. Cardoons, radicchio, fresh wasabi, burdock, and Jerusalem artichokes have all found places in my cooking repertoire.

Although most local grocery stores do a good, even great, job with produce, these markets and greengrocers specialize in fruits and veggies and make it their business to bring you the best of what the Pacific Northwest has to offer.

There's a lot to showcase in a state quilted with diverse growing regions that produce everything from **cranberries** (☞ *p.* 81), horseradish, daikon, chickpeas, olives, and persimmon to fennel, **wild mushrooms** (☞ *p.* 187), and juniper berries. Although plenty of Portlanders these days meet their household fruit and vegetable needs via **community supported agriculture** (☞ *p.* 148), local **farmers markets** (☞ *p.* 169), farm stands, and by digging in the dirt to **grow their own** (☞ *p.* 179), these Portland greengrocers do the work for you.

Berry Good Produce

♥ 5523 SE 28th Ave, Portland **☎** 503-234-7288 **◷** M–Sa 9am–7pm, Su 9am–6pm

Berry Good Produce fills a niche, with fresh produce within walking distance of Reed College. Almost everything's still in the crate, pallet, or box that it arrived in at this small, open-air shop except for a small selection of refrigerated items such as Rose Valley butter and Tillamook cheese. There's also duck and squirrel food (nut- and grain-based) that you can purchase to feed the neighboring Crystal Springs Rhododendron Garden critters – if you can sneak it past the volunteers.

Cherry Sprout Produce Market

✆ www.cherrysprout.com
♥ 722 N Sumner St, Portland **☎** 503-445-4959 **◷** M–Sa 9am–8pm, Su 10am–7pm

You won't find any $3 tomatoes in Cherry Sprout Produce Market's produce coolers. That's because Cherry Sprout is dedicated to keeping its abundant produce selection affordable. Here you'll find produce and non-perishables (there's a particularly good selection of Mexican dried spices and chilies), with a nod to snacks, sweets, and sodas for students of nearby Jefferson High School.

This small, brightly painted community market is a joy to shop in. There's an old piano by the door if you're feeling inspired, and kumquats by the register if you want something quick and healthy. The focus is on local, seasonal, and organic, but Cherry Sprout has something for everyone. There are always big bags of

NEW SEASONS MARKET

The produce is fantastic at New Seasons Market. Since 1999, this locally owned and operated business with nine locations in and around the Portland area has been showcasing local, farm-direct produce from farms such as Gathering Together Farm, Columbia Gorge Fruit, and Johansen Ranch.

Beyond an impressive selection of fruits and vegetables, New Seasons Markets boast well-stocked cheese, meat, and deli counters; many beers and wines; in house bakeries; regular front-of-store tastings; and home goods and wellness departments. New Seasons favors specialty local, organic, and health foods, but you'll also find conventional items on the shelves.

♀ Arbor Lodge: 6400 N Interstate Ave, Portland ♪ 503-467-4777 ♀ Cedar Hills Crossing: 3495 Cedar Hills Blvd, Beaverton ♪ 503-641-4181 ♀ Concordia: 5320 NE 33rd Ave, Portland ♪ 503-288-3838 ♀ Fisher's Landing: 2100B SE 164th Ave, Vancouver, WA ♪ 360-760-5005 ♀ Happy Valley: 15861 SE Happy Valley Town Center Dr, Happy Valley ♪ 503-558-9214 ♀ Hawthorne: 4034 SE Hawthorne Blvd, Portland ♪ 503-236-4800 ♀ Mountain Park: 3 SW Monroe Pkwy, Lake Oswego ♪ 503-496-1155 ♀ Orenco Station: 1453 NE 61st Ave, Hillsboro ♪ 503-648-6968 ♀ Progress Ridge: 14805 SW Barrows Rd, Suite 103, Beaverton ♪ 503-597-6777 ♀ Raleigh Hills: 7300 SW Beaverton-Hillsdale Hwy, Portland ♪ 503-292-6838 ♀ Sellwood: 1214 SE Tacoma St, Portland ♪ 503-230-4949 ♀ Seven Corners: 1954 SE Division St, Portland ♪ 503-445-2888

🕐 All locations 8am–10pm every day
🔗 www.newseasonsmarket.com

cut collards and mustard greens in the produce section; okra, smoked meats, and premade foods in the freezers; and basic home supplies.

It's clear from the moment you walk through the door of the small market that Cherry Sprout is a labor of love.

Kruger's Farm Market

🔗 www.krugersfarmmarket.com
♀ 17100 NW Sauvie Isl. Rd, Portland ♪ 503-621-3489
♀ 2310 SE Hawthorne Blvd, Portland ♪ 503-235-0314
♀ 7316 N Lombard Ave, Portland ♪ 503-289-2535
🕐 Seasonal hours for all locations, call ahead

The farm meets the city at Kruger's Farm Markets. The 150-acre Kruger Farm on Sauvie Island, just twelve miles north of Portland at the confluence of the Willamette and Columbia Rivers, has as its major draw its u-pick berries and seasonal crops, including strawberries, blueberries, marionberries, boysenberries, tomatoes, pumpkins, and more, and its seasonal events. There are also u-cut flowers – they kindly loan you clippers and buckets. The farm is open to the public with a farm store in the barn filled with seasonal fruits, vegetables, and other local goods. And throughout the spring, summer, and early fall Kruger hosts all sorts of barbecues and events (live music on Thursday nights in the summer) with tasty food and drink carts and trucks on premises, including **Captured by Porches** beer, wood-fired pizza, barbecue, burgers, and more. Dogs are allowed but must be on leash at all times. That keeps the fifty free-range chickens happy. Kruger's two outdoor tented city farm stands in Southeast and North Portland are also well stocked with fresh, local produce and open seasonally from spring through early fall.

PORTLAND PICKLING

Oddly enough, the author of *The Joy of Pickling*, Linda Ziedrich, rarely craves pickles, favoring fresh, raw food over preserved. Her son drew her into the pungent and puckery world of dilly beans and bread and butters when he developed a powerful taste for pickles.

Concerned with the unhealthy preservatives and additives in store-bought pickles, Ziedrich decided to pickle some fruits and vegetables from her family's farm near Portland. While pickling for her family and researching recipes for *The Joy of Pickling*, Ziedrich, who has a bachelor's degree in anthropology, became fascinated with pickles.

"Every single country has a pickle they're known for," she says. "There is so much sentimental value attached to pickles." By pickles, she refers to all pickled foods, not just cucumbers – Korean *kimchi* (spicy fermented Asian cabbage and/or vegetables), Russian pickled tomatoes, Indian chutneys, French cornichons, Scandinavian pickled herring, Southern watermelon pickles.

For supplies and inspiration to make pickles at home, check out **Mirador Community Store** (☞ p. 166). Mirador sells everything you need for pickling and canning foods, including pressure and water bath canners, canning jars, widemouth funnels, jar lifters, lid steriizers, stoneware crocks, and cheesecloth.

Proper Eats Market & Cafe

See page 94

Raw Raw Raw Produce

⊘ *www.rawrawrawproduce.com*
📍 735 NW 21st Ave, Portland 📞 503-221-3004
🕐 M–Sa 9:30am–7pm, Su 10am–7pm

Since 2005 Raw Raw Raw Produce has owned and managed the produce department in **City Market**. Many times over the years when I've stopped by, something in the coolers has inspired me to write a local food story. Some items go for Nob Hill prices, while others are more in line with farmers market costs.

The hand-misted produce selection at Raw Raw Raw Produce is mostly local, organic, and farm-direct – and it's always inspiring. Think "living" lettuce (hydroponically grown and still alive in water when you buy it), watermelon radishes, Oregon black truffles nestled in small bowls of uncooked rice, and a wide rainbow of fresh produce that you may or may not have seen before. There's usually fresh local tofu available for bulk purchase in a small bucket of water by the greens. Raw Raw Raw is all about its outstanding selection and dedication to small local farms.

CRANBERRIES

Despite the widely held belief that cranberries only grow on the shores of New England, Oregon is the fourth-largest cranberry producer in the country, with more than 2,700 acres of cranberry bogs. Most of the cranberry plants originally cultivated in Oregon grew from cuttings of East Coast plants shipped over at the turn of the twentieth century.

A vast majority of the state's cranberry bogs are located in southern Oregon, where the sandy, acidic soil, and mild climate are ideal for cultivation.

The cranberry, along with the Concord grape and the blueberry, is native to North America; in fact, wild cranberries were an important part of the early Pacific Northwest Indians' diet. Pemmican, a staple for long trips, was a mixture of dried meat, fat, and cranberries that was pounded, shaped into cakes, and sun dried.

In late spring, the light pink cranberry flowers bloom and twist back, looking similar to the head and bill of a crane. This is how the cranberry got its name – a linguistic evolution from "craneberry." In the late summer and early fall, local cranberry bogs appear crimson with ripe berries. More than 98% of Oregon cranberries are water harvested: the bogs are flooded, the berries float to the top, and they're mechanically picked.

OREGON'S RIVERS, LAKES, AND COAST produce geoducks, oysters, clams, Dungeness crab, sturgeon, salmon, crawfish, and more. Portland is definitely baited and hooked, but be forewarned that you might have to do a little work to reel in the good stuff. Portland's saltwater and freshwater bounty doesn't always translate to good, fresh catch at restaurants and markets, but rest assured that if you follow my recommendations throughout this chapter you won't be disappointed.

If you want to catch your own, there are plenty of spots to do so (be sure to get the proper permit from the **Oregon Department of Fish and Wildlife,** ☞ *p.* 88). Since living in Portland, I've learned to catch and cook crawfish, dig for clams, shuck oysters and fish for lake crappie. I've also learned the dangerous techniques of cracking and eating a Dungeness crab with nothing but bare hands.

If the late James Beard had his way, Portland would be swimming in seafood options due to our proximity to the Pacific Coast. His love of our state's rich coastal bounty rings loud and clear in his 1964 classic *Delights and Prejudices*: "Those busy days on the Oregon Coast left their mark on me, and no place on earth, with the exception of Paris, has done as much to influence my professional life."

ABC Seafood Market

♀ 6509 SE Powell Blvd, Portland ☎ 503-771-5802 🕐 9:30am–8:30pm every day

Every time I visit ABC Seafood Market, I am pleasantly surprised by the cleanliness and against-all-odds order in the tiny shop that's home to more than ten fish tanks holding everything from live crawfish, spot prawns, and tilapia to geoducks, periwinkle clams, crab, and lobster. There are some frozen (sea cucumber, pompano, and cuttlefish) and fresh whole/fillet options (bass, lingcod, and catfish), but most people visit ABC Seafood Market for the live tanks. There's also a tiny produce, beer, wine, and non-perishables section in the back.

Fubonn Shopping Center

🔗 *www.fubonn.com*
♀ 2850 SE 82nd Ave, Suite 80, Portland ☎ 503-517-8877 🕐 9am–8pm every day

Fubonn Shopping Center's claim to fame is that it's "the largest Asian shopping center in Oregon." The center is stocked with everything from a travel agency to music stores, book shops, and shoe shops, and the fluorescent-lit Fubonn is enormous on its own. Imagine all of the small Asian markets you've ever been to and multiply them by ten. Sometimes this translates to a more diverse selec-

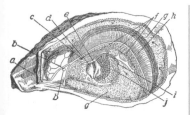

OYSTERS

Every time I'm in Newport I make a point to stop by **Oregon Oyster Farms**. It doesn't seem like a trip to the coast without picking up a sack of oysters on ice – usually the small and slightly sweet Kumamotos.

Oregon Oyster Farms (OOF), on Newport's Yaquina Bay, mainly cultivates sweet and mild Pacific oysters as well as cherished Kumamoto oysters. Oysters require brackish water – a mixture of fresh water and seawater – and the farm's five hundred acres in Yaquina Bay provide the ideal mixture of fresh water from the Yaquina River and Pacific seawater.

Oregon Oyster Farms was established in 1907 to supply oysters to downtown Portland's **Dan & Louis' Oyster Bar**, and today OOF mainly wholesales to restaurants throughout the United States and Asia. They make biweekly trips to the Portland International Airport, sending oysters to such places as the **Grand Central Oyster Bar & Restaurant** in Manhattan, which usually orders 100 to 150 dozen oysters a week. Locally, you can find OOF oysters at **EaT: An Oyster Bar** and other restaurants.

Each week, OOF purchases sev-

tion, but sometimes it just means a lot more bottles of Sriracha hot sauce and bags of dried rice noodles on the shelf.

The seafood department is truly diverse. Here you'll find fresh and frozen pompano, largemouth bass, bonito, tilapia, farmed sturgeon, rabbitfish, and butterfish. In the large adjacent fish tanks are manila clams, lobster, Pacific oysters, and crab. It's not the cleanest fish market, and there isn't much information available about the seafood, but if the bottom line is most important, Fubonn's seafood is cheap.

Other things to check out at Fubonn: every part of the pig and duck; a diverse selection of produce, including chayote, green daikon, yali pear, opo, and nagaimo root; and an enormous supply of fresh, frozen, and dried noodles.

Newman's Fish Company in City Market

𝒫 *www.newmansfish.com*
♥ 735 NW 21st Ave, Portland ☎ 503-227-2700
🕐 M–Sa 9:30am–7pm, Su 10am–7pm

Looks can be deceiving at independently owned Newman's Fish Company in Nob Hill's **City Market** (☞ *p.* 90). Seafood is delivered daily (from the wholesale North Portland division of Newman's Fish Company) and the case is often on the light side with fresh catch projected to sell in a couple days. Even though the case can sometimes look skimpy, rest assured that most of Newman's seafood is straight off the boat – wild and fresh or frozen at sea. You'll rarely find farmed fish here.

Newman's Fish got its start in Eugene in the late 1800s, and in the mid-1980s John Cleary brought Newman's to Portland with four markets. Today Newman's Fish Company

eral million oyster larvae from a nearby hatchery. The larvae look like tiny black pinpricks on the shells after three days in the tank. The "good sets," the shells with the most healthy larvae attached, are woven into braided ropes and suspended from wooden floats in the bay; most will survive. The "bad sets" are thrown to the bottom of the bay, where about 50% make it.

In Oregon, from July until the fall rains start, Xin Liu and Tom Ragghianti, farm co-owners since 1998 – recommend consumers cook their oysters. When the water temperature rises just one degree, bacteria levels increase substantially.

At the OOF storefront, customers can choose from Pacific and Kumamoto oysters (in the shell or shucked), oyster cocktails, smoked oysters, steamer clams, oyster seasonings, and other products.

Oregon Oyster Farms
📍 6878 Yaquina Bay Rd, Newport
📞 541-265-5078
🔗 www.oregonoyster.com
🕐 9am–5pm every day

in City Market and the North Portland Newman's Fish Company wholesale warehouse continue to thrive along with two Newman's businesses in Eugene.

At Newman's Fish Company in City Market the case reflects the season, although you'll almost always see scallops, shrimp, squid, and smoked and pickled fish along with whatever's fresh. Come for halibut in March, Copper River salmon at the end of May, crawfish in June, and Oregon albacore tuna in July. Pink grouper, swordfish, rockfish, albacore tuna, and black cod are also often available, as are live Maine lobster, live Northwest Dungeness crab, mussels, and various oysters and clams.

All of the smoked and cured fish (including smoked salmon collar, wild sockeye lox, smoked trout, and smoked sturgeon) is prepared in the 1,000-pound-capacity smoker at Newman's wholesale warehouse in North Portland. A visit to the warehouse on an early weekday morning is a who's-who of Portland restaurants, as crates of fresh fish are brought in, cleaned, cut, and loaded onto restaurant-labeled crates and into delivery trucks. On a recent trip to the warehouse, I saw crates for **Andina Restaurant**, **Paley's Place**, **Castagna**, **3 Doors Down Café**, **Lincoln Restaurant**, **Ned Ludd**, **Park Kitchen**, and **Bluehour**. Impressive stuff.

On Saturdays and Sundays at Newman's City Market, you'll usually find whole fish, often lane snappers or smelt – in addition to weekend specials like house-made crab cakes, salmon burgers, and seafood sausage (a delicious mince of scallops, lox, rockfish, dill, and cayenne). If you're craving something that you don't see, let someone behind the counter know and they'll custom order it for you. But

JOHN CLEARY

PRESIDENT, NEWMAN'S
FISH COMPANY'S
PORTLAND DIVISION

Number of Portland restaurants to which Newman's purveys: 80+.

Some of Newman's loyal customers: Bluehour, Andina Restaurant, Castagna, Clyde Common, 3 Doors Down Café, Paley's Place, Simpatica Catering & Dining Hall.

Delivery minimum: $100.

What Cleary does most mornings: Haggles on the phone with fish processors around the country for the best quality and price.

What Cleary was doing when I met him: Switching back and forth between various land lines and his cell phone, trying to bring his four main halibut brokers down in price for Southeast Alaskan halibut.

The price of fish goes up: When the processor's phone rings a lot.

The price of fish goes down: When the processor's phone doesn't ring a lot.

Biggest seller: Halibut, with 3,000 to 4,000 pounds sold a week.

Most perishable item: Squid.

Size of North Portland warehouse: Ten thousand square feet.

Cleary's favorite way to get fish: Overnight air cargo.

How that fish is packed: In 100-lb. boxes with gel packs and liners.

don't ask anyone at Newman's to shuck your oysters on the spot: they're far too busy for that.

Pacific Seafood

www.pacseafood.com
9 3380 SE Powell Blvd, Portland 503-233-4891
M–F 9am–6pm

I remember thinking that I'd found a gem the first time I stepped inside this tiny sixty-plus-year-old fish market on SE Powell. Now I know that the market is a storefront for the very large seafood company Pacific Seafood Group with facilities throughout the West Coast and worldwide distribution. That doesn't negate the quality of the fresh and frozen fish, but it does make it feel a little less special.

At Pacific Seafood, you'll usually find fresh wild sturgeon, catfish, albacore tuna, cod, and snapper in the case along with scallops, shrimp, oysters, and mussels. In the small freezer, there are lobster tails, crawfish, squid steak, and soft-shell crab. There's also a smoked fish case stocked mainly with vacuum-packed salmon.

Uwajimaya

www.uwajimaya.com
9 10500 SW Beaverton–Hillsdale Hwy, Beaverton
 503-643-4512
M–Sa 8am–10pm, Su 9am–9pm

Any time I'm in Beaverton, I swing by Uwajimaya. It's the kind of place where I always buy more than I plan to. There's a **Kinokuniya Bookstore**, a travel agency, a cosmetics shop, and a restaurant in the Uwajimaya complex, but the heart of the matter, as far as I'm concerned, is the market's food and drink. I'm particularly fond of the tea aisle, dried mush-

Creole

Acadia
- 📍 1303 NE Fremont St, Portland
- 📞 503-249-5001
- 🔗 *www.creolapdx.com*

Peruvian

Andina Restaurant
- 📍 1314 NW Glisan St, Portland
- 📞 503-228-9535
- 🔗 *www.andinarestaurant.com*

Mexican

Autentica
- 📍 5507 NE 30th Ave, Portland
- 📞 503-287-7555
- 🔗 *www.autenticaportland.com*

Gluten-free rice flour batter

Corbett Fish House
- 📍 5901 SW Corbett Ave, Portland
- 📞 503-246-4434
- 📍 Hawthorne Fish House
  343 SE Hawthorne Blvd, Portland
- 📞 503-548-4434
- 🔗 *www.corbettfishhouse.com*

Oysters

Dan & Louis' Oyster Bar Restaurant
- 📍 208 SW Ankeny St, Portland
- 📞 503-227-5906
- 🔗 *www.danandlouis.com*

Oysters, Creole, and Cajun

EaT: An Oyster Bar
- 📍 3808 N Williams Ave, Portland
- 📞 503-281-1222
- 🔗 *www.eatoysterbar.com*

Classy, old-school Portland

Genoa
- 📍 2832 SE Belmont St, Portland
- 📞 503-238-1464
- 🔗 *www.eatoysterbar.com*

Rustic French with plenty of seafood

St. Jack
- 📍 1610 NW 23rd Ave, Portland
- 📞 503-360-1281
- 🔗 *www.stjackpdx.com*

Fish and chips

Horse Brass Pub
- 📍 4534 SE Belmont St, Portland
- 📞 503-232-2202
- 🔗 *www.horsebrass.com*

Authentic sushi and ramen

Mirakutei
- 📍 536 E Burnside St, Portland
- 📞 503-467-7501
- 🔗 *www.mirakuteipdx.com*

High-end sushi

Murata Restaurant
- 📍 200 SW Market St, Suite 105, Portland
- 📞 503-227-0080

Crawfish

My Brother's Crawfish
- 📍 8220 SE Harrison St, Portland
- 📞 503-774-3786
- 🔗 *www.mybrotherscrawfish.com*

French/Northwest

Paley's Place
- 📍 1204 NW 21st Ave, Portland
- 📞 503-243-2403
- 🔗 *www.paleysplace.net*

Thai

Pok Pok
- 📍 3226 SE Division St, Portland
- 📞 503-232-1387
- 🔗 *www.pokpokpdx.com*

High-end and mid-range local seafood

Roe and Block & Tackle
- 📍 3113 SE Division St, Portland
- 📞 503-236-0205
- 🔗 *www.blockandtacklepdx.com*

Big-ass sushi

Saburo's Japanese Sushi House
- 📍 1667 SE Bybee Blvd, Portland
- 📞 503-236-4237
- 🔗 *www.saburos.com*

Creative sushi

Yoko's
- 📍 2878 SE Gladstone St, Portland
- 📞 503-736-9228

Go to
SEAFOOD
Spots

DIY DUNGENESS

If you're craving crab and want to catch your own, head to the coast and rent some crab pots. You'll need an Oregon Department of Fish and Wildlife shellfish license ($7 for the year for Oregon residents, $20.50 for nonresidents), a measuring device, and some bait. Most bait and tackle shops at the coast sell licenses and rent out or sell crab pots or rings. Fish carcasses are the most common bait.

Dungeness crabbing is usually best on the coast from late summer until mid-February, when the bays and estuaries fill up with rainwater and the crabs head out for deeper, saltier ocean water. Recreational crabbers can catch up to twelve male Dungeness crabs a day that are a minimum of five and three-quarter inches wide across the back. Female crabs, which can be determined by a broad tail flap on their underside, must be returned to the water unharmed.

Resident crab cleaners and cookers can be found at most docks. For a small fee they will gut, clean, and steam or boil your crabs so that you can eat them there or reheat them at home. For a list of sites where shellfish licenses are sold, check the **Oregon Department of Fish and Wildlife website** (www.dfw. state.or.us) or call 800-720-6339. Most bays, estuaries, piers, and jetties are open year round, but inquire about special regulations.

room section, miso cooler, kimchi assortment, produce section filled with jackfruit and bitter melon alongside baskets of lemongrass and green papaya, and the sake and Asian beer selection.

And of course, the seafood. Since 1998 this Asian megastore has been feeding delicious fresh, often sushi-grade, seafood to Portlanders. The tanks alone are reason to make the trek to Uwajimaya: live geoduck, Dungeness crab, Maine lobster, tilapia, oysters, and cherrystone and razor clams are ready to be netted and cleaned. Over at the fresh case, there's a wide selection of sushi-grade fish, as well as whole and filleted fish. There's also plenty of prepared sushi and sashimi if you want to grab and go. If you can't find a particular cut or type of fish, check out the extremely diverse frozen seafood selection.

Uwajimaya stands out for its selection, sourcing (there are more local and seasonal offerings here than you'll find at any other Asian shop in town), and aesthetic. It's clean, nicely lit with hanging lamps, and has colorful art and information every step of the way. Don't know what that sticky, strange-looking stuff called natto in the frozen aisle is? There's a card fastened to the freezer door that spells out all you wanted to know about natto and then some in terms of history and preparation.

LAMPREY

Chances are you've never sunk your teeth into the slimy, scaleless, oily flesh of a lamprey. The jawless but toothy creature looks like an eel but is in fact a species similar to hagfish. Believe it or not, it's a Pacific Northwest culinary and cultural icon, but you won't find it in local restaurants or markets anytime soon. In 2002 the commercial harvest of lampreys was banned in Oregon due to a plummeting population caused by overfishing, pollution, and man-made water barriers.

Even though it's considered a delicacy throughout much of Europe, Dale Nelson, a former fisheries biologist for the **Oregon Department of Fish and Wildlife** (ODFW), admits he hasn't tried lamprey.

"It was once described to me as a tough and chewy cross between liver and duck," he says. But he knows many Pacific Northwest Native American elders liken lamprey to fish candy. "Younger tribal folks don't care for it because they haven't grown up with it," he says, "while the elders, who were raised on lamprey, consider it a treat."

Tribal preparation of lamprey is often a two-part process. First, the lamprey is boiled in order to rid it of excessive fat, and then it can be barbecued, baked, simmered in a stew, or air dried.

For thousands of years, Pacific Northwest Native American tribes have depended on the lamprey. Kelly Dirksen, fish and wildlife program manager for the **Confederated Tribes of the Grand Ronde**, an Oregon confederation consisting of 26 different tribal linguistic groups, organizes annual summer lamprey harvesting trips to Willamette Falls in Oregon City. Like salmon, lampreys are anadromous, returning from the sea to their freshwater spawning sites in the spring and early summer.

"When we're out there fishing, I think about how these tribes used to have to hunt for deer, forage for camas, and source all kinds of other plants and animals in order to survive," he says. "Then at certain times of the year they could travel to Willamette Falls or other nearby falls and waterways and simply pluck a seemingly endless supply of lamprey right off the rocks."

Harvesting lampreys is no longer such an easy process. "It's dangerous," Dirksen says. "You're hurtling heavy currents. The water traveling over the falls now is warm surface water because of the hydro plant. All of the nutrients in this warm water make for an overgrowth of slippery algae. It's extremely difficult to get a footing."

Highly regulated personal-use lamprey harvest is only open for a couple months every summer. Lamprey catch must be recorded daily and reported to the ODFW. To apply for a free personal-use harvest permit and a possession permit, contact ODFW's Clackamas office (503-657-2000) and then head down to the east side of Willamette Falls, the only permissible spot for Oregon lamprey fishing.

ONE OF THE BEST PARTS of Portland's food markets is decentralization. Yes, we have megashops and big boxes just like everywhere else (although thanks to smart urban growth boundaries, not so many close to the city), but small and specialized is Stumptown credo. Shops with handpicked, and often house-made, food and drink can be found in most neighborhoods – places where it's possible to build relationships with the owners, employees, and other customers; places where what you sacrifice in selection you often gain in quality and flavor.

Portlanders often favor baskets over carts in such shops because they make more sense in cramped quarters. An added bonus is that food and drink often gets more attention when you carry it. It's sniffed, ogled, touched, and often talked about. Growing and producing food takes time – so should selection.

Although there are some amazing one-stop specialty food shops included here, Portland is often monomaniacal when it comes to food. Think salt shops, spice shops, meat shops, bottle shops. The specialty food shops in this chapter are here because of their variety. More specific specialty food shops – **cheese** (☞ *p*. 33), **chocolate** (☞ *p*. 39), **produce** (☞ *p*. 78) – are covered in their respective chapters.

If you want the perfect picnic, these are great spots to check out.

City Market

📍 735 NW 21st Ave, Portland 📞 503-221-3007 🕐 M–Sa 9:30am–7pm; Su 10am–7pm

I don't go to City Market all that often. It's not because I don't appreciate its live seafood tanks, "living" greens, house-made pasta, and house-cured meats. The reason I don't get to City Market as much as I'd like to is because I live across the river. My loss.

Home to **Raw Raw Raw Produce** (☞ *p*. 80), **Newman's Fish Company** (☞ *p*. 84), **Chop Butchery and Charcuterie** (☞ *p*. 65), and **Pastaworks** (☞ *p*. 93), City Market's full of all sorts of tasty, and often spendy, treats. At Pastaworks, every local and imported cheese has its own description handwritten atop it in the cooler, and there's an incredible low- to highbrow wine selection along with lots of packaged imported specialty foods, not to mention fresh house-made pasta and pasta sauces. Check out the Pastaworks pasta machine close to Chop's meat counter. I've never seen such a tall one with so many different cuts.

Although City Market is spendy (and its clientele isn't in the habit of price checking), I believe that you get what you pay for. At least I always have.

The Woodsman Market

www.woodsmantavern.com/market

📍 4529 SE Division St, Portland 📞 971-373-8267 🕐 9am–7pm every day

This teeny tiny market, located next to **The Woodsman Tavern**, shares the same owner (Duane Sorenson of **Stumptown Coffee**) and stretch of SE Division as the namesake restaurant. Don't go here expecting to fill your mesh re-usable shopping bag to the brim, but do go here for some specialty treats like cured meats from **Chop and Fino in Fondo**, farm fresh local produce, bread from **Little T Bakery**, a small but super tasty selection of local and international cheeses, precious chocolate bars, beer, wine, and more. Everything in the store is handpicked, including chocolate pudding in Mason jars, gin marmalade, and local sea salt. There are yummy sandwiches and soups available to go from the counter.

Elephants Delicatessen

www.elephantsdeli.com

📍 115 NW 22nd Ave, Portland 📞 503-299-6304 🕐 M–Sa 7am–7:30pm; Su 9:30am–6:30pm
📍 812 SW Park Ave, Portland 📞 503-546-3166
   🕐 M–F 6:30am–7:30pm, Sa 9am–8pm, Su 11am–6pm
📍 5885 SW Meadows Rd, Lake Oswego 📞 503-620-2444 🕐 M–F 6:30am–5pm
📍 625 SW 5th Ave, Portland 📞 503-467-4084 🕐 M–F 6am–3pm
📍 7000 NE Airport Way, Portland Airport 📞 503-937-1090 🕐 5am–9pm every day
📍 877 SW Taylor St, Portland 📞 503-937-1073 🕐 11am–8:30pm every day

Elephants Delicatessen has been in business since 1979, and like a good elephant, it's been slowly growing for many years as a PDX catering and food and drink depot. What sets Elephants apart is its ready-made selection. The Northwest Elephants is the largest location by far, with the most diverse offerings. In fact, the Northwest Elephants usually feels like a food festival taste pavilion. Slow-roasted meat is being carved over here, ganache is being spread over there, wine is being poured up front, and there are always plenty of employees on the floor to keep up with the bustling business.

The Northwest Elephants has a hot window stacked with steaming, bubbling trays of oven-baked foods: lasagna bolognese, traditional meatloaf, squash enchiladas with tomatillo sauce, and more. There's also a wood-fired oven cranking out specialty pizzas and a grill cooking up everything from burgers and sliders to grilled fish. The deli serves more than twenty cured meats from purveyors such as **Framani** and **Salumi**. And the bar shakes specialty cocktails and serves hot and cold breakfast, lunch, and dinner.

Beyond Elephants' ready-to-eat foods, available at all locations, most locations carry a decent supply of standard grocery store fare (wine, beer, soda, bulk olives, packaged specialty foods) as well as kitchen and entertaining supplies. All Elephants locations are great for food/drink splurges, edible gifts, and picnic supplies, but I wouldn't consider any location a one-stop shop unless you just planted a row of money trees.

Foster & Dobbs Authentic Foods

www.fosteranddobbs.com
📍 2518 NE 15th Ave, Portland 📞 503-284-1157 🕐 M–Sa 7am–8pm, Su 8am–6pm

The moment you walk into this tiny Northeast specialty food and drink shop, you'll be noticed. Foster & Dobbs owners Luan Schooler and Tim Wilson and their employees are charmingly attentive and eager to talk with customers about everything from the impressive cheese and meat counter (favoring domestic and international farmstead cheeses) to the colorful array of Spanish-centric imports and delicacies.

Schooler and Wilson can often be found in the shop stocking and prepping the cases and shelves and preparing the small in house food and drink menu: beer and wine, cheese and cured meat plates, sandwiches, and various dine-in specials throughout the year such as fondue for two.

Foster & Dobbs tends to showcase a lot of lowbrow turned highbrow foods: dried-on-the-cob, hand-milled grits from South Carolina; spendy dog biscuits with potato flour and amaranth; and slow-ground Virginia peanut butter. In other words, the packaged, non-perishable section feels more boutique than market. To that tune, Foster & Dobbs is a great spot for special occasion shopping and foodie gifts. There are other markets nearby to round out a more comprehensive shopping trip.

The shop regularly hosts wide-ranging events, including wine tastings, chocolate-making classes, and pickling demonstrations. Check out the Foster & Dobbs website for more event information.

Luce

www.luceevents.blogspot.com
📍 2138 & 2140 E Burnside St, Portland 📞 503-236-7195 🕐 11am–10pm every day

John Toboada's (chef-owner of **Navarre**) specialty foods corner store/café/events space is all about less is more Italian-style. The twenty-plus-seat black and white checkered floor café serves all sorts of tasty antipasti, fine wines, soups, salads, housemade pasta, steaks, and more. It's the kind of place you go for a bite to eat and then leave with a bag full of unusual honeys (bergamot, chestnut ...), true balsamic vinegar, fennel pollen, and imported pasta.

Martinotti's Café & Deli

www.martinottis.ypguides.net
📍 404 SW 10th Ave, Portland ☎ 503-224-9028 🕐 M–F 8:30am–7:30pm, Sa 10am–6pm

At the thirty-plus-year-old Martinotti's Cafe & Deli, you'll find crate upon crate of Italian wines, big jars of black licorice candies, and more types of packaged panforte than you can shake an imported Italian breadstick at. But the deli counter is definitely the hub. It's where you'll find a mouth-watering assortment of cheeses, olives, salads, and cured meats, including mortadella and braunschweiger. The rest of the cramped corner shop, filled with small tables and chairs so you can stay a while, is well worth perusing too. Just watch your step because the small paths between wine crates, shelves, and tables aren't too forgiving.

Pastaworks

www.pastaworks.com
📍 3731 SE Hawthorne Blvd, Portland ☎ 503-232-1010 🕐 M–Sa 9:30am–7pm, Su 10am–7pm
📍 35 NW 21st Ave, Portland (in City Market) ☎ 503-221-3002
🕐 M–Sa 9:30am–7pm, Su 10am–7pm
📍 Evoe at 3735 SE Hawthorne Blvd, Portland ☎ 503-232-1010 🕐 W–Su noon–7pm

I can remember just about everything I've ever purchased from the SE Hawthorne Pastaworks: house-made duck gizzard confit, locally grown Fuyu persimmons, house-cured bacon, locally foraged morels, Oregon-grown wild rice, pork fat–wrapped local bison, and locally produced Arbequina olive oil.

Surprisingly, that doesn't even come close to the magic encased in Pastaworks. The meat counter is always impressive, with house-made wild boar bacon, guanciale, pancetta, lomo, and lardo. The produce cooler in the center of the shop is stocked at different points throughout the year with everything from locally grown artichokes, Padrón peppers, radicchio, and cardoons to Hood River Pink Lady apples and Comice pears. The wine selection is outstanding and wide ranging, with all sorts of hard-to-find Italian varietals. And the deli is filled with tasty ready-to-eats.

Pastaworks prices range from precious (that sixteen-month aged Italian prosciutto will set you back a few bucks) to affordable. My favorite pit stop Pastaworks snack is a small Italian salametti secchi and a golden and crusty house-baked roll.

Since summer 2008, the attached restaurant, **Evoe**, helmed by chef Kevin

Gibson, has been serving up delicious food and wine. The shoe box-sized restaurant showcases a constant flux of Pastaworks' top ingredients in dishes written on the big chalkboards behind the bar.

At Evoe, be a good kid and share. An appetizer, meat or cheese plate, salad, and main plate make a great meal for two. The fresh, local, and delicious Oregon spot prawns, served with a nutty romesco sauce and side of lightly dressed frisée, are so good you'll be compelled to order a second plate. Gibson removes the head and antennae before grilling, but keeps the shell intact, sometimes along with bright orange eggs, which are even sweeter and juicier than the prawn.

For the house bocadillo de jamón, Gibson slices paper-thin, fat-ribboned pieces of jamón (dry-cured Spanish ham) from a whole pig's leg – hoof and all – and serves it simply with butter or olive oil on a whole grain mini-baguette.

Evoe's greatest house bargain: Buy a bottle of wine next door from Pastaworks' fantastic selection and pay a $5 corkage fee at Evoe. This is a steal compared to the usual Portland restaurant markup. There are also glass pours, draft or bottled beer, still and sparkling water, and seltzer available.

Proper Eats Market & Cafe

www.propereats.org

9 8638 N Lombard Ave, Portland **☎** 503-445-2007 **🕑** 9am–10pm every day

Proper Eats Market & Cafe reminds me of the cooperative living housing at my college. That on-campus housing always smelled like good food, people wore scarves and wraps around their hair and drank herbal tea from jars, and there was a communal vibe fueled by plenty of interesting conversation, community activism, and a lively kitchen. That's Proper Eats.

Located across the street from the historic **St. Johns Twin Cinema & Pub**, Proper Eats hosts everything from First Amendment–themed film screenings to open-mic nights and saved-seed swaps. The crowd is a mixed bag, with plenty of stray University of Portland kids.

At the front of the business is the tiny market packed with unusual, mostly organic, Oregon-grown fruits and vegetables. In the fall, you're likely to find quince, medlar, and jujubes, and in the summer, local rhubarb, berries, and string and shell beans. The bulk section is great, with grains and cereals, spices in Mason jars, and liquid bulk, including oils and honeys.

The open kitchen is the heart of Proper Eats and provides food and drink (including beer and wine) for the raggle-taggle dining room with a small rug-strewn stage in the back for all sorts of live events. There are tasty raw, vegan, and vegetarian options on the menu, along with plenty of salads, soups, and sandwiches. My favorite thing to order at Proper Eats is the house Reuben made with local **It's Alive!** sauerkraut, caramelized onions, vegan sauce, **Dave's Killer Bread** (☞ *p.* 17), and house-marinated tempeh.

Sheridan Fruit Company

🔗 *www.sheridanfruit.com*

📍 409 SE Martin Luther King Jr Blvd, Portland 📞 503-236-2114

🕐 M–Sa 6am–8pm, Su 6am–6pm; *Grill:* M–F 11am–5pm

Starting in the early 1900s, Produce Row was the east riverside area of Portland known for fresh fruits and vegetables. This skinny industrial flank – roughly defined as south of East Burnside Street, west of SE 12th Avenue, and north of the **Oregon Museum of Science and Industry** – was home to numerous produce markets, fruit stands, and wholesalers for much of the twentieth century, including Sheridan Fruit Company.

In 1916 John Sheridan founded the Sheridan Fruit Company. In 1946 the Paleo brothers bought the business and it remained an outdoor produce market (in what is today the parking lot) until 1961, when they moved the business back into its present building. At this time, groceries were added and, soon after, a meat department.

These days Sheridan Fruit Company is a wholesaler and full-service grocery store with a large meat and cheese department, an impressive dry bulk section, domestic and microbrew beer, a decent selection of wine, and, of course, a fresh and colorful assortment of fruit and vegetables year round. In other words, it's a wonderful, family-owned, one-stop grocery store.

If you're in the neighborhood and want something freshly grilled, stop by the Sheridan grill in the market's parking lot for char-cooked burgers, brats, and more. Order your food from the grill to go or eat it at one of the several outdoor tables.

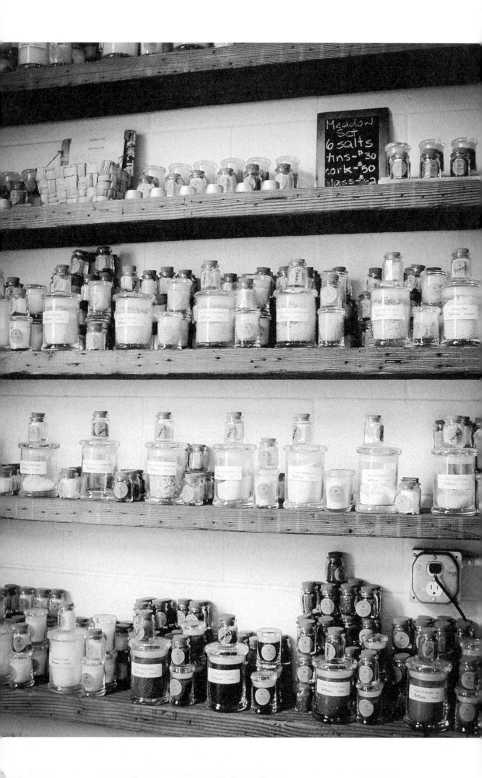

LOOK AT A KITCHEN'S SPICE RACK and you'll learn a lot about the household and its cooks. I tend to think of kitchen spice and salt in the same way that I think of seed packets for the home gardener – relatively inexpensive small parcels with big results. Portland gardens grow wild with herbs and spices in the spring and summer – oregano, basil, fennel, mint, cilantro, dill, chilies, and much more – but in the fall as the leaves change colors and the rain returns, many of these flavorsome plants, if not plucked from the ground, wither and die. It's time for a return to our indoor spice racks.

Most people get their year round spices and salts wherever they do the rest of their grocery shopping, but Portland has a few shops, in addition to countless ethnic markets, that specialize in both and are worth the extra trip. Considering the homogenization of supermarket salts and spices, the extended warehousing time that they often endure, and the fillers and additives dumped into many of them, it's nice to buy spices and salts from small specialty markets if you can.

Caribbean Spice Market

📍 4516 NE 42nd Ave, Portland 📞 503-493-2737
🕐 M noon–8pm, Tu–Sa 10:30am–8pm, Su 11am–5:30pm

Caribbean Spice Market is loud in more ways than one, with its bright red, yellow, and green painted cinderblock exterior and front door alarm that sounds every time someone enters or exits.

If you want to find ingredients that will push you into new culinary terrain, Caribbean Spice Market should top your list. Walking through the aisles, you'll find unusual foods such as ukazi, uda, and wollo, and sacks of semolina, farina, plantain, and fufu flour. Down another aisle are red palm oils, okra dust for thickening gumbos and stews, and lots of jars and sacks of jerk seasonings and other brazen herbs and spices. The freezers in the side room are stocked with everything from cuts of goat meat, oxtails, and cow feet to cassava leaves and roasted and frozen breadfruit.

The Herb Shoppe

🔗 www.theherbshoppe.net
📍 3327 SE Hawthorne Blvd, Portland 📞 503-234-7801
🕐 M–F 11am–7pm, Sa 10am–6pm, Su noon–5pm

Although the focus at this small Hawthorne shop is medicinal herbs, there's a small section dedicated to culinary herbs and salts, with roughly one hundred big glass jars filled with everything from parsley, lemon balm, and juniper berries to spearmint, stevia, and chamomile. There is also a small teapot section. Gather what you want in bulk and pay by the ounce at the counter.

The Meadow

www.atthemeadow.com

📍 3731 N Mississippi Ave, Portland 📞 503-288-4633, 888-388-4633
🕐 Su–Th 10am–6pm, F–Sa 10am–7pm

Mark Bitterman opened The Meadow in the summer of 2006 as a small floral shop with a decent section of specialty salts that he'd acquired during years of travel. The small North Mississippi shop is now home to more than ninety salts; a wall of hard-to-find wines, ciders, and twenty-plus bitters and vermouths; more than three hundred types of chocolate bars; edible flowers such as acacia, apple blossoms, hibiscus; and more. Yes, more. It's the kind of place where you crouch down to see what's on a low shelf and discover what Mark Bitterman deems "a game-changing soy sauce." Then you turn ninety degrees and discover a tin of the Bittermans' favorite anchovies.

There is a wooden table toward the back of the shop nestled in the wine section that's usually topped with a taster or two for you to nibble or sip on – a local hard cider, a just-in deep sea salt from Kona reminiscent of champagne, or a rare Icelandic sea salt slowly evaporated and chock-full of minerals and flavor.

The Meadow regularly hosts classes in the evenings on everything from Himalayan salt block cooking to an introduction to artisan salt or salted caramels. These small classes usually cost $15–$20 and fill up fast. Go to The Meadow's website to sign up or to check out their growing online selection of six hundred-plus salt products.

The Meadow is one of the best places in town to take a food-loving Portland visitor. It's an incredibly unique shop filled with all sorts of edible souvenirs. Also check out Mark Bitterman's books: *Salted*, which is a field guide to the world of artisan salt; and his latest, *Salt Block Cooking;* and the next time you're in New York stop by his West Village outpost of The Meadow.

Penzeys Spices

www.penzeys.com

📍 11322 SE 82nd Ave, Portland 📞 503-653-7779 🕐 M–Sa 10am–6pm, Su 11am–5pm
📍 120 NW 10th Ave, Portland 📞 503-227-6777 🕐 M–Sa 10am–6pm, Su 11am–5pm
📍 11787 SW Bvtn–Hills Hwy, Beaverton 📞 503-643-7430 🕐 M–Sa 10am–6pm, Su 11am–5pm

The Wisconsin-based Penzeys Spices (with more than sixty U.S. locations) carries over 250 herbs and spices. The burlap sack décor at Penzeys is minimal, and spice sections are broken up by crates. Toward the back, there's a big map that employees have stuck with flag-topped pins denoting where various spices are sourced from – a marjoram flag in Egypt, a green cardamom flag in Costa Rica.

Every herb and spice is in glass, easy-to-open, apothecary jars to encourage smelling and looking. When your nose grows weary from comparing white, green, and black cardamom pods, or you feel the tickle of a sneeze from Indian black peppercorns, you can grab one of the many small jars filled with roasted coffee beans and do as the label says: inhale and "refresh your palate."

In addition to whole and ground single spices, there are mixes and blends such as Krakow nights spice blend (a peppery seasoning for meats), corned beef spices, and breakfast and bratwurst sausage seasonings. Complimentary recipe cards are placed all around the shop, in addition to literature on herb and spice basics, history, and cooking tips.

Once or twice a week, Penzeys receives shipments of spices cultivated mainly within one hundred miles of the equator, which is regarded as the best spice-growing area in the world. Culinary school students, restaurateurs, and food business entrepreneurs can be found sniffing around the store in hot pursuit of the latest arrival.

Go to SPICY FOOD Spots

Classic sichuan

Taste of Sichuan
- 16261 NW Cornell Rd, Beaverton
- 503-629-7001
- www.tasteofsichuan.com

Hot wings

Fire on the Mountain
- 4225 N Interstate Ave, Portland
- 503-280-9464
- 1708 E Burnside St, Portland
- 503-230-9464
- 3443 NE 57th Ave, Portland
- 503-894-8973
- www.portlandwings.com

Sichuan style

Lucky Strike
- 3862 SE Hawthorne Blvd, Portland
- 503-206-8292
- www.luckystrikepdx.com

Korean worth the drive

Nak Won Korean Restaurant
- 4600 SW Watson Ave, Beaverton
- 503-646-9382

Thai street food

Pok Pok
- 3226 SE Division St, Portland
- 503-232-1387
- www.pokpokpdx.com

Authentic Thai

Red Onion
- 1123 NW 23rd Ave, Portland
- 503-208-2634
- www.redonionportland.com

Izakaya hotspot

Tanuki
- 8029 SE Stark St, Portland
- 503-477-6030
- www.tanukipdx.com

Thai drinking food

Whiskey Soda Lounge
- 3131 SE Division St, Portland
- 503-222-0102
- www.whiskeysodalounge.com

'**M SURPRISED THAT THERE AREN'T MORE** vegan and vegetarian options in Portland. Yes, most restaurants, cafés, and markets make concessions, but few cater exclusively to vegans and vegetarians, although since this book first came out, there are definitely some new additions. That said, Portland is home to the only vegan strip mall I know of (☞ **Food Fight!** *below*). In addition, Portland has its own vegetarian club, a nearby raw food festival, and even a master vegetarian program. Here are some spots to check out.

Back to Eden Bakery

www.backtoedenbakery.com
2217 NE Alberta St, Portland · 503-477-5022 · 9am–10pm every day

Back to Eden Bakery isn't just for vegans. It's also a go-to spot for folks with various food allergies and sensitivities to gluten, soy, dairy, and sugar. It feels like a hipster root cellar, as in: everything is DIY, local, healthful, and handmade, from the tasty cashew tarts, mini cakes, and vegan soft serve to the cobbled-together décor. Even non-vegan, non-restricted eaters will be happy here, with all sorts of lovingly made treats to choose from, often made with things you've never heard of but will end up devouring. Don't let the *Portlandia*-ness steer you away. Back to Eden Bakery is sweet (and savory!), earnest, and 100% delicious.

Food Fight! Vegan Grocery

www.foodfightgrocery.com
1217 SE Stark St, Portland · 503-233-3910 · 10am–8pm every day

Food Fight! Vegan Grocery is devoted to vegan convenience foods – TV dinners, fake meats, sodas, snacks – but you'll also find fresh fruits, vegetables, and hearty bulk items. They're passionate about promoting small, local food producers, hence the sacks of **Cellar Door Coffee** (☞ *p.* 117), roasted just a few blocks away. There's a mural of militant vegetables on the wall and tables out front if you want to eat your plantain chips in peace between the vegan tattoo shop and vegan retail clothing shop. The vegan strip mall that houses Food Fight! is home to four other vegan businesses: **Sweetpea Baking Co.**, **Scapegoat Tattoo**, **Red and Black Cafe**, and *Herbivore* magazine's retail shop.

Papa G's Vegan Organic Deli

www.pappags.com
2314 SE Division St, Portland · 503-235-0244 · M–Sa 11am–8pm, Su noon–8pm

I may be an omnivore, but I recognize a killer salad bar when I see one. Papa G's

OTA TOFU

Ota Tofu's small Southeast Portland workspace smells malty and slightly sweet, like milk-soaked cereal. Every day Ota Tofu makes several types of fresh tofu, *age* (deep-fried tofu cutlets or pouches), and soy milk. The employees transform the soybeans using stainless-steel machines to grind, pressure-cook, press, and cut the tofu.

Since 1918 this family business has focused on the local market. Ota's tofu is unpasteurized, so the shelf life is brief, and flavor and consistency are not always uniform. Ota uses a flavor-rich, refined form of *nigari* (the traditional tofu solidifier, extracted from seawater) to set the tofu, rather than a chemical compound, which favors higher yields over flavor. The result is tofu that really sets Ota apart. You can find packages of Ota Tofu in such markets as **Sheridan Fruit Company**, **People's Food Co-op**, **Anzen**, **Fubonn Shopping Center**, **Uwajimaya**, and **New Seasons Market**.

♀ 812 SE Stark St, Portland
☎ 503-232-8947
🕐 M–Sa 9am–5pm

Vegan Organic Deli's salad bar includes watermelon radishes, hijiki seaweed, golden beets, and more, and they also offer a hot counter, made-to-order sandwiches (including a wild rice tempeh Reuben and a spicy barbecue tofu sandwich), and grab-and-go foods like pizza rolls and tofu walnut balls. It's the kind of place where culinary discoveries await: house-made dairy-free kefirs, nut and hemp milks, cashew "yogurt" made with coconut, and raw sunflower seed "cheese," which crumbles like ricotta. Whether or not you're vegan, Papa G's is a worthy stop.

Sweetpea Baking Co.

🔗 *www.sweetpeabaking.com*
♀ 1205 SE Stark St, Portland   ☎ 503-477-5916
🕐 M–Sa 8am–6pm, Su 9am–5pm

Sweetpea Baking Co. is best known for two things: its $10 all-you-can-eat Southern-style Sunday brunch buffet (fresh-squeezed orange juice and coffee included) and a sweet and savory vegan bakery case. There's even vegan cheesecake.

Just like **Red and Black Cafe** around the corner, Sweetpea is a nice, low-key neighborhood hangout for breakfast, lunch, and then some. For lunch, there are premade sandwiches and usually a couple of soups. The coffee is **Stumptown** (☛ *p.* 123), the tea is **Townshend's** (☛ *p.* 136), and the open kitchen is all vegan, from its herby focaccia down to its cinnamon scones. There are great vegan bagel spreads like fake bacun scallion. On Saturdays, come for a vegan doughnut. Sweetpea started off as a wholesale business, and in addition to the bakery café, you can still find Sweetpea baked goods in shops, restaurants, and cafés around town.

Go-to VEGAN/VEGETARIAN Spots

Healthy light

Blossoming Lotus
- 1713 NE 15th Ave, Portland
- 503-228-0048
- www.blpdx.com

Plenty of creative Chinese inspired veg dishes available 'til late

The Baowry
- 8307 N Ivanhoe St, Portland
- 503-285-4839

Bar with vegan food

Bye & Bye
- 1011 NE Alberta St, Portland
- 503-281-0537
- www.thebyeandbye.com

Frenchy bistro with loads of fresh, seasonal veggie dishes

Cocotte
- 2930 NE Killingsworth St, Portland
- 503-227-2669
- www.cocottepdx.com

Higher-end veggie fare

Natural Selection
- 3033 NE Alberta St, Portland
- 503-288-5883
- www.naturalselectionpdx.com

Romantic veggie-centric

The Farm Café
- 10 SE 7th Ave, Portland
- 503-736-3276
- www.thefarmcafe.com

Vegan barbecue food cart

Homegrown Smoker Natural Barbecue
- Mississippi Marketplace, Portland
- www.homegrownsmoker.wordpress.com

Vegan café

Proper Eats Market & Cafe
- 8638 N Lombard Ave, Portland
- 503-445-2007
- www.propereats.org

Italian by night

Portobello Vegan Trattoria
- 1125 SE Division St, Portland
- 503-754-5993
- www.portobellopdx.com

Ethiopian vegetarian meals

Queen of Sheba
- 2413 NE Martin Luther King Jr Blvd, Portland
- 503-287-6302
- www.queenofsheba.biz

Cooperative vegan food and drink

Red and Black Cafe
- 400 SE 12th Ave, Portland
- 503-231-3899
- www.redandblackcafe.com

Southern-style vegan brunch buffet and more

Sweetpea Baking Co.
- 1205 SE Stark St, Portland
- 503-477-5916
- www.sweetpeabaking.com

Lots of Mexican vegetarian and vegan options

Taqueria Los Gorditos
- 50th Ave and SE Division St, Portland
- 503-875-2615
- 1212 SE Division St, Portland
- 503-445-6289
- NW Davis St, between 9th and 10th Aves, Portland
- 503-805-5323

Hipster vegetarian/vegan meals

Vita Café
- 3023 NE Alberta St, Portland
- 503-335-8233
- www.vita-cafe.com

Regional Mexican with plenty of veg

Xico
- 3715 SE Division St, Portland
- 503-548-6343
- www.xicopdx.com

DRINK

AS A GENERAL RULE, Portland beer is hoppy, full-flavored, and strong – a lot of beer brewed here has an alcohol content of 7% or higher. One explanation is that hops grow in the Northwest. For that reason, brewers flock here, and the next thing you know, Portland has fifty-plus breweries within city limits – more than any other city in the world. Beer is huge in Portland.

Several years ago, a homebrewer friend of mine visited from Cincinnati with the intention of visiting as many breweries as possible while in town. It was my duty to be tour guide. I don't think my friend realized just what a huge undertaking it would truly be to visit (and of course, to drink at) each and every one. We didn't even come close. My friend's biggest impression when all was said and drunk: Portland beer is amazing and hoppy.

This chapter primarily covers Portland breweries and brewers, but I've also included some of my favorite beer bars and bottle shops. There are also loads of brew festivals that take place every year in Portland. Check out **Food and Drink Events** (☞ *p.* 174) for those.

Alameda Brewhouse

www.alamedabrewhouse.com
4765 NE Fremont St, Portland ☎ 503-460-9025
Su–Th 11am–11pm, F–Sa 11am–midnight

Alameda Brewhouse brews beer to write home about. Some of Alameda's standout beers include the Klickitat Pale Ale, the Siskiyou Golden Ale, the Black Bear XX Stout, and the Wilshire Wheat Ale. They brew in fairly small batches and are stingy about distribution, so if you want to choose from Alameda's full hoppy, malty selection, you'll have to make the trek to the brewhouse.

The menu is a good read (grilled ahi, skewered prawns and scallops, bacon-wrapped filet mignon), but in my experience it doesn't translate to the plate. Go for the beer. Also keep in mind that Alameda Brewhouse is a neighborhood family depot and there are usually plenty of kids around.

Belmont Station and Biercafe

www.belmont-station.com
4500 SE Stark St, Portland ☎ 503-232-8538
Store: M–Sa 10am–10pm, Su noon–9pm; *Biercafe:* noon–11pm every day

Belmont Station generally has about twelve hundred international, national, and local beers in stock. In addition to beer, Belmont sells hard cider, mead, sake, wine, soda, and more. The shop also sells classic beer steins, mugs, and other beer paraphernalia.

The Belmont Station Biercafe (appropriately located) has an amazing selection as well. Just like some of the better pubs in town, when a keg blows here, it's always replaced with something different. Belmont Station is all about diversity, with a tilt toward craft local and international beers. Top sellers at the shop and biercafe are the hoppy local beers, and co-owner and manager Carl Singmaster guesses that 90% of the inventory is 6% or higher in alcohol content. Singmaster used to co-own Belmont Station and Biercafe with the late, legendary Don Younger of Portland's **Horse Brass Pub**.

If you want to get the most out of your visit to Belmont Station, stop by during its once- or twice-a-week free tastings.

BridgePort Brewing Co.

www.bridgeportbrew.com
BridgePort Brewpub and Bakery, 1313 NW Marshall St, Portland 503-241-3612
Tu–Th 11:30am–11pm, F–Sa 11:30am–midnight, Su–M 11:30 am–10pm

BridgePort Brewing Co. is the oldest craft brewery in Oregon. Located in a one-hundred-plus-year-old former rope factory in Northwest Portland, what began as a small microbrewery is now a 100,000-barrel-a-year business, with distribution in eighteen states. BridgePort beers, including ESB, Blue Heron Pale Ale, Black Strap Stout, and Ropewalk Amber, are never force carbonated and are always naturally conditioned in the bottle, keg, or cask.

Renovations in 2005 improved the space, but I doubt I'm the only one who misses the former raw, old, brick and ivy space that was BridgePort. The alehouse feels much more corporate now, though it does still have some character – specifically, its beer.

Bridgetown Beerhouse

915 N Shaver St, Portland 503-477-8763
M–Th noon–10pm, F–Sa noon–11pm,
Su noon–9pm

This small North Portland bottle shop opened in early 2009. The square-shaped shop has several coolers filled with a mishmash of two hundred different beers. Maybe there's some method to the madness, but it's hard to tell.

Most of Bridgetown Beerhouse's beer is stateside microbrews, and a lot is from the Pacific Northwest. You'll also find plenty of domestics such as Pabst Blue Ribbon and other canned beers. Owner Mike Waite often ages beer in an

Go to PUBS Spots WITH A GOOD BEER SELECTION

Apex
📍 1216 SE Division St, Portland
📞 503-273-9227
🌐 www.apexbar.com

Bazi Bierbrasserie
📍 1522 SE 32nd Ave, Portland
📞 503-234-8888
🌐 www.bazipdx.com

Belmont Station and Biercafe
📍 4500 SE Stark St, Portland
📞 503-232-8538
🌐 www.belmont-station.com

Bailey's Taproom
📍 213 SW Broadway, Portland
📞 503-295-1004
🌐 www.baileystaproom.com

Concordia Ale House
📍 3276 NE Killingsworth St, Portland
📞 503-287-3929
🌐 www.concordia-ale.com

EastBurn
📍 1800 E Burnside St, Portland
📞 503-236-2876
🌐 www.theeastburn.com

Green Dragon
📍 928 SE 9th St, Portland
📞 503-517-0660
🌐 www.pdxgreendragon.com

Henry's Tavern
📍 10 NW 12th Ave, Portland
📞 503-227-5320
🌐 www.henrystavern.com

Higgins Bar
📍 1239 SW Broadway, Portland
📞 503-222-9070
🌐 www.higgins.ypguides.net

Horse Brass Pub
📍 4534 SE Belmont St, Portland
📞 503-232-2202
🌐 www.horsebrass.com

Moon and Sixpence
📍 2014 NE 42nd Ave, Portland
📞 503-288-7802

Produce Row Café
📍 204 SE Oak St, Portland
📞 503-232-8355
🌐 www.producerowcafe.com

Saraveza
📍 1004 N Killingsworth St, Portland
📞 503-206-4252
🌐 www.saraveza.com

old bank vault in the back of the shop and stocks it only when the flavor is just right. Check out the website for tastings and events.

Captured by Porches Brewing Company

🌐 www.capturedbyporches.com
📍 40 Cowlitz #B, St. Helens. Check the website for a full listing of the brewery's beer buses parked in several neighborhoods throughout town.
📞 971-207-3742 (call for a tasting or brewery tour).

This brewery isn't technically in Portland, but it's still a Portland DIY institution. Captured by Porches Brewing Company started off as brewer-owner Dylan Goldsmith's small home-brew club in Portland. Goldsmith crafted good, hoppy, barrel-conditioned beer and delivered kegs right to the porches of Portlanders.

These days, the brewery is located in a two thousand-square-foot brewery in St. Helens. Captured by Porches beers include Invasive Species IPA, Red Emma Amber Ale, and lots of seasonal brews, including a spring kölsch, a fall dunkelweizen, and a winter porter.

You can find Captured by Porches unfiltered and barrel-conditioned beer at the **Horse Brass Pub**, **Belmont Station and Biercafe** (☞ p. 104), **Red and Black Cafe**, **The Waypost**, **Davis Street Tavern**, **The Know**, **Leisure Public House**. The brewery's mobile public house buses park in various locations year round, pulling tasty Captured by Porches beer.

Deschutes Brewery and Public House

🌐 www.deschutesbrewery.com
📍 210 NW 11th Ave, Portland 📞 503-296-4906
🕐 Su–Tu 11am–10pm, W–Th 11am–11pm, F–Sa 11am–midnight

This popular Bend brewery opened its Port-

|||||||||||||||||||||||||||||||||||||||||||||||||||||||||||||||||||

BREWERIES

Varied and balanced beers
Breakside Brewery
♀ 820 NE Dekum St, Portland
☏ 503-719-6475
♀ 5821 SE Int'l Way, Milwaukie
☏ 503-719-6475
🔗 *www.breakside.com*

Sour beer
Cascade Brewing
♀ 939 SE Belmont St, Portland
☏ 503-265-8603
🔗 *www.cascadebrewing.com*

Ten barrel brewery
Coalition Brewing Co.
♀ 2724 SE Ankeny St, Portland
☏ 503-894-8080
🔗 *www.coalitionbrewing.com*

Unfiltered craft brew
Burnside Brewing Company
♀ 701 E Burnside St, Portland
☏ 503-946-8151
🔗 *www.burnsidebrewco.com*

|||||||||||||||||||||||||||||||||||||||||||||||||||||||||||||||||||

BOTTLE SHOPS

500-plus ales and lagers
The Beer Mongers
♀ 1125 SE Division St, Portland
☏ 503-234-6012
🔗 *www.thebeermongers.com*

150 beers and ciders
Hop Haven Beer Bar and Bottle Shop
♀ 2130 NE Broadway, Portland
☏ 503-287-0244

Barbecue + beer in house or to-go
Bottles Beer Bar and Bottle Shop
♀ 5015 NE Fremont St, Portland
☏ 503-287-7022
🔗 *www.bottlesnw.com*

Sellwood beer and wine shop
Portland Bottle Shop
♀ 7960 SE 13th Ave, Portland
☏ 503-232-5202
🔗 *www.pdxbottleshop.com*

land brewpub in the Pearl in 2008. It produces all Deschutes seasonal and year round brews, including Mirror Pond Pale Ale, Black Butte Porter, and Green Lakes Organic Ale in twelve-barrel batches. In 2009 the Portland brewery was granted Oregon Tilth organic certification.

Huge wooden beams and rafters, tall ceilings, and big neon signs dominate the often packed beer hall located just up the road from the downtown **Powell's City of Books**. There are sixteen taps, featuring Deschutes standbys as well as various seasonal and experimental beers that you can't find elsewhere. The menu's classic pub fare often has a twist (Thai hot wings, steamer clams in a Mirror Pond Pale Ale butter sauce, wild mushroom ragout), and it's loaded with local, seasonal ingredients. I recommend a hot pretzel knot with bubbly cheese fondue alongside a hoppy Deschutes ale or IPA.

F. H. Steinbart Co.

🔗 *www.fhsteinbart.com*
♀ 234 SE 12th Ave, Portland ☏ 503-232-8793
🕐 M–W 8:30am–6pm, Th–F 8:30am–7pm, Sa 9am–4pm, Su 10am–4pm

F. H. Steinbart Co., founded in 1918, is one of the oldest wine and beer supply houses in the nation. It's also one of my favorite Portland businesses. Over the years, I've been to Steinbart countless times. Sometimes I buy small – a packet of champagne yeast – and sometimes I buy big – a five-gallon carboy. Sometimes I rent – a cider press – and sometimes I just wander the aisles and soak it all up. Only brewers, vintners, and drink enthusiasts work at Steinbart, and these folks never tire of talking potables.

The malt room houses more than one hundred bulk malts, the wine aisles are crowded

Alameda Brewhouse
📍 4765 NE Fremont St, Portland
📞 503-460-9025
🔗 www.alamedabrewhouse.com

Breakside Brewery
📍 820 NE Dekum St, Portland
📞 503-719-6475
📍 5821 SE Int'l Way, Milwaukie
📞 503-719-6475
🔗 www.breakside.com

Burnside Brewing Company
📍 701 E Burnside St, Portland
📞 503-946-8151
🔗 www.burnsidebrewco.com

Cascade Brewing Barrel House
📍 939 SE Belmont St, Portland
📞 503-265-8603
🔗 cascadebrewingbarrelhouse.com

The Commons Brewery
📍 1810 SE 10th Ave, Portland
📞 503-343-5501
🔗 www.commonsbrewery.com

BridgePort Brewpub
📍 1313 NW Marshall St, Portland
📞 503-241-3612
🔗 www.bridgeportbrew.com

Deschutes Brewery and Public House
📍 210 NW 11th Ave, Portland
📞 503-296-4906
🔗 www.deschutesbrewery.com

Hair of the Dog Brewing Company
📍 61 SE Yamhill St, Portland
📞 503-232-6585
🔗 www.hairofthedog.com

Hopworks Urban Brewery
📍 2944 SE Powell Blvd, Portland
📞 503-232-4677
📍 Bikebar: 3947 N Williams Ave
📞 503-287-6258
🔗 www.hopworksbeer.com

Upright Brewing
📍 240 N Broadway #2, Portland
📞 503-735-5337
🔗 www.uprightbrewing.com

Widmer Gasthaus Pub
📍 929 N Russell St, Portland
📞 503-281-3333
🔗 www.widmer.com

with wine bases and purees, and the soda aisle is filled to the brim with botanicals and extracts. Steinbart equipment, ingredients, and literature are all a giant ode to DIY. On more than one occasion, I've seen novice brewers and vintners head to the front desk and pull out their bottles of problematic brews and wines for expert Steinbart staff opinions. Staff members will sniff, make pained, pinched faces, and offer sage advice.

In addition to all the supplies (carboys, cappers, barrels, bottles), ingredients (hops, vinegar mothers, wine and beer yeast), and advice, Steinbart hosts monthly classes on beginning to advanced beer and wine making and other topics. They're quite affordable, at $25 or less per person.

Hair of the Dog Brewing Company

🔗 www.hairofthedog.com
📍 61 SE Yamhill St, Portland 📞 503-232-6585
🕐 Tu–Th 11:30am–8pm, F–Sa 11:30am–10pm, Su 11:30am–8pm

Several times a year, this enigmatic and revered Southeast brewery hosts special beer sales, and once a year they host FredFest – an annual spring/summer birthday celebration for local renowned beer writer Fred Eckhardt. Beyond these annual events, Hair of the Dog Brewing Company is an incredible specialty brewery, founded circa 1993, with delicious, hard-to-find-elsewhere beers.

Some of the most popular Hair of the Dog brews include Ruth (an American ale), Adam (a dessert beer), Fred (a ten-hop variety), and Doggie Claws (a barley wine). Hair of the Dog brews only a small amount of their high-impact beer (most are 10% alcohol or more) and each bottle has a unique bottling number. The brewery specializes in unusual and sometimes new beer styles, and several Hair of the Dog beers are bottle-conditioned. Stop by the industrial Southeast tasting room to sample a solid selection of them.

Hopworks Urban Brewery

℘ *www.hopworksbeer.com*

📍 2944 SE Powell Blvd, Portland 📞 503-232-4677

🕐 Su–Th 11am–11pm, F–Sa 11am–midnight

📍 Bikebar: 3947 N Williams Ave, Portland 📞 503-287-6258

🕐 M–Th 11am–11pm, F–Sa 11am–midnight, Su 11:30am–8pm

Months before Hopworks Urban Brewery (HUB) opened, I was chomping at the bit. Along with other lucky Portlanders, I'd been drinking Hopworks Urban Brewery beers since the fall of 2007 at various pubs and restaurants around town, and they were good. Very good – especially the IPA.

Hopworks owner Christian Ettinger didn't plan to open the doors to a brewpub several months after wholesaling kegs to local establishments, but that's the way it worked out. According to Ettinger, the Hopworks production facility took a lot less time to build than the large upstairs brewpub. It's a good thing it did because it was genius marketing. Folks enjoyed the delicious local mystery brew served at top Portland pubs, and from there the buzz about Hopworks built. Ettinger teamed up with his architect father, and Hopworks Urban Brewery opened in March 2008.

At Hopworks Urban Brewery, there are always ten beers on tap and two cask beers. Standards include HUB Lager, Crosstown Pale Ale, Velvet ESB, Hopworks IPA, Survival Stout, and Deluxe Organic Ale. There are also always four seasonals on tap, which keeps the brewers and customers happy. In 2009 HUB began

bottling some of its beers in twenty-two-ounce bottles.

The menu is good pub fare, especially the tasty half-pound burgers, thin crust pizza, and nacho french fries. Hopworks is a kid magnet, with designated kid areas, coloring books, and free pizza dough for kids to play with at the tables.

Reusing is a big part of HUB's culture, and in addition to using all sorts of old kegs and brewery equipment inside and outside the building as functional décor, they use spent fry oil from the restaurant upstairs to fuel the brew kettle and delivery truck. In late September of 2009, HUB hosted its first annual Biketoberfest – an all-day food, drink, music, and bike festival open to anyone who rode their bike to get there. HUB is super bike-friendly – there's a bicycle repair stand by the entrance and you can buy a new bike tube at the bar with your beer. HUB Bikebar opened in North Portland in the summer of 2011.

John's Market

🔗 *www.johnsmarketplace.com*
📍 3535 SW Multnomah Blvd, Portland 📞 503-244-2617 🕐 M–F 7am–10pm, Sa–Su 8am–10pm

Founded in 1923, this Multnomah Village neighborhood market has an enormous beer and wine selection. Choose from 800 domestic and imported bottled beers, 400 wines, and one hundred kegs. Although you can purchase meats and cheeses from the attached **Multnomah Deli** (same owners) and shop for basic market foods and produce, the incredible selection of beer and wine is what it's all about. Check out the regular Friday night wine tastings and other events.

Laurelwood Public House and Brewery

🔗 *www.laurelwoodbrewpub.com*
📍 5115 NE Sandy Blvd, Portland 📞 503-282-0622
   🕐 M–Th 11am–10pm, F 11am–11pm, Sa 10am–11pm, Su 10am–10pm
📍 6716 SE Milwaukie Ave, Portland 📞 503-894-8267 🕐 Su–Th 11am–10pm, F–Sa 11am–11pm
📍 Laurelwood Half Court Pub: 1 North Center Court St, Portland 📞 503-235-8771
   🕐 Open during events at the Moda Center

I've always enjoyed the beer at Laurelwood Public House and Brewery. Head brewer Chad Kennedy brews everything from Hop Monkey IPA and Mother Lode Golden Ale to Organic Free Range Red and Organic Tree Hugger Porter at the NE Sandy location, although there are several Laurelwood public houses and restaurants around town. Food at all locations focuses on pub grub such as nachos, pizza, quesadillas, burgers, steak, and fish and chips. This is a very kid-friendly spot.

Lucky Labrador Brewing Company

www.luckylab.com

- **Brew Pub:** 915 SE Hawthorne Blvd, Portland 503-236-3555
  - M–Sa 11am–midnight, Su noon–10pm
- **Beer Hall:** 1945 NW Quimby St, Portland 503-517-4352
  - M–W 11am–11pm, Th–Sa 11am–midnight, Su noon–10pm
- **Public House:** 7675 SW Capitol Hwy, Portland 503-244-2537
  - M–Sa 11am–midnight, Su noon–10pm
- **Tap Room:** 1700 N Killingsworth St, Portland 503-505-9511
  - M–W 11am–11pm, Th–Sa 11am–midnight, Su noon–10pm

The beer at Lucky Labrador Brewing Company is good, and there are always at least eight Lucky Lab brews (Black Lab Stout, Dog Day IPA, Crazy Ludwig's Alt, Hawthorne Best Bitter, Reggie's Red, and more) on tap in addition to a cask pump, nitro tap, and guest tap. The food is different at each location and ranges from sandwiches and salads to bento and pizza.

Yes, this is the place to head if you want to drink with your dog. Although you can't bring your pooch inside, all four Lucky Lab pubs have big outdoor areas where you can drink good beer and hold a leash. Inside and out, Lucky Lab has a low-key beer hall feel, with tall ceilings, long communal tables, and minimal décor.

For those who want to save a little cash, check out Miser Monday at the **Hawthorne Brew Pub** and Tightwad Tuesday at the **Multnomah Village Public House** and the **Quimby Street Beer Hall**. One of Lucky Lab's latest endeavors is solar beer. Check out the website to learn more.

The Mash Tun Brewpub

www.themashtunbrewpub.com

- 2204 NE Alberta St #101, Portland 503-548-4491
  - M–Th 4pm–midnight, F 4pm–1am, Sa 10am–1am, Su noon–1am

The Mash Tun Brewpub is a good spot to grab a beer and a bite to eat. It serves Mash Tun beer along with beers from other breweries.

The draw at Mash Tun is the space. Tucked away on a side street of Alberta, this indoor/outdoor hangout has a pool table, free jukebox, darts, and a nice back patio. It's a comfortable, low-key hangout in an area that's known for pushing out the low-dough to make way for expensive new joints. The food is also good and there's a lot to choose from – a notch above standard brewpub fare with some good vegetarian options.

McMenamins Pubs

www.mcmenamins.com

- Black Rabbit Restaurant at Edgefield: 2126 SW Halsey St, Troutdale 503-492-3086
  - 7am–10pm every day
- Kennedy School: 5736 NE 33rd Ave, Portland 503-288-2192 *Courtyard Restaurant*:
  7am–1am every day; *Cypress Room*: M–F 4pm–1am, Sa–Su noon–1am
- Greater Trumps: 1520 SE 37th Ave, Portland 503-235-4530
  - M–Th 4pm–midnight, F–Sa 4pm–1am, Su 4pm–midnight
- White Eagle Saloon: 836 N Russell St, Portland 503-282-6810
  - M–Th 11am–1am, F 11am–2:30am, Sa noon–2:30am, Su 4pm–11pm
- Fifteen additional locations *(see website for details)*.

If I have friends or family visiting Portland, chances are good that at some point we'll find ourselves at a McMenamins. No matter which one you visit (my favorites are the **Kennedy School**, **Edgefield**, **Greater Trumps**, and **White Eagle Saloon**), there's sure to be some history and lots of funky art to soak up. McMenamins is known for restoring and renovating historic buildings (chapels, schools, hotels, and dance halls) and incorporating lots of artwork and murals into their cobbled-together, usually historic spaces.

McMenamins is difficult to categorize. What started in the 1980s as a family business is now twenty-four breweries and fifty-seven Oregon and Washington establishments. It all started with beer, and today the company's two hundred-plus beers are brewed in six-barrel batches.

McMenamins brews poured at its wide-ranging establishments (hotels, bars, movie theaters, music venues, and more) include the Terminator Stout, the hoppy and top-selling Hammerhead, the slightly sweet Ruby, and the Black Rabbit Porter. Although McMenamins distills spirits, roasts coffee, and crafts wine and soda as well, beer is the draw.

Old Lompoc Brewery

⌨ www.lompocbrewing.com

 ♀ **New Old Lompoc:** 1616 NW 23rd Ave, Portland ☎ 503-225-1855 🕔 11am–2am every day
 ♀ **Hedge House:** 3412 SE Division St, Portland ☎ 503-235-2215
   🕔 Su–M 11:30am–11pm, Tu–Sa 11:30am–midnight
 ♀ **Fifth Quadrant:** 3901 N Williams Ave, Portland ☎ 503-288-3996
   🕔 M–Th 11am–midnight, F–Sa 11am–1am, Su 11am–11pm
 ♀ **Sidebar:** 3901-A N Williams Ave, Portland ☎ 503-288-3997 🕔 F 4–9pm, Sa noon–5pm
 ♀ **Oaks Bottom Public House:** 1621 SE Bybee Blvd, Portland ☎ 503-232-1728
   🕔 M–Sa 11:30am–midnight, Su 11:30am–10pm

All Old Lompoc Brewery locations are good, solid, low-key spots, but my favorite
was the **New Old Lompoc** in Northwest Portland before the 2013 renovations
because it has the most history and a nice indoor/outdoor space. Each location
features the Old Lompoc beer lineup, including Fool's Golden Ale, Codor Pale
Ale, Centennial IPA, Lompoc Strong Draft, and Sockeye Cream Stout, as well as
many seasonal brews.

Old Lompoc locations serve plenty of lighter beers – in Portland 5% alcohol
content is considered light – in addition to the heavier stouts, porters, and IPAs.
Old Lompoc's newest outpost is **Sidebar** on North Williams, just around the corner from **Fifth Quadrant** bar. Sidebar is an Old Lompoc tasting room that specializes in a variety of the brewing company's barrel-aged, specialty beers.

Mactarnahan's Taproom

⌨ www.portlandbrewing.com

 ♀ 2730 NW 31st Ave, Portland ☎ 503-228-5269
   🕔 M 11am–9pm, Tu–Th 11am–10pm, F 11am–11pm, Sa noon–11pm, Su noon–9pm

I went to this brewpub a couple times when it was still the "founded in 1986"
Portland Brewing Company – before it was acquired by Pyramid Breweries. Pyramid Breweries' Mactarnahan's Taproom is definitely not a spot you just stum-
ble upon. Get directions before heading to this out-of-the-way industrial Northwest brewery.

There is a lot of history in the huge old building, as well as twelve beers on tap,
including MacTarnahan's Amber Ale, Sling Shot Pale Ale, and Summer Grifter
IPA. There's heaps of indoor seating, with a fireside dining room, plus an outdoor
patio. The menu is standard pub fare with some standout rotisserie dishes and
applewood-grilled fare.

Rogue Ales

🔗 *www.rogue.com*

📍 **Rogue Distillery & Public House:** 1339 NW Flanders St, Portland 📞 503-222-5910
🕐 Su–Th 11am–midnight, F–Sa 11am–1am

📍 **Green Dragon Bistro & Brewpub:** 928 SE 9th Ave, Portland 📞 503-517-0660
🕐 Su–W 11am–11pm; Th–Sa 11am–1am

📍 **Rogue Ales at Portland International Airport** 📞 503-282-2630
🕐 W–M 5am-midnight, Tu 5am–6pm

Although there are thirty-eight taps at **Rogue Distillery & Public House**, the beer isn't brewed here. The brewing takes place in Newport (but they do operate a distillery out of the location; ☞ *p.* 130). The space includes indoor and outdoor seating, but most people sit at the bar in front of the impressive tap lineup of Rogue beers and usually a few guest microbrews. Rogue is based in Newport but now has several pubs and brewpubs in Portland and throughout Oregon and Washington.

Rogue's **Green Dragon** in Southeast Portland is a great place for beer snobs. Some beers you might find on tap (although the taps do constantly change): Ninkasi Total Domination, Captured by Porches Porter, Lagunitas Brown Shugga, and Walking Man Walking Stick Stout. If you really want to impress your beer-loving friends, take them to one of the pub's many Meet the Brewer nights, where beer is the topic of the hour.

The beer selection at Green Dragon – nineteen taps and loads of bottles and cans – is incredible, the food is good, and the bar is stocked with plenty of local spirits. If service is slow, which can happen when the bistro is busy, I recommend ordering at the bar and heading outside to one of several picnic tables or the big patio.

Saraveza

🔗 *www.saraveza.com*

📍 1004 N Killingsworth St, Portland 📞 503-206-4252 🕐 W–M 11am–midnight.

Saraveza is a multipurpose space: bottle shop, pub, beer swag museum. You'll find over two hundred bottles for sale (to enjoy in house or to go) in the old-school beer coolers up front, ten rotating taps pouring mostly craft American and Belgian brews, tables collaged and epoxied with beer caps, and delicious British food to the tune of meat and vegetable pasties. Cheesehead owner Sarah Pederson turns on Packer games on game days.

The staff at Saraveza is extremely friendly and knowledgeable. I often end up trying something new here, and I almost always like it (their Caesar salad is incredible). Saraveza also hosts lots of beer-soaked events – beer release parties, tastings with local brewmasters, cheese and beer tastings, and more. Check their website for a detailed schedule.

Tugboat Brewing Company

⊘ www.d2m.com/tugwebsite
♀ 711 SW Ankeny St, Portland   ✆ 503-226-2508
   ◐ M 5pm–10pm, Tu–Th 4pm–midnight, F–Sa 4pm–1am

This tiny brew company in downtown Portland specializes in British-style strong ales, with two-barrel batches and fifteen taps that are heavy on house hoppy beers and stouts. There's often live jazz here, too. If you need entertaining, there are lots of books and board games available to use at the pub.

Upright Brewing Company

⊘ www.uprightbrewing.com
♀ 240 N Broadway, Suite 2, Portland   ✆ 503-735-5337
   ◐ *Tasting room:* F 4:30pm–9pm, Sa–Su 1pm–6pm

Housed in the Leftbank Project, Upright Brewing Company brews beers in the traditional French and Belgian farmhouse style. Beers are named with numbers – 4, 5, 6, 7 – which denote the specific gravity of the beer's wort. They are often aged in wine barrels.

You can find Upright Brewing Company's beers on tap at fine establishments around town including **Belmont Station and Biercafe** (☞ *p.* 104), **EastBurn, Concordia Ale House, Saraveza** (☞ *p.* 114), and **Bailey's Taproom.**

Widmer Brothers Brewing Company

⊘ www.widmerbrothers.com
♀ Brewery: 929 N Russell St, Portland   ✆ 503-281-2437 *(call ahead for tours).*
♀ Gasthaus Pub: 955 N Russell St, Portland   ✆ 503-281-3333 **◐** *Dining room:* Su–Th 11am–10pm,
   F–Sa 11am–11pm; *Bar:* Su–Th 11am–10:30pm, F–Sa 11am–11pm

If the conversation includes Portland beer, chances are good that brothers Kurt and Rob Widmer's brewery will get air time. This epic Portland brewery has been pumping out the good stuff since 1984. Although best known for its Hefeweizen, Widmer also produces Drop Top Amber, Broken Halo IPA, and other craft brews. Widmer also brews limited release beers, including the Collaborator Series, which is brewed in conjunction with the Oregon Brew Crew – a local home brew association.

SE Portland bar pouring all hard cider all the time

Bushwhacker Cider

♀ 1212-D SE Powell Blvd, Portland

☎ 503-445-0577

🔗 www.bushwhackercider.com

Bottled and kegged hard cider made from local apples at this cidery and public taproom

Reverend Nat's Hard Cider

♀ 1813 NE 2nd Ave, Portland

☎ 503-567-2221

🔗 www.reverendnatshardcider.com

Wine country bottled and kegged hard cider from

Wandering Aengus Ciderworks/Anthem Cider

♀ 4070 Fairview Indust. Dr SE, Salem

☎ 503-361-2400

🔗 www.wanderingaengus.com

🔗 www.anthemcider.com

🕐 Very limited tasting room hours; call ahead

English-style bottled hard ciders

Portland Cider Company

☎ 503-908-7654

🔗 www.portlandcider.com

French-style, farm fresh bottled hard cider

E.Z. Orchards

♀ 5504 Hazel Green Rd NE, Salem

☎ 503-393-1506

🔗 www.ezorchards.com

Walla Walla Valley apple hard cider

Blue Mountain Cider Company

♀ 235 E Bdwy Ave, Milton-Freewater

☎ 541-938-5575

🔗 www.drinkcider.com

One thing that sets Widmer apart from other breweries is the yeast that they use. Widmer has been brewing with the same German Altbier yeast strain that Kurt brought back to Portland from Bavaria in the early 1980s. The Altbier yeast strain is so important to the integrity of Widmer beer that strains of it are stored at labs at Oregon Health & Science University and in Chicago, New Hampshire, and the United Kingdom.

Another thing that sets Widmer apart is their premium quality hops. Every year, the Widmer brew team heads to Yakima, Washington, to inspect various lots of local hops and select the ones that they want to brew with. In addition to Washington hops, Widmer uses varieties grown in Oregon and the Nelson variety from New Zealand.

You can find Widmer beers at their **Gasthaus Pub** across the street from the brewery, as well as at local bars and restaurants across town and nationwide. Visit the Gasthaus Pub in the summer and you can sit outside with an industrial view of the Fremont Bridge, the train tracks, and the Willamette River. The Gasthaus Pub serves classic German fare – schnitzel, sauerbraten, sausages, and then some.

GET THE JITTERS just thinking of the volume of coffee regularly imbibed in Portland – hipster baristas grind and pull thousands of shots a day from locally roasted beans. Portland coffee is spectacular and to be quite honest, the sheer selection can be intimidating. Step into a Stumptown Coffee Roasters café and you're likely to see an $85 per pound roast on the board among a list of other high-quality, locally roasted, farm-direct, and, for the most part, less expensive beans.

Portland is one of the most advanced coffee cities in this country. Stumptown Coffee Roasters is based here and there are loads of roasters and microroasters in town – forty-plus.

If you think that being a barista in Portland is an easy high school or college job, put that notion behind you. Baristas, as well as coffee roasters, are superstars in this city, just like roller derby girls, and the only way to get into the world of coffee in Portland is by doing something crazy like learning how to roast coffee in your backyard grill. Coffee is king.

Boyd Coffee Company

www.boyds.com
📍 19730 NE Sandy Blvd, Portland ☎ 503-666-4561 🕐 M–F 7:30am–4pm

Boyd Coffee Company is the oldest coffee company in Portland, founded in 1900 by New Zealand-born American immigrant Percival Dewe Boyd. Owned today by third- and fourth-generation members of the Boyd family, Boyd Coffee Company offers more than 650 coffee and food items and is headquartered on thirty acres east of Portland. Boyd's coffee, espresso, rare estate coffees, and teas fall under several Boyd brands such as Italia D'Oro, Coffee House Roasters, and Boyds Coffee, and are served at Boyd Coffee cafés and at restaurants and food-service operations throughout the country.

Cellar Door Coffee

www.cellardoorcoffee.com
📍 2001 SE 11th Ave, Portland ☎ 503-234-7155 🕐 7am–7pm every day

Cellar Door Coffee owners Andrea Pastor and Jeremy Adams started roasting coffee with a popcorn popper in their kitchen in 2005, and they have been professionally roasting since 2007. It's a classic Portland DIY story – no slogging away for another roaster, just lots of reading, note taking, and trial and error.

Cellar Door's mostly fair trade and organic beans are roasted in the basement of the Southeast café, which opened in early 2008. The coffee is available brewed in house or by the bag at the café, as well as at several other restaurants and cafés around Portland, including **Gravy**, **Food Fight!**, and **Market of Choice**. Cellar Door's café cup is French-pressed, its espresso is available as a blend or single origin, and there are usually quiches, scones, pastries, and bagels behind the counter.

Coava Coffee Roasters

  www.coavacoffee.com
  1300 SE Grand Ave, Portland   503-894-8134
    M–F 6am–6pm, Sa 7am–6pm, Su 8am–6pm

According to Matt Higgins, owner of Coava Coffee Roasters, the word "coava," pronounced "ko-vuh" means "green coffee" in old Turkish. Higgins takes his green bean very seriously. In addition to traveling to Panama to train competition circuit baristas and being a United States Barista Competition-certified judge, he roasts beans in an old carriage house in his North Portland backyard. Higgins serves his mostly single-origin coffees at his southeast tasting room and also delivers them to nearby businesses including **Red E Café** and **Coffeehouse Five**. Contact Higgins at *matt@coavacoffee.com* to arrange Coava cuppings and other coffee events.

Courier Coffee

  www.couriercoffeeroasters.com
  923 SW Oak St, Portland   503-545-6444   M–F 7am–5pm, Sa–Su 9am–4pm

Most days the Courier Coffee guys begin their bicycle delivery routes at the crack of dawn and then roast in the backyard Southeast roasting house once deliveries are through. Thirty-two-year-old Joel Domreis has been roasting and bike delivering his Courier Coffee in Portland since 2005. The first year and a half Domreis did everything solo: roasting, bagging, delivering, communicating, and

troubleshooting with clients. He now has one full-time and one part-time employee.

On average, Courier's San Franciscan steel drum roaster – located in their roasting facility: a converted garage behind a house on SE Hawthorne – roasts 10,000 pounds of coffee annually. Courier roasts everything from Sumatra Sulawesi, and medium roast Ethiopian to Bolivian Cenaproc cooperative coffee.

Courier does pregrind, but they'd much rather deliver whole bean coffee. It's all about freshness and flavor, which is why the company has an uncommon buyback agreement. If the coffee goes past its prime, Courier – not the client – eats the cost.

You don't have to own a business to have Courier Coffee delivered to your front door – all it takes is a phone call. You can also enjoy Courier Coffee at the downtown cafe a block away from **Powell's City of Books** and buy bagged Courier Coffee at **Two Tarts Bakery**, **New Seasons Market**, and other spots around town.

K&F Select Fine Coffees

www.kandfcoffee.com
2706 SE 26th Ave, Portland 503-238-2547
M–F 6am–6pm, Sa–Su 7am–6:00pm

K&F Select Fine Coffees president and CEO Don Dominguez founded this coffee company, which now has twenty-plus employees, with his father in 1983. The company now roasts more than one hundred varieties and blends of coffee and recently rolled out its BellaSelva line of organic coffee.

Kobos Coffee

www.kobos.com
2355 NW Vaughn St, Portland 503-222-2302
M–F 6am–6pm, Sa 8am–6pm, Su noon–5pm
200 SW Market St, Portland 503-221-0418
M–F 6am–5pm

David and Susan Kobos founded Kobos Coffee in 1973, and since then the company has grown into fifty-plus coffees and espressos.

Stumptown by expert baristas
Albina Press
4637 N Albina Ave, Portland
503-282-5214
5012 SE Hawthorne Blvd, Portland
503.282.5214

Vacuum pots and award-winning blends from top roasters
Barista
539 NW 13th Ave, Portland
503-274-1211
1725 NE Alberta St, Portland
529 SW 3rd Ave, Unit 110, Portland
www.baristapdx.com

Bootstraps blends and single origin
Cellar Door Coffee
2001 SE 11th Ave, Portland
503-234-7155
www.cellardoorcoffee.com

Coffee geeks with Stumptown
Coffeehouse Northwest
1951 W Burnside St, Portland
503-248-2133

Great coffee and no pretense
The Fresh Pot
4001 N Mississippi Ave, Portland
503-284-8928
3729 SE Hawthorne Blvd, Portland
503-232-8928
724 SW Washington St, Portland
www.thefreshpot.com

Coffee, tea, hookahs, and dessert
The Pied Cow Coffeehouse
3244 SE Belmont St, Portland
503-230-4866

Live music, good coffee, and desserts in an old Victorian house
Rimsky-Korsakoffeehouse
707 SE 12th Ave, Portland
503-232-2640

Italian ristretto-style
Spella Caffé
520 SW 5th Ave, Portland
503-752-0264
www.spellacaffe.com

Go to MICRO-ROASTER Spots

High quality coffee roasting and brewing equipment

Clive Coffee
📍 79 SE Taylor St, Portland
☎ 503-784-3464
🔗 www.clivecoffee.com

Specialty roasts and pour-overs worth the wait

Extracto
📍 2921 NE Killingsworth St, Portland
☎ 503-281-1764
📍 1465 NE Prescott, Suite B, Portland
☎ 503-284-1380
🔗 www.extractocoffee.com

Aeropress advocates and Southern Hemisphere focused coffee

Heart Roasters
📍 2211 E Burnside St, Portland
☎ 503-206-6602
📍 537 SW 12th Ave, Portland
☎ 503-224-0036
🔗 www.heartroasters.com

Educational classes, DIY coffee roasting, and more

Mr. Green Beans
📍 3932 N Mississippi Ave, Portland
☎ 503-288-8698
🔗 www.mrgreenbeanspdx.com

Single-origin, blends, pour-overs, and $1.50 cups of French press

The Red E Café
📍 1006 N Killingsworth St, Portland
☎ 503-998-1387
📍 721 NW 9th Ave, Portland
☎ 503-819-9755
🔗 www.theredecafe.com

Quality roasts, dapper baristas, and excellent espresso

Sterling Coffee Roasters
📍 417 NW 21st Ave, Portland
☎ 503-248-2133
📍 1951 W Burnside St, Portland
☎ 503-367-6943
🔗 www.sterlingcoffeeroasters.com

Innovative blends and oak-aged beans from around the world

Water Avenue Coffee
📍 1028 SE Water Ave 145, Portland
☎ 503-808-7083
🔗 www.wateravenuecoffee.com

You can find Kobos Coffee in restaurants such as **Acadia, Bijou Café, Bob's Red Mill, Dots Café, Helser's, Meriwether's,** and **Zell's,** and in markets such as **Market of Choice, Stroheckers,** and **Phil's Uptown Meat Market** (☞ p. 72). Kobos's top-selling coffees include a Columbian and African Bistro Blend, its Sulawesi-grown Celebes Kalossi Coffee, and its Columbian Supremo Coffee.

Nossa Familia Coffee

🔗 www.familyroast.com
📍 1319 NW Johnson St, Portland ☎ 503-719-6605
🕐 M–F 7am–4pm, Sa 8am–4pm

Augusto Carvalho Dias Carneiro, co-owner of Nossa Familia Coffee (the only family-traded coffee in Portland), grew up in Rio but spent holidays on his family's coffee farm eight hours west of Rio. His fondest childhood memories include early morning horseback riding with his grandpa through the coffee fields.

These days Carneiro is based in Portland, and he imports about 5% of his family farm's Brazilian coffee (about 80,000 pounds a year) to roast for Nossa Familia Coffee. Nossa's various coffees are all named after Carneiro's family – Ernesto's Family Roast, Teodoro's Italian Roast, Augusta's Certified Organic, Mathilde's French Roast, and Camila's Certified Organic. In 2004, Nossa Familia Coffee won the highly sought after Cup of Excellence award.

You can find Nossa Familia coffees at their café at the nonprofit **Ethos** on North Killingsworth (along with tea and snacks for kids and adults) and at **New Seasons Market** (☞ p. 79), **People's Food Co-op** (☞ p. 63), **Food Front Cooperative Grocery** (☞ p. 62), **Hollywood Farmers**

Market (☞ *p.* 172), **Lents International Farmers Market** (☞ *p.* 172), and other locations around town.

Portland Roasting Coffee Company

⌥ www.portlandroasting.com
♥ 340 SE 7th Ave, Portland ☎ 503-236-7378, 800-949-3898

I think it's safe to say that most Portlanders don't know much about Portland Roasting Coffee Company (PRCC), even though it's been roasting great coffee locally since 1996. Maybe it's the fact that it doesn't operate a retail location, or maybe it's the fact that Portland Roasting isn't as hip and closely monitored by the media as Stumptown and other local roasters. Whatever the reason, I think its coffee and ethics deserve more attention.

PRCC owner Mark Stell says that his company focuses not only on fair trade practices but on "friendly fair trade" practices, combining fair trade with increased social responsibility. On average, PRCC pays its coffee growers 30% more than fair trade agreements require for its one million–plus pounds of coffee brewed annually. The company is also active in supporting education, health care, and infrastructure in areas from which it sources coffee.

Stell owns a coffee farm in Tanzania situated next to the Ngorogoro Conservation Area. The farm is 1,000 acres but only 160 of these are currently devoted to coffee. For the last few years the farm has produced two shipping containers of coffee per harvest used exclusively for PRCC's Tanzania brew. In the future, as the farm produces more, they will distribute the excess to other roasters. When Stell and his brothers bought the farm three years ago it employed just twelve farm workers; PRCC now has seventy full-time Tanzanian employees on staff.

If you want to participate in a free Portland Roasting Coffee Company cupping (afternoons Monday through Friday), call the office at least twenty-four hours in advance. Cuppings usually accommodate up to ten people and last about an hour at the 18,000-square-foot Southeast Portland roasting facility, which was previously a popcorn roasting facility. You can buy PRCC coffee on their website and in many shops, markets, and restaurants throughout the Pacific Northwest and beyond.

Ristretto Roasters

🔗 *www.ristrettoroasters.com*
📍 3808 N Williams Ave, Portland 📞 503-288-8667 🕐 M–Sa 6:30am–6pm, Su 7am–6pm
📍 555 NE Couch St, Portland 📞 503-284-6767 🕐 M–Sa 6:30am–8pm, Su 7am–6pm
📍 2181 NW Nicolai St, Portland 📞 503-227-2866
　🕐 M–F 6:30am–6pm, Sa 7:30am–6pm, Su 8am–4pm
📍 1355 NW Everett St, Portland 📞 971-279-4708 🕐 M–F 6am–6pm, Sa–Su 7am–6pm

Din Johnson has been roasting coffee for fourteen years and owns the four-shop-strong Ristretto Roasters. He opened his original Northeast location with its glass-enclosed roasting room in 2005 and his North Portland café in 2008, which *Food & Wine* calls "a wine bar, but for coffee lovers." Ristretto usually has several roasts available, ranging from medium to dark. Keep an eye out for free Ristretto events, including semiregular cuppings, at the large North Portland café.

Spella Caffé

🔗 *www.spellacaffe.com*
📍 520 SW 5th Ave, Portland 📞 503-752-0264 🕐 M–F 7:30am–3:30pm

There are a lot of great food and drink carts in Portland, and Spella Caffe – now a brick-and-mortar destination – got its start as one. The reason: Andrea Spella. Spella, who is part Italian and part Polish, drinks ten to fifteen shots of espresso every day. He claims it helps him sleep. Says Spella with a smile, "I guess I'm just wired differently." In 2010 Spella opened his brick-and-mortar cafe serving the same great coffee.

Spella's signature classic Italian roast coffee is roasted in small eleven-pound batches and pulled ristretto style with an old-school piston machine, as opposed to a modern pressurized pump espresso machine. There's no walking away from the machine, or even chitchatting much with customers, while a Spella espresso is in the works. The end result is a perfectly extracted cup of coffee with beautiful crema.

In addition to expertly prepared coffee, Spella serves from-scratch chai, hand-shaken iced drinks (Spella doesn't like blenders), small-batch Stella Gelato made in Eugene, and all sorts of tasty baked goods – authentic biscotti, quickbreads, and cookies – prepared by a loyal customer and librarian at downtown's Central Library. At the café, you can buy half-pound sacks of coffee to take home. Spella also serves wholesale accounts with local restaurants, cafés, and offices around town.

St. Johns Coffee Roasters

www.stjohnscoffee.com
8445 N Ivanhoe St, Portland 503-445-2249

St. Johns Coffee Roasters' organic, fair trade, and sometimes direct trade coffee is roasted in small batches. You can purchase St. Johns Coffee Roasters coffee at the roastery, **Proper Eats Market & Cafe** (☞ *p.* 94), at **Food Front Cooperative Grocery** (☞ *p.* 62), at **Linnton Feed and Seed**, and at the **Cedar Mill**, **St. Johns**, and **Milwaukie** farmers markets. If you'd like to have St. Johns Coffee delivered in the early morning to your doorstep, all you have to do is call and submit an order. Current zip codes in the delivery zone include 97203, 97217, and 97211.

Stumptown Coffee Roasters

www.stumptowncoffee.com
4525 SE Division St, Portland 503-230-7702 M–F 6am–7pm, Sa–Su 7am–7pm
3356 SE Belmont St, Portland 503-232-8889 M–F 6am–7pm, Sa–Su 7am–7pm
128 SW 3rd Ave, Portland 503-295-6144 M–F 6am–7pm, Sa–Su 7am–7pm
1026 SW Stark St, Portland 503-224-9060 M–F 6am–7pm, Sa–Su 7am–7pm
100 SE Salmon St, Portland 503-467-4123 M–F 10am–4pm

Stumptown Coffee Roasters is synonymous with Portland. Since 1999 this local institution has been roasting and serving up delicious wholesale and retail beans and brew. The company's adherence to strict quality control, farm-direct sourcing, and small-batch artisanal roasting has been emulated by shops and roasters across the nation.

For the past few years Stumptown has helped the coffee growers it works with travel to Portland and Seattle for its popular Meet the Producers events, which include talks, tastings, and slideshows. According to Stumptown's head of operations, Matt Lounsbury, it's often very emotional for the growers to see their coffee labeled with the name of their farm and town sold in cafes and shops. It's usually a first.

Coffee drinkers outside of Portland and Seattle can now sip on Stumptown coffee that's been roasted in Brooklyn in the company's café in Manhattan's **Ace Hotel**. But Stumptown Coffee isn't planning to take over the country. The majority of its wholesale accounts are located within a forty-five-minute drive from Portland. With five coffee shops in town and two roasting facilities, Stumptown services approximately two hundred local wholesale accounts.

Free cuppings are open to the public at the **Stumptown Annex** on SE Belmont every day at 11am and 3pm. Stumptown employees are required to go to at least two employee or café cuppings a week – it keeps them up to snuff with the usual in house lineup of thirty coffees.

World Cup Coffee & Tea

www.worldcupcoffee.com
1740 NW Glisan St, Portland ☏ 503-228-4152 ◷ M–F 6:30am–8pm, Sa–Su 7am–7pm
1005 W Burnside St (Powell's City of Books), Portland ☏ 503-228-4651
9am–11pm every day

I've probably been to the **Powell's City of Books** World Cup Café more than any other café in Portland. I love it. I love the coffee, the window-seat people watching, and of course, I love the books that you're allowed to bring in from the bookstore and check out with a perfectly roasted cup of Yirgacheffe. This is the stuff my dreams are made of.

In 1993 World Cup began roasting, and in 1999 it opened its first café – the NW Glisan location. World Cup keeps a blog with frequently updated cupping notes on their various roasts, which are often crafted from organic green beans sustainably sourced (often farm-direct) from around the world.

ZBEANZ

www.zbeanz.com
☏ 503-452-1078

Doreen and Stanley Zemble founded their Portland coffee roasting company, ZBEANZ, in 2004. These days, ZBEANZ coffees can be found at **Baker & Spice** (☞ *p. 13*), **Market of Choice**, the **Beaverton** and **Hillsdale farmers markets**, and other spots around town.

I N PORTLAND, you'll find plenty of delicious, naturally sweetened, alternative sodas ready to bubble you up. And lucky for you, some are made from local herbs and farm-fresh fruits. The best in house soda selection in town is at **Kenny & Zuke's Delicatessen** downtown. **Rocket Fizz** (535 SW 6th Ave, Portland; 503-222-0711; *www.rocketfizz. com*) also has all sorts of fizzylifters. If you head north of Portland, just a hop and skip across the river into Vancouver, you'll find **Pop Culture** (1929 Main St, Vancouver, WA; 360-750-1784; *www.drinkpopculture.me*), which has a huge selection of old-school and new-school sodas in the cooler. And if you keep north to Seattle there's a lot of soda happening up there from **Jones Soda** (800-656-6050; *www.jonessoda.com*) to **DRY Soda Co.** (888-379-7632; *www.drysoda.com*).

Crater Lake Soda

www.craterlakesoda.com
503-731-3715

Crater Lake Soda is the youngest soda company in Portland. Crater Lake's bottled and draft sodas are free from high-fructose corn syrup, and flavors include root beer, orange cream, lemon lime, and vanilla cream.

Hotlips Soda

www.hotlipssoda.com
503-224-2069

Hotlips Soda is one of the more standout bubblies in town because the sustainably minded pizza parent company (Hotlips Pizza) uses local fruits and berries for its seasonal soda. Hotlips Soda got its start at the company's pizza spots but now can be found bottled in restaurants and markets throughout the Pacific Northwest. I love the fresh fruit flavor of these sodas, including boysenberry, apple, pear, raspberry, and blueberry.

Thomas Kemper Soda Co.

www.thomaskemper.com
503-517-8636

Thomas Kemper Soda Co., one of the older soda companies in town, was founded in 1990. Although best known for its root beer, Thomas Kemper brews all sorts of sweet and bubbly sodas, all of which are now made with cane sugar rather than high-fructose corn syrup.

IN RECENT YEARS, Portland has seen a huge revival in small craft distilleries. In fact, there's an area in Southeast Portland that is so dense with distilleries it's now referred to as Distillery Row. In this town of DIY booze entrepreneurs, you'll find everything from single malt whiskey, absinthe, and aquavit to organic vodka, Douglas fir spirits, and eaux-de-vie. In 2011 almost 12% of Oregon's liquor sales were of Oregon-made distillates.

Although there is no definitive answer as to why Oregon boasts nearly fifty distilleries – many of which are in Portland proper – while neighboring Washington state has fewer than thirty, there is plenty of speculation. The fact that a one-year distillation license costs $100 in Oregon while a similar license runs $2,000 in Washington (Washington recently added a $100 craft distillation license that's a step in the right direction) might play a part. Probably more significant, however, is the passion and skill-sharing of distillers who have paved the way for years in Oregon.

According to Joy Spencer of the Oregon Liquor Control Commission, Oregon liquor sales continue to grow annually. Oregon, bolstered by the Oregon Distillers Guild and an award-winning past, has nowhere to go but up with craft spirits. If you would like to locate a particular Oregon spirit, the OLCC website maps liquor store locations where you can source it and gives you store hours and contact info as well as the amount of bottles in stock at each location: ℰ *www.Oregon-LiquorSearch.com.*

Artisan Spirits

📍 1227 SE Stark St, Portland 📞 503-781-2357 (*call to schedule a tasting or tour*)

Artisan Spirits is located at the northern end of Distillery Row, this small-batch distillery crafts Apia Artisan Vodka (made with raspberry blossom honey from Buzzing Canyon Apiary in Estacada) and Martin Ryan Handmade Vodka (made from Columbia Valley Syrah grapes). Artisan Spirits co-owner Ryan Csansky says of the Martin Ryan, "The end result is . . . a truly unique vodka. A spirit with terroir."

In 2009, Artisan welcomed Gwydion Stone, founder of The Wormwood Society Absinthe Association and maker of Marteau Absinthe. In upcoming years, Stone plans to expand his line of absinthe to include a series of historically correct regional styles. You can find Artisan Spirits vodkas and Marteau Absinthe at fine liquor stores, bars, and restaurants around town, particularly **Uptown Liquor Store** and **Pearl Specialty Market and Spirits**.

JUNIPER BERRIES

Juniper berries are famously distilled with other botanicals in gin, but they have many culinary uses. They're cooked in game dishes; ground and mixed into marinades, stuffings, and sauces; and tossed whole into sauerkraut.

The Western juniper tree (*Juniperus occidentalis*), native to the Northwest, is a dominant part of the Central and Eastern Oregon landscape – as ubiquitous as sagebrush and cattle. Jim Bendis, proprietor of Bendistillery in Bend, says, "The reason I started Bendistillery in 1995 is because of juniper berries. There are so many gnarly juniper trees around Bend, and I wanted to find some kind of use for them."

In the beginning Bendis, along with family and friends, made seasonal trips east into Oregon cattle country to collect the berries. "Late October and early November are usually the best times to go. The berries are the bluest and juiciest then. You can tell by the chalky color on the outside," Bendis says.

His Cascade Mountain gin is clean and flavorful with few botanicals present aside from juniper berries. The company also distills Desert Juniper gin, which amps up the juniper content for those craving more of the berry's peppery sweetness.

Bendistillery
📍 1470 NE 1st St #800, Bend
📞 541-318-0200
🔗 *www.bendistillery.com*

Bull Run Distilling Company

🔗 *www.bullrundistillery.com*
📍 2259 NW Quimby St, Portland 📞 503-224-3483
🕐 W–Su noon–6pm

Former House Spirits co-owner Lee Medoff and Patrick Bernards launched Bull Run in the spring of 2010 in Northwest Portland with two 800-gallon stills, the largest stills in the state. In their small tasting room just off NW 23rd Avenue you can sample their tasty and expertly crafted Medoyeff Vodka, Pacific Rum, Aria Dry Gin, Temperance Trader Straight Bourbon Whiskey made by other distillers, and in a year or so their own Oregon whiskey.

Clear Creek Distillery

🔗 *www.clearcreekdistillery.com*
📍 2389 NW Wilson St, Portland 📞 503-248-9470
🕐 M–Sa 9am–5pm

Clear Creek Distillery proprietor Steve McCarthy is a perfectionist, and it shows in his work. Clear Creek's award-winning, labor-intensive twenty-plus eaux-de-vie, brandies, grappas, liqueurs, whiskeys, and more, are some of the most intricate spirits out there. Many of the distillery's spirits are made with fruit from the McCarthy family's pear and apple orchards in the Mt. Hood area. Clear Creek uses German copper pot stills, French oak barrels, and Swiss and Alsatian techniques. McCarthy was only the second American eau-de-vie distiller when he started distilling in the 1980s.

A particularly popular Clear Creek creation is its single malt whiskey, which sells out every year within days of its release. McCarthy says, "We are increasing production every year, hoping someday to get to the point where we can

Prohibition era with a twist
The Woodsman Tavern
📍 4537 SE Division St, Portland
📞 971-373-8264
🔗 www.woodsmantavern.com

Bitters inclined
Clyde Common
📍 1014 SW Stark St, Portland
📞 503-228-3333
🔗 www.clydecommon.com

Portland history and classic cocktails
Huber's
📍 411 SW 3rd Ave, Portland
📞 503-228-5686
🔗 www.hubers.com

Lucy Brennan originals
Mint
📍 816 N Russell St, Portland
📞 503-284-5518
🔗 www.mintand820.com

Refined crafty cocktails
Kask
📍 1215 SW Alder St, Portland
📞 503-241-7163
🔗 www.grunerpdx.com/kask

Old-school classics
Secret Society Lounge
📍 116 NE Russell St, Portland
📞 503-493-3600
🔗 www.secretsociety.net

Classy drinks and house bitters
Teardrop Cocktail Lounge
📍 1015 NW Everett St, Portland
📞 503-445-8109
🔗 www.teardroplounge.com

Expert classic and Tiki-style cocktails
Rum Club
📍 720 SE Sandy Blvd, Portland
📞 503-467-2469
🔗 www.rumclubpdx.com

Classics with and without a twist in hip old saloon space
Interurban
📍 4057 N Mississippi Ave, Portland
📞 503-284-6669
🔗 www.interurbanpdx.com

fill the pipeline and maybe lay a few barrels down for an eight-, ten-, or twelve-year-old."

Clear Creek Distillery is open for tours by appointment on Saturday at 9am, 11am, and 1pm. Tastings and sales are available during regular hours with no appointment necessary. Clear Creek spirits can be found at the distillery, as well as in any local bar, restaurant, or liquor store worth its salt.

Eastside Distilling

🔗 www.eastsidedistilling.com
📍 1512 SE 7th Ave, Portland 📞 503-926-7060
🕐 M–Thur noon–5pm, F noon–7:30pm, Sa 11am–6pm, Su noon–5pm

Since 2009 this Distillery Row business has been crafting small batch spirits including Burnside Bourbon, Double Barrel Bourbon, Cherry Bomb Whiskey, Portland Potato Vodka, Below Deck Rums (including the Coffee Rum made with cold-brewed coffee and molasses), and various holiday liqueurs. They moved to their current location in 2011.

House Spirits Distillery

🔗 www.housespirits.com
📍 2025 SE 7th Ave, Portland 📞 503-235-3174
🕐 W–Sa noon–6pm, Su noon–5pm

Even though House Spirits Distillery crafts several different spirits, Aviation Gin is by far its most well known. It's a very good gin, full of all kinds of bright botanicals, juniper berries, cardamom, coriander, and lavender. Founder-owner Christian Krogstad runs the show at this Southeast Portland distillery co-owned by NFL legend Joe Montana that got its start in 2004. House Spirits produces Aviation Gin, Volstead Vodka, two Krogstad Aquavits, a barrel-aged whiskey, and an apothecary line that includes ouzo and rum in their 4,500-square-foot Southeast Portland distillery. If you'd like to tour the distillery, stop by for one of the year round Saturday tours or call to schedule one. While you're there be sure to visit the **Apothecary Tasting Room** next door to try various limited-production house spirits.

Indio Spirits

⨁ *www.indiospirits.com*
📍 7272 SW Durham Rd #100, Portland
☎ 503-620-0313 *(call for tour and tasting info)*

Since 2004 Indio Spirits distillery has been in Cottage Grove with headquarters in Portland. Indio's infused vodkas incorporate locally sourced flavors, along with plenty of unusual combinations like lemongrass lime. Indio's Silver Edition Vodka is triple-filtered via charcoal-activated coconut husks, which allows the rye to come through sweet and clean. Indio Spirits also offers a three-year-aged batch of rum and cocktail mixes, including an all-natural concoction with red hibiscus.

New Deal Distillery

⨁ *www.newdealdistillery.com*
📍 900 SE Salmon St, Portland ☎ 503-234-2513
🕐 W–F 1pm–4pm, Sa–Su noon–5pm

Tom Burkleaux and Matthew Vanwinkle decided somewhat radically in 2002 to start a local vodka business even though neither had any distillation experience. In 2004 New Deal Distillery flipped the "open" sign. At that point vodka was uncharted territory in Portland.

New Deal currently has several vodkas and gins on the market – including New Deal Vodka, Portland 8 Vodka, and their red pepper-infused

---

ANDERS JOHANSEN

OF **DOLMEN DISTILLERY**

Anders Johansen has a fondness for arcane spirits. So arcane, in fact, that he's made a business of crafting mead and distilling it into one of Oregon's more interesting libations: **Worker Bee Honey Spirits.**

A self-described "geeky" homebrewer in the 1980s and a professional brewer for Pyramid Breweries and Deschutes Brewery in the '90s, Johansen is now a local distiller and the sole proprietor of Dolmen Distillery. His dad kept honeybees for years, so once Johansen began homebrewing, he began making home-crafted mead. The idea for honey spirits followed a few years later when Johansen had twenty gallons of his own oak-aged mead that, he says, "was too good to toss but not quite good enough to bottle." He realized he could distill it, and in 2005 Worker Bee Honey Spirits buzzed onto Oregon liquor store shelves. Johansen knows of no other retail American-made honey spirits.

Dolmen Distillery, located in an old well shed on the Johansen family's seventy-five-acre farm outside of McMinnville, has been a one-man and one-spirit operation since day one. Dolmen's most important tool of the trade is, of course, the honey. Each 375-milliliter bottle of Worker Bee requires roughly two and a half pounds of honey.

→ **DOLMEN DISTILLERY**, *continued*

Johansen works closely with a Yamhill County beekeeper who cultivates clover, blackberry, and boysenberry honeys.

Johansen has been experimenting with darker, more flavorful honeys in recent years, including one of his favorites, meadowfoam (made with a Pacific Northwest ground cover), which is often compared to butterscotch. He's also experimenting with eucalyptus, rutabaga, buckwheat, and various tropical honeys, which he hopes to fine-tune and market one day.

Worker Bee is 80 proof, crystal clear, and subtly sweet, but it is difficult to source. In Portland, Lloyd Center Liquor Store and Uptown Liquor Store frequently stock Worker Bee Honey Spirits throughout the year.

Dolmen Distillery
📍 PO Box 732, McMinnville
📞 541-977-5812
🔗 *www.dolmen.arbre.us*

Hot Monkey Vodka – along with several organic liqueurs that they craft in partnership with LOFT Organic Liqueurs in San Francisco. The distillery also offers seasonal spirits, such as basil-infused vodka, available for sale exclusively from its tasting room.

Although New Deal imports their base neutral spirits, they impart unique character and flavor via their stills and final distillation process – a method that, according to Burkleaux, was all about learning by doing. They do it well.

Rogue Distillery & Public House
🔗 *www.rogue.com*
📍 1339 NW Flanders St, Portland 📞 503-222-5910
🕐 Su–Th 11am–midnight, F–Sa 11am–1am; tours offered M–F 2pm or by special request.

An offshoot of Oregon's legendary Rogue Ales, Rogue Distillery started distilling in Portland in 2003. They quickly gained market success and industry accolades for their spirits. Although still best known for craft beer, Rogue's successful spirits include a hazelnut-spice rum (Rogue founder Jack Joyce's favorite), dark rum, white rum, and spruce gin. The rum is distilled in Portland, and the gin in Newport.

Sub Rosa Spirits
🔗 *www.subrosaspirits.com*
📞 503-476-2808

Mike Sherwood's complex, savory Sub Rosa Tarragon Vodka and Sub Rosa Saffron Vodka, which can be found throughout the West Coast, started out as a kitchen experiment at his home in Dundee. Sherwood infused vodka with every spice he had in the house until he came up with the perfect combinations.

Each botanical – there are eight in the saf-

DOUGLAS FIR EAU-DE-VIE

Pine and fir essences are typically harnessed for their olfactory properties rather than for their taste, but for more than a decade Stephen McCarthy, proprietor of Portland's renowned **Clear Creek Distillery**, has been tinkering with the sweet, earthy flavors of the Douglas fir. His Eau de Vie of Douglas Fir was unveiled in 2005 and now lines liquor store shelves throughout the Pacific Northwest and beyond.

McCarthy first came across *eau de vie de bourgeons de sapins d'Alsace* in a book among a list of exotic eaux-de-vie. He notes, "At that time the distillery and eau-de-vie in general were only a glimmer in my eye, so it got filed away somewhere in my mind. When I worked my way through most of the obvious eau-de-vie – pear, kirsch, etc. – I started to think about slightly crazier stuff. There was no reason to try to duplicate the sapin d'Alsace the spruce tree that covers the hills of the Vosges Mountains. Our iconic conifer is the Doug fir. So, why not?"

The process of creating Clear Creek's Eau de Vie of Douglas Fir begins with the distillation of Oregon wine (mainly Chardonnay and Pinot noir) into high-proof grape spirits, which McCarthy describes as "basically brandy, but more like grape Everclear." This grape spirit is used for some of Clear Creek's other liqueurs and they also fortify some local vintners' wine into port with it.

The Douglas fir tips, which Clear Creek employees harvest annually from McCarthy's family land just north of Mount Hood, are soaked in the grape spirit in stainless tanks for a week, after which the spirit is redistilled. This fixes the flavor and aroma but removes all the color. After redistilling, the crew adds additional Douglas fir tips to the eau-de-vie to steep again for a few days to a few weeks. This process develops the flavor and results in slight coloration. It is then bottled and sent out to be enjoyed.

Pop-up brunch from Nik Woidek with housemade bacon, kimchi and cheap booze

Kenton Club
- 2025 N Kilpatrick St, Portland
- 503-285-3718
- www.kentonclub.com

Gastropub savory and French 75s

Interurban
- 4057 N Mississippi Ave, Portland
- 503-284-6669
- www.interurbanpdx.com

Cajun-creole and Bloody Mary bar

The Parish
- 231 NW 11th Ave, Portland
- 503-227-2421
- www.theparishpdx.com

Schnitzel, Bi Bim Bop and unusual Bloody Marys

Tasty n Alder
- 580 SW 12th Ave, Portland
- 503-621-9251
- www.tastynalder.com

1-hour plus wait for daily killer brunch

Tasty n Sons
- 3808 N Williams Ave, Portland
- 503-621-1400
- www.tastyntasty.com

All wood-fired weekend brunch

Ned Ludd
- 3925 NE M.L. King Blvd, Portland
- 503-288-6900
- www.nedluddpdx.com

Always a wait southern brunch Portlandia-style

Screen Door
- 2337 E Burnside St, Portland
- 503-542-0880
- www.screendoorrestaurant.com

Farm-fresh omelets and fresh baked treats daily

Toast
- 5222 SE 52nd Ave, Portland
- 503-774-1020
- www.toastpdx.com

fron and three in the tarragon – is infused separately in 190-proof vodka that's been passed through an activated carbon filter several times to extract any lingering off-flavors. Then the infusion is blended with 90-proof vodka, hand-bottled, and labeled. There are no artificial flavors, sweeteners, or colors here – just fresh and dried herbs and spices. And because there are so many fresh ingredients involved, every batch is a little different.

Sub Rosa Tarragon vodka and Saffron vodka can be found in many Portland liquor stores. It's regularly stocked in Portland at **11th Avenue Liquor Store**, **Uptown Liquor Store**, and **Lloyd Center Liquor Store**, and is shaken and stirred in plenty of specialty cocktails in restaurants and bars around town.

ALTHOUGH TEA ISN'T QUITE AS POPULAR in Portland as coffee, it does have a long and varied history here. Portland is home to many of the country's tea bigwigs, including **Tazo Tea**, **Stash Tea**, **Oregon Chai**, **Kombucha Wonder Drink**, and more – along with loads of smaller importers, tea houses, and even a man who calls himself the **Tea Monk** (☞ *see below*). If you want to grow your own, *Camellia sinensis* can even be grown here.

Foxfire Teas

www.foxfireteas.com
⚲ 2505 SE 11th Ave #105, Portland ☎ 503-288-6869 🕑 W–F 10am–6pm, Sa 10am–4pm

Prior to opening their first tea shop in Portland in 2004, Katherine Losselyong was a massage therapist and Quinn Losselyong was working for the Portland Business Alliance. But once the tea bug hit, they both left their day jobs and jumped headlong into the tea business. They haven't looked back.

Foxfire Teas sells a lot of Pu-erh – the Pinot noir of teas – along with Earl Grey and other premier black, green, white, and herbal teas. Seasonal favorites include lapsang souchong and ginger in the fall and winter and Jamaican red bush in the spring and summer. Teas are sold by the ounce in brown paper resealable bags.

One thing that you won't find at Foxfire is decaffeinated tea. According to Quinn, they've never been able to source any from their tea brokers that has satisfactory flavor. His advice: If you want a decaffeinated brew, resteep your tea. The second cup or pot will have drastically less caffeine than the first.

In addition to in house retail sales, Foxfire services fifty wholesale accounts with various restaurants, cafés, and bars in Portland and beyond. If you order $50 or more worth of tea, Foxfire will deliver to your doorstep.

Heavens Tea and Sacred Arts Center

www.heavenstea.com
☎ 503-230-0953

When you make an appointment with the **Tea Monk** (a. k. a. owner Paul Rosenberg) of Heavens Tea and Sacred Arts Center, some of the teas you'll have the opportunity to taste are so deep and elemental in flavor that they seem to transport you to another place.

Heavens Tea and Sacred Arts Center in Southeast Portland is a great place to kick back and unwind. The indoor and outdoor tasting rooms are loaded with incense, candles, shrines, and offerings, as well as all sorts of tea (including one from a 1,000-year-old Yunnan Province tree). The indoor tea room is filled with

sacred art from various centuries and has a tiny burl table with pillows for seats on an Oriental rug. Tea time with the Tea Monk is all about talking, laughing, and sharing stories over round after round of rare teas.

With the Tea Monk, you might sip tea from 200-foot tall trees; tea from 1,500-year-old trees; tea that tastes like the essence of root, bark, and leaf from one steeping to the next. With many aged Pu-erhs – which Rosenberg specializes in along with aged oolong teas – you can get more than twenty steepings. Each steeping brings something new to the cup.

If you'd like to attend a Tea Monk tasting – which can last up to three hours, costs $15 to $65, and is limited to seven people – check out the website. Some of Rosenberg's popular tastings include rare oolongs of Taiwan and China, aged teas of China, young Pu-erhs, and his full moon tea tasting.

The Jasmine Pearl Tea Merchants

⋄ www.thejasminepearl.com
♀ 724 NE 22nd Ave, Portland ♪ 503-236-3539 ◑ M–F 10am–6pm, Sa 11am–5pm

Since 2004 the Jasmine Pearl Tea Merchants have specialized in single estate selections and unique flavor blends of certified organic loose leaf teas and herbal tisanes. The price range is wide: from $2 to $100 per ounce. Jasmine Pearl teas can be found at coffeehouses, restaurants, spas, and natural grocery stores throughout Portland. Andrea Spella serves Jasmine Pearl's chai at **Spella Caffé** (☞ *p.* 122), and he claims that it's the best chai in town. Jasmine Pearl's tasting room is small and open by appointment only. Call for a private tea tasting. Jasmine Pearl tea and teaware is also available on their website.

Tao of Tea

⋄ www.taooftea.com
♀ 3430 SE Belmont St, Portland ♪ 503-736-0119 ◑ M–Sa 11am–10pm, Su 11am–9pm
♀ 239 NW Everett St (Portland Classical Chinese Garden), Portland ♪ 503-224-8455
  ◑ 10am–4:30pm every day

The warm bamboo and stone decor of Tao of Tea makes it a perfect place for good conversation or introspection. This isn't the kind of place where you'll find everyone gabbing on cell phones or working on their computers.

The tea list, or rather tea *book*, reads like poetry. You're sure to find something you'll like, from several raw and cooked Chinese Pu-erhs to Taiwanese oolongs and Indian chais. There's also some good globe-trotting food like veggie dumplings, salad rolls, Indian flatbread, samosas, and steamed tofu topped with matcha and cayenne.

The Tao of Tea inside the Portland Classical Chinese Garden's Tower of Reflections is one of Portland's most beautiful teahouses. Keep in mind, however, that you have to pay admission to the garden ($8.50 for adults, $7.50 for seniors, $6.50 for students) in order to visit this two-story classic teahouse that serves all sorts of tea and food. Check out the Tao of Tea website for events.

Tea Chai Té

www.teachaite.com

📍 734 NW 23rd Ave, Portland 📞 503-228-0900
🕐 9am–10pm every day

📍 3403 SE Hawthorne Blvd, Portland
📞 503-233-4221 🕐 Su–Th 9am–8pm, F–Sa 9am–9pm

📍 7983 SE 13th Ave, Portland 📞 503-432-8747
🕐 9am–9pm every day

Apart from its teas, Tea Chai Té ranks high on my list because of its cozy second-floor nooks, creaky floor, big comfy couch, outdoor deck, and mismatched tables and chairs.

Tea Chai Té's one hundred–plus varieties of loose leaf tea, available hot or iced, are on display on the wall by the register in small glass canisters so that you can see and smell them. Beyond tea, there's house-made kombucha and bubble tea, as well as lots of baked

KOMBUCHA

WONDER DRINK

Steve Lee has blazed an American tea trail. In 1972 he co-founded **Stash Tea**, and in 1994 he helped form **Tazo Tea** and **Teaports**, a company that provided Russia with imported tea after the fall of the Soviet Union. Lee's latest leafy venture is the Portland-based Kombucha Wonder Drink, which he founded in 2001.

Kombucha is a fermented, sweetened tea first brewed in China more than four thousand years ago. The unique flavors of kombucha have been compared to cider, champagne, and Moselle wine. It's a sweet and slightly sour effervescent tonic that blends the flavor of tea with a yeasty tartness.

"There are hundreds of theories as to the origins of kombucha," Lee says. "Discerning myth from truth is tricky. I think someone simply left a cup of brewed tea out for a while – it attracted yeast and bacteria and became what we know as kombucha."

Kombucha Wonder Drink's Portland facility brews the tea in 300-gallon stainless steel tanks. The concentrate (fermented with starters from Siberia, Nepal, and China) is poured into tea, and light carbonation is infused via carbonation stones. The kombucha is then filtered and bottled.

Lee likens the buzz surrounding kombucha to energy drinks in the

CONTINUES ➤

→ **KOMBUCHA WONDER DRINK**, *continued*

1980s. "Energy drinks entered the market in 1987, and now they are a billion-dollar business," he says. Since the beginning, Kombucha Wonder Drink has struggled to keep up with demand. You can often find the Oregon Tilth-certified organic beverage in natural food stores, upscale grocery stores, coffeehouses, restaurants, and bars around the country.

Kombucha Wonder Drink
⚲ 1321 NE Couch St, Portland
☎ 503-224-7331, 877-224-7331
⚟ *www.wonderdrink.com*

goods such as cookies, brownies, and cakes. In addition to all sorts of green, white, black, and herbal teas (many of which are organic and/or fair trade) for sale in house or online, there are some beautiful pots, presses, and mugs for sale.

TeaZone & Camellia Lounge

⚟ *www.teazone.com*
⚲ 510 NW 11th Ave, Portland ☎ 503-221-2130
🕐 M–W 8am–9pm, Th–F 8am–midnight, Sa 10am–midnight, Su 10am–9pm

TeaZone is a small teahouse and retail space with lots of tea accessories and a substantial tea menu. Tea service is nice here, with all the bells and whistles, and you will find plenty of standbys as well as some rare and precious teas. There are loads of iced and bubble teas available. In the back of the building is Camellia Lounge, a low-lit cocktail lounge with regular art shows and live music and the same full tea menu as TeaZone.

Townshend's Alberta Street Teahouse

⚟ *www.townshendstea.com*
⚲ 2223 NE Alberta St, Portland ☎ 503-445-6699
🕐 9am–10pm every day
⚲ 3531 SE Division St, Portland ☎ 503-236-7772
🕐 9am–10pm every day
⚲ 4301 NE Sandy Blvd (inside Whole Foods), Portland 🕐 8am–7pm every day

The wholesale and retail loose leaf tea selection at Townshend's Albert Street Teahouse is impressive. Teas that you normally wouldn't find in a café, such as unusual oolongs and Darjeelings, come in all sorts of varieties along with the standard brews. Some of Townshend's pots arrive over a candle warmer so that the tea stays warmed to optimal temperature. There's comfy seating, with big chairs and couches and indoor and outdoor tables, including one topped with a permanent chessboard. Townshend's offers their teas on their website as well.

Steven Smith Teamaker

🔗 *www.smithtea.com*

📍 1626 NW Thurman St, Portland 📞 503-719-8752 🕐 M–F 9am–5pm, Sa 11am–5pm

Steven Smith of Steven Smith Teamaker, a boutique tea company specializing in high-quality full leaf, small batch tea with a retail shop on NW Thurman in Portland, has been working with the same local spearmint growers since the mid-1970s – Don, Monty, and Marvin Mills of **Mills Mint Farm** in Stanfield, Oregon.

In the mid-'70s Smith was a co-owner of Stash Tea before it was sold in 1993 to Yamamotoyama in Japan. At that time Smith and the other Stash owners and employees purchased field run mint (unprocessed mint directly from the farm) from the Mills family and cleaned it in what is now **¡Oba! Restaurante**, but which was then Stash Tea headquarters. They cleaned the mint for their tea and also sold mint to Lipton Tea and Celestial Seasonings.

Says Smith, "We cleaned mint there and stored some of it across the street in the Maddox Transfer building before they called the area the Pearl District. I think it should have been named the Mint District for the way it smelled back then."

After selling Stash in the early 1990s, Smith started Tazo Tea in his home kitchen. He sold Tazo to Starbucks in 1999 and continued to work there until 2006. In late 2009 Smith opened his newest tea endeavor – Steven Smith Teamaker – in the brick building next to the Northwest **Olympic Provisions**. Here he does things like experiment with aging teas in Pinot noir and whiskey barrels. Smith takes his teas very seriously. Lucky for us.

All of Smith's spearmint to this day comes from Mills Mint Farm. If you'd like to try Mills's local leaves they are blended in Smith's Fez tea – a combination of Mao Feng China green tea, Oregon spearmint, and Australian lemon myrtle leaves.

When asked why Smith still works with Mills, he answers succinctly, "Flavor, appearance, aroma, overall approach to business, and long-standing relationship."

FOLKS HAVE BEEN PLANTING WINE GRAPES throughout Oregon since the 1970s, but it wasn't until relatively recently that the region began getting more and more attention for its wines, particularly its Pinot Noir, Pinot Gris, Chardonnay, Viognier, Riesling, and Pinot Blanc. The shops included in this chapter all carry a good to great selection of local wine, and some even specialize in local producers.

Portland is lucky to have so many diverse wine shops in every quadrant. According to **Cork** owner Darryl Joannides, one reason Portland is fortunate with wine selection is that there are so many wine distributors in town. It doesn't hurt that Portland is also home to many urban wineries and is surrounded by a diverse and productive wine country.

Blackbird Wine Shop

www.blackbirdwine.com
♥ 4323 NE Fremont Ave, Portland ☎ 503-282-1887
🕐 Tu–W 2pm–8pm, Th 2pm–9pm, F–Sa noon–9pm, Su 2pm–7pm

This hip little wine shop rocks the $10 to $30 bottles, with a focus on small to midsize producers from around the world. Blackbird doesn't have a huge selection, but everything on the shelves is quality. There is also a cheese counter in the back of the shop, a separate business that slices and wraps cheese to go or serves cheese plates with **Little T American Baker** bread (☛ *p.* 22) to eat in house at a table or at the window bar. Blackbird tasters and glass pours go well with the cheese plates. There's funky art on the walls, a polished concrete floor, and good music. Friday-night tastings are popular.

Boedecker Cellars

www.boedeckercellars.com
♥ 2621 NW 30th Ave, Portland ☎ 503-288-7752
🕐 Sa–Su 1pm–5pm *(call ahead for private tours and tastings)*

Since 2003 Athena Pappas and Stewart Boedecker have been making award-winning, highly reputable wine at Boedecker Cellars. And even though their facility is smack-dab in the middle of Oregon's many wine-growing regions, it also happens to be in a forklift-ridden and train-tracked industrial part of Northwest Portland. As you approach Boedecker Cellars, rather than seeing the more typical rolling hills, flocks of birds, and idyllic countryside that accompanies travel to many wineries, you'll see loading docks and a sign that reads "Caution: hot molten zinc." At Boedecker Cellars the needle scratches the record and wine gets real.

Boedecker specializes in Pinot Noir and Chardonnay but also produces Pinot

Blanc, Pinot Gris, rosé, and Grenache. Depending on the time of year, there are usually several different Boedecker Pinot Noirs available, ranging from the Athena Pinot Noir and the Stewart Pinot Noir to various single vineyard options. When Boedecker and Pappas first started blending Pinots together, they realized that they had two very different palates and styles, so they decided to create two different blends.

According to Pappas, "Stewart's Pinot Noir is a very classic Pinot Noir. It's a red fruit, pretty blend, with good acidity that's going to sit in the cellar a long time. And I don't know why I like this, maybe it's because I grew up eating lamb and other big foods, but I like the bigger Pinot Noir. I like a lot of spice and a little more oomph to it."

Boedecker Cellars has a hard time keeping up with demand. From late September until early November, the grapes from the ten or so vineyards the winery sources from are delivered to Boedecker. The crew starts by making wine for eight to ten hours per day and later increases production to fourteen to sixteen hours per day.

Boedecker Cellars keeps their crew busy pretty much year round, doing everything from visiting vineyards and checking on the fruit to processing the harvested fruit, making wine around the clock, and conducting blending trials. Stop by the urban winery during tasting room hours to sample Boedecker wines and get a tour of the facility.

Cork

🔗 *www.corkwineshop.com*
📍 2901 NE Alberta St, Portland 📞 503-281-2675 🕐 Tu–Sa 11am–7pm

Cork is run by a first-rate chef. Darryl Joannides was chef-owner of the much-missed **Assaggio** before he opened Cork in 2006. So in addition to a great selection of wine, Cork also offers a selection of high-quality chocolates, bulk olive oil, aged balsamic vinegar, craft beer, and more. Joannides has worked harvests in Sonoma, helped out with Carlton Winemakers Studio's first vintage, and regularly makes his own wine at home. His passion for wine translates into Cork's stellar wine selection.

But just because Cork is run by a wine expert doesn't mean that you need to be shy about buying less-expensive wines. The majority of bottles displayed on crates and shelves throughout the shop are $20 or less, and Joannides promises that you'll always find at least twenty wines that are less than $10. Yes, there are some splurges, but you don't need a fat wallet to be taken seriously here.

Stop by Cork for Friday night drop-in tastings. Joannides also hosts regular multicourse food and wine pairings. Go to Cork's website for event and tasting information. Also, be sure to check out the Cork Club lifetime membership benefits include store discounts and invitations to member-only events.

E&R Wine Shop

www.erwineshop.com
6141 SW Macadam Ave, Suite 104, Portland
503-246-6101
Tu–F 10am–6:30pm, Sa 9:30am–6pm, Su 2pm–5pm

This classy wine shop is only five minutes south of downtown Portland. Wine is presented on wrap-around shelves and organized mostly by region, including California, Oregon, Italy, France, Germany, Chile, and Portugal. There are also several rare (and pricey) limited quantity Austrian wines.

Toward the back of the shop there's an impressive port and dessert wine selection near a table stacked with all sorts of for sale wine books. Buy any six bottles of wine at E&R and get 10% off; buy twelve bottles or more and get 15% off. Most bottles are in the $10 to $60 range, but you'll find plenty of more spendy bottles as well.

Every Day Wine

www.everydaywine.com
1520 NE Alberta St, Portland 503-331-7119
Tu–Sa 2pm–10pm

Most of the wine at this small neighborhood wine shop is $10 to $20. The selection isn't huge, but service is friendly, knowledgeable, and there's zero snob quotient. In fact, Every

MAKE YOUR OWN WINE

Making fruit and flower wines at home is easy and can cost next to nothing. All you need is fruit, flowers, a food-grade bucket, a carboy, and some old wine bottles or cider jugs. The process, from crushing to bottling, takes nine months to a year.

Portland wine- and beer-making supply house **F.H. Steinbart Co.** (☞ p. 107) can shave off some time at the start. Steinbart carries fruit wine bases and purées with recipes (pear, berry, or apple) for those who don't want to mash and strain their own.

If you're starting from scratch, you'll need fruit and/or flowers. The Willamette Valley is chock-full of fruit much of the year, and anything that is not rotten or insect-riddled is wine-ready. Some ideas: Volunteer for a harvest party with the nonprofit **Portland Fruit Tree Project** (☞ p. 184) and, in addition to helping harvest and distribute to hunger relief agencies fruit that would otherwise go to waste, you get to take home a small sack of fruit yourself. You can also pay to pick at a berry-, fruit-, or veggie-picking farm; Sauvie Island is popular, but farms and orchards on the mainland can be less expensive.

If you'd like to make wine from flowers, there are many edible varieties out there, though be sure to get them from a location that you know has not been sprayed with chemicals. Common wine flowers

CONTINUES ➧

→ **MAKE YOUR OWN WINE**, *continued*
include rose petals, elderflowers, violets, red clover blossoms, and daylilies.

Wines are sweetened using any number of natural sources, but the most common are cane sugar, honey, agave syrup, maple sugar, sorghum, rice syrup, and molasses.

As for supplies and equipment, you'll probably have to buy at least one or two items to start making wine at home, but you can usually cobble together most of the essentials for less than the cost of a decent bottle at a restaurant. Here are some standard supplies and their typical cost: **carboy** ($25–$30), **air lock** ($1), **food-grade bucket** ($10–$20), **cheesecloth or reusable filter** ($5–$10), **wine yeast** ($1 per packet), new or used **wine bottles and corks or old juice jugs** fitted with a rubber or cork stopper ($5–$20 for a dozen), and **clear vinyl tubing** ($2.50).

It's wise to ask around before you buy; people frequently treat winemaking as a hobby, and after a few short months their equipment is stored away, waiting to be handed off. If you can't find it for free, **F.H. Steinbart Co.** (☞ p. 107) and **Mirador Community Store** (☞ p. 166) both carry a variety of fermentation equipment: stoneware crocks, books, cheesecloth, bottles, and more.

For recipes, consult the dozens of books or websites on the topic. I use Sandor Ellix Katz's basic fruit wine recipe in *Wild Fermentation* for all sorts of DIY wines, but there are loads of other recipes out there.

Day Wine is so approachable that there is even a house dog that might nuzzle up and give you some love while you check out the wall of wine.

There are about three hundred wines to choose from all of which you can take home or drink in house at the bar or at a table for a $5 corkage fee. Sample some of what the shop has to offer at a Friday night tasting. Keep in mind that Every Day Wine doesn't serve food, though you're welcome to bring your own snacks.

Great Wine Buys

⌘ *www.greatwinebuys.com*
📍 1515 NE Broadway, Portland ☎ 503-287-2897
🕐 M–Sa 10:30am–7pm, Su noon–5pm

This neighborhood wine shop has been in business since 1985. Great Wine Buys is packed with a lot of local Pinot noir along with all the usual suspects in terms of regions and varietals. The cozy shop has more than two hundred local wines as well as seven hundred international wines. Stop by on Friday nights from 5pm to 7:30pm and on Saturdays from 2pm to 5pm for wine tastings.

Hip Chicks Do Wine

⌘ *www.hipchicksdowine.com*
📍 4510 SE 23rd Ave, Portland ☎ 503-234-3790
🕐 11am–6pm every day

Be sure to closely follow the sandwich boards to this industrial Southeast Portland winery or you might get lost. Depending on when you visit, you may see one of the owners – Laurie Lewis and Renee Neely – hosing out barrels in the parking lot the winery shares with **Hair of the Dog Brewing Company** (☞ *p.* 108), or conducting blending trials in the wine-making space adjacent to the tasting room.

Each year this small Portland winery produces five thousand cases of its fifteen all-vegan wines, made from Washington and Oregon grapes. All Hip Chicks Do Wine wines are available to try and buy at the tasting room. In addition to sampling wine there is a small gift shop with other local food and drink, plus various wine-related products.

Liner & Elsen

🔗 *www.linerandelsen.com*
📍 2222 NW Quimby St, Portland 📞 503-241-9463, 800-903-9463 🕐 M–Sa 10am–6pm

Liner & Elsen is one of the more reputable wine shops in Portland, and has been since 1990, with frequent accolades from national publications such as *Gourmet* and *Bon Appétit*. Although the shop looks small, there is a lot to choose from here: the shop offers over two thousand wines.

Bottles are arranged by region on floor-to-ceiling shelves that wrap around the store. Wine regions are represented by maps lining the walls, and there's a small refrigerated section up front. If you're looking for a Pinot noir, expect to find bottles ranging from $10 to $100. Tilt your head up to the tip-top shelves and check out the empty bottles of extra-special wines collected over the years.

Owner Bob Scherb keeps the shop's focus on the juice of the vine, but you can also purchase Riedel stemware, wine books, wine keys, and other wine-centric products. And even though the shop is located in parking-nightmare Northwest Portland, Liner & Elsen shares a small lot with adjacent businesses out front. Check out the website for regular shop tastings and events.

Old and new world Rhone varietals
Alchemy Wine Productions
📍 3315 SE 19th Ave Suite F, Portland
📞 503-893-4659
🔗 *www.alchemywineproductions.com*

Several excellent small wineries
SE Wine Collective
📍 2425 SE 35th Place, Portland
📞 503-208-2061
🔗 *www.sewinecollective.com*

Pinot noir and Syrah with curated cheese
Clay Pigeon Winery
📍 815 SE Oak St, Portland
📞 503-206-8117
🔗 *www.claypigeonwinery.com*

Hip tasting lounge, a full, bold line, and regional food pairings
ENSO Winery
📍 1416 SE Stark St, Portland
📞 503-683-3676
🔗 *www.ensowinery.com*

Rhône inspired wines from Sauvage wine bar
Fausse Piste Winery
📍 537 SE Ash St, Portland
📞 503-807-5565
🔗 *www.faussepiste.com*

Over a dozen approachable wines
Hip Chicks Do Wine
📍 4510 SE 23rd Ave, Portland
📞 503-234-3790
🔗 *www.hipchicksdowine.com*

French barrel fermented wines
Jan-Marc Wine Cellars
📍 2110 N Ainsworth St, Portland
📞 503-341-4531
🔗 *www.janmarcwinecellars.com*

Full-bodied reds from Washington grapes
Seven Bridges Winery
📍 2303 N Harding Ave, Portland
📞 503-203-2583
🔗 *www.sevenbridgeswinery.com*

Mt. Tabor Fine Wines

www.mttaborfinewines.com

📍 4316 SE Hawthorne Blvd, Portland ☎ 503-235-4444

🕐 Tu–Th 10am–6:30pm, F 10am–7:30pm, Sa 11am–6pm

Most of the wine at this small Southeast Portland wine shop is $8 to $30. Even though the space is tight, there is great diversity, with a focus on small particularly Northwest producers. There is also plenty of great European wine to choose from.

Don't forget to take a peek in the small back room, which houses most of the Italian wine, champagne and sparkling wine, and some stemware for sale. If you are looking to sample wine, stop by for Friday-night tastings from 4pm to 7:30pm with a fee of $10 to $25.

Oregon Wines on Broadway

www.oregonwinesonbroadway.com

📍 515 SW Broadway, Portland ☎ 503-228-0126, 800-943-8858 🕐 M–Sa noon–8pm

This small downtown wine shop and wine bar keeps it local with mostly Oregon and Washington wines, so you'll find a lot of Pinot noir, Syrah, Viognier, Cabernet, and Chardonnay. The only bottles that aren't local are some sparkling wines and champagnes. If you're after local Pinot noir, Oregon Wines has a large selection. With downtown real estate, however, comes downtown prices: most bottles are $20 and up with the majority in the $30 to $50 range.

Buy wine to go or take a seat at a table or at the bar, and try some of the more than thirty wine pours. In the evenings Oregon Wines often hosts live music.

Portland Wine Merchants

www.portlandwinemerchants.com

📍 1430 SE 35th Ave, Portland ☎ 503-234-4399

🕐 Tue–Th 10am–6:30pm, F 10am–8pm, Sa 10am–6:30pm, Su noon–5pm

Since 1993 Portland Wine Merchants has carried local wines as well as imports. Stop in every Friday night for informal tastings from 4:30pm to 7:30pm. Tastings are usually $15 and feature five wines ranging from big reds made in the U. S. to Bordeaux wines to sparkling wines.

Vino

🖉 *www.vinobuys.com*

📍 137 SE 28th Ave, Portland 📞 503-235-8545

🕐 Tu–Th 10:30am–5:30pm, F 10:30am–8pm,
Sa 10:30am–6:30pm, Su noon–5pm

Vino is a friendly, diverse, and affordable shop with most bottles priced $6 to $20. The colorful space, filled with light from big windows, is arranged by region with a focus on wines from Oregon, Washington, California, Italy, France, and Spain. There are some handwritten tasting notes posted here and there, all of which are highly informative. There are several tables up front for Vino's Friday night tastings, which take place from 4:30pm to 8pm.

Vinopolis Wine Shop

🖉 *www.vinopoliswineshop.com*

📍 1025 SW Washington St, Portland 📞 503-223-6002

🕐 M–W 10am–6pm, Th–F 10am–7pm,
Sa 10am–6pm, Su noon–5pm

Vinopolis is the largest wine shop in Portland, and it can certainly be overwhelming in terms of presentation. Most wine is stacked in boxes or crates around the shop, while only some of it is on shelves. Luckily the space is well lit and the staff is very attentive. Crowding the entrance is a vast and impressive selection of local Pinot noir along with many French wines, while the far reaches of the back room hold a wide variety of German wines. These are some of the most substantial sections, but you'll find most of the world's wine regions represented.

There is a lot to read throughout the shop thanks to posted wine notes that often include Robert Parker points. Stop by for Vinopolis

Go-to WINE BARS Spots

Ambonnay
📍 107 SE Washington St, Portland
📞 503-575-4861
🖉 *www.ambonnaybar.com*

Bar Avignon
📍 2138 SE Division St, Portland
📞 503-517-0808
🖉 *www.baravignon.com*

Bin 2I
📍 5011 NE 21st Ave, Portland
📞 503-284-4445
🖉 *www.bin21pdx.com*

Coppa
📍 417 NW 10th Ave, Portland
📞 503-295-9536
🖉 *www.vinoparadiso.com*

Cork Screw Wine Bar
📍 1665 SE Bybee Blvd, Portland
📞 503-239-9463
🖉 *www.corkscrewpdx.com*

The Hop & Vine
📍 1914 N Killingsworth St, Portland
📞 503-954-3322
🖉 *www.thehopandvine.com*

M Bar
📍 417 NW 21st Ave, Portland
📞 503-228-6614
🖉 *www.mbarpdx.com*

Pour Wine Bar & Bistro
📍 2755 NE Broadway, Portland
📞 503-288-7687
🖉 *www.pourwinebar.com*

Remedy
📍 733 NW Everett St, Portland
📞 503-222-1449
🖉 *www.remedywinebar.com*

Vie de Boheme
📍 1530 SE 7th Ave, Portland
📞 503-360-1233
🖉 *www.viedebohemepdx.com*

tastings on Fridays from 4pm to 7pm and Saturdays from noon until the bottles run out.

Shaker and Vine

ℊ *www.shakerandvine.com*

⚑ 2929 SE Powell Blvd, Portland ☎ 503-231-8466

◉ Tu–W 3pm–10pm, Th 3pm–11pm, F 3pm–midnight, Sa 2pm–midnight, Su 3pm–9pm

It's not often you find a happening wine shop and bar in the same business strip as a bowling alley, doughnut shop, and mani/pedi shop. Shaker and Vine has more than five hundred wines to sample in house or to go from around the world, many of which are local and organic.

Shaker and Vine features live music most evenings in the bar along with free pool, foosball, darts, and other games in the game room. There's zero snob factor. There's food available in house (highbrow and lowbrow cheese and snacks), but you can also bring your own food.

The Wine Cellar
Neighborhood Tasting Room & Shop

ℊ *www.portlandwinecellar.com*

⚑ 525 NW Saltzman Rd, Portland ☎ 503-643-5655 ◉ Tu 11am–6pm, W–Sa 11am–9pm

Although this wine shop is a little out of the way (ten minutes west of downtown) and a little hard to find (at the back of a not-visible strip mall) the Wine Cellar has a couple things going for it. There are many organic and small-producer wines in house as well as regular, well-attended Friday and Saturday tastings that are free with a bottle purchase. When visiting, watch for The Wine Cellar in the back of the renovated warehouse a music school shares the same address at the front of the building.

Zilla Sake House

ℊ *www.zillasakehouse.com*

⚑ 1806 NE Alberta St, Portland ☎ 503-288-8372 ◉ 3pm–10pm every day

OK, so sake isn't wine, but this sake bar is just too good to miss. Since 2007 this small, low-lit sake and sushi house has been serving one of the largest and most impressive selections of sake in Portland. There are more than eighty cold and hot sakes to choose from, with plenty of filtered, unfiltered, sweet, and dry options, along with a full bar and sake cocktails. All the sakes are well explained and accessible. There's often live music at Zilla as well; call ahead or check the website for events.

ACKNOWLEDGEMENTS INTRODUCTION FOOD DRINK RESOURCES INDEX

COMMUNITY SUPPORTED AGRICULTURE (CSA) has been growing in popularity for years in the greater Portland area. To become a CSA member at a local farm, you pay a fee up front and sometimes agree to volunteer on the farm in return for your supply of that farm's goods. CSA orders usually include a weekly supply of produce, and sometimes meat or dairy. If this sounds good to you, sign up fast – most local CSAs have waiting lists months before their season commences.

The cost of a Portland-area CSA membership generally ranges from $200 to $1,000 a season, and most seasons run from spring or summer through fall or early winter. Some farms offer discounts and scholarships for those in need.

CSAs are constantly opening and closing, so for the most up-to-date information, please visit the PACSAC website (&www.portlandcsa.org), where you'll find advice on choosing a CSA as well as a list of other Oregon CSA farms.

I've decided to leave out "organic," "organic practices," and "certified-organic" when describing these CSAs because this is a constantly shifting issue for farmers. Contact the farms directly to find out what their current growing practices are.

47th Avenue Farm

&www.47thavefarm.com
Base Camp: 6632 SE 47th Ave, Portland 503-777-4213
Luscher Farm: 125 Rosemont Rd, Lake Oswego

Grows: Vegetables and herbs.
Delivery/Pickup: At Base Camp, bus accessible at Luscher Farm.
Season: Summer share: May–October; winter share: November–April.

Abundant Harvest

&www.abundantharvest.biz
PO Box 714, North Plains 971-205-2203

Grows: Vegetables, fruits, herbs, and flowers at Dos Sequoias Farm and New Earth Farm.
Delivery/Pickup: Farm pickup and pickup in Southeast Portland.
Season: Summer share: May–October; winter share: November–April.

Artisan Organics

www.artisanorganics.net

5910 SE Davis Rd, Hillsboro ☎ 503-270-6689

Grows: Vegetables, tree fruit, eggs, and lamb.

Delivery/Pickup: Farm pickup and pickup sites in Portland at Legacy Emanuel Hospital and Health Center in Northwest Portland, and Legacy Good Samaritan Hospital and Medical Center in Northwest Portland.

Season: Summer share: June–October; fall share: October–December.

Rising Stone Farm

www.risingstonefarm.com

Lovena Farm: 9311 SE Stanley Ave, Milwaukie ☎ 503-916-9576

Grows: Vegetables, herbs, and berries.

Delivery/Pickup: Farm pickup and pickup at SE 30th Ave and Belmont St.

Season: May–October.

Big Leaf Farm

www.bigleaffarm.com

29644 SE Weitz Ln, Eagle Creek ☎ 503-367-8124

Grows: Vegetables, fruit, herbs, and eggs.

Delivery/Pickup: Farm pickup and sites in Southeast Portland and Oregon City.

Season: May–October.

Birds & Bees Community Farm

20495 S Geiger Rd, Oregon City ☎ 503-655-7447

Grows: Free-range eggs, honey, fruit, herbs, and vegetables.

Delivery/Pickup: Farm pickup.

Season: Forty-three-week share spread over twelve months.

Braeside Farms

www.braesidefarmscsa.com

PO Box 1141, Estacada ☎ 503-630-5861

Grows: Greens mix, salad mix, vegetables, herbs, fruit, chicken, rabbit, lamb, beef, pork, honey, and eggs.

Delivery/Pickup: Farm pickup and home delivery.

Season: Year-round shares.

City Garden Farms

⊘ www.citygardenfarms.com
♥ 4319 SE Bybee Blvd, Portland ☏ 503-730-0981

Grows: Vegetables. Eggs and meat are available for an additional fee.
Delivery/Pickup: Pickup sites in Northeast and Southeast Portland.
Season: June–October.

Creative Outlet Nursery & Farm LLC

⊘ www.creativeoutletnurseryandfarm.blogspot.com
♥ 11602 NE 192nd Ave, Brush Prairie, WA ☏ 360-608-2137

Grows: Vegetables, herbs, strawberries, flowers, and eggs.
Delivery/Pickup: Farm pickup and pickup sites in Vancouver, Washington.
Season: June–October.

Dancing Roots Farm

⊘ www.dancingrootsfarm.com
♥ 29820 E Woodard Rd, Troutdale ☏ 503-695-3445

Grows: Vegetables, herbs, flowers, and some fruit. Eggs are available for an additional fee.
Delivery/Pickup: Farm pickup or pickup sites in Northeast Portland Piedmont neighborhood.
Season: May–November.

Diggin' Roots Farm

⊘ www.digginrootsfarm.com
♥ 11934 SE Beckman Ave, Mollala ☏ 503-759-3969

Grows: Vegetables, fruit, chestnuts, berries, herbs, eggs, chicken, and lamb.
Delivery/Pickup: Pickup in Milwaukie.
Season: May–October.

French Prairie Gardens

www.fpgardens.com

♥ 17673 French Prairie Rd, St. Paul ☎ 503-633-8445

Grows: Fifteen fruits, including berries, apples, and peaches; twenty different vegetables, flowers, and herbs.

Delivery/Pickup: Farm pickup and pickup sites in Northeast Portland, Southeast Portland, Beaverton Farmers Market, Wilsonville, and optional business drop-off sites.

Season: June–October.

Gaining Ground Farm

www.gaininggroundfarm.com

♥ 21480 NE Laughlin Rd, Yamhill ☎ 503-662-5251

Grows: Vegetables, herbs, and flowers. Eggs and local wine available for an additional fee.

Delivery/Pickup: Farm pickup and pickup sites in Beaverton and Northeast Portland.

Season: June–October.

Garden at Van Schepen Vineyards

www.blizzardwines.com/csa

♥ 29495 SW Burkhalter Rd, Hillsboro ☎ 360-904-1668

Grows: Grapes, vegetables, fruits, herbs, and flowers.

Delivery/Pickup: Vineyard pickup and pickup sites in Hillsboro, Northwest Portland, and Salem. Special arrangements available.

Season: June–mid-October.

Gee Creek Farm

www.geecreekfarm.com

♥ 1606 NW 215th Circle, Ridgefield, WA ☎ 360-887-0463

Grows: Vegetables and fruit.

Delivery/Pickup: Farm pickup and pickup at some Portland farmers markets.

Season: June–November.

Helsing Junction Farm

⌕ *www.helsingfarmcsa.com*
♀ 12013 Independence Rd, Rochester, WA ✆ 360-273-2033

Grows: Vegetables, fruits, herbs, and flowers.
Delivery/Pickup: Deliveries in the Hawthorne, Fremont, and Alberta areas.
Season: June–October.

Hidden Oasis CSA, LLC

♀ 5410 NE 229th Ct, Vancouver, WA ✆ 360-256-6896

Grows: Vegetables, herbs, shiitake mushrooms, Asian pears, blackberries, apples, plums, and flowers.
Delivery/Pickup: Farm pickup and pickup at various Vancouver, Washington locations.
Season: Summer share: April–mid-October; winter share: limited, bi-weekly.

Hood River Organic Cooperative CSA

⌕ *www.hoodriverorganic.com*
♀ PO Box 1550, 4780 Oregon 35, Hood River ✆ 341-354-2111

Grows: Cremini and portobello mushrooms, vegetables, herbs, garlic, flowers, asparagus, berries, fruit, wild and exotic mushrooms, eggs, and bread.
Delivery/Pickup: Home delivery in Portland, Hood River, and The Gorge. Drop-off sites for rural customers.
Season: Year-round and seasonal shares.

Hunters' Greens Farm

⌕ *www.huntersgreens.com*
♀ 11116 NE 156th St, Brush Prairie, WA ✆ 360-256-3788

Grows: Vegetables. Flower shares, meat, and eggs are available for an additional fee.
Delivery/Pickup: Farm pickup and pickup sites at Fisher's Landing C-Tran and in Vancouver, Washington.
Season: June–October.

Kookoolan Farms LTD

www.kookoolanfarms.com

📍 15713 Hwy 47, Yamhill 📞 503-730-7535

Grows: Salad greens, braising greens, pod and shell peas, green and shell beans, root vegetables, potatoes, tomatoes, several different peppers, eggplants, broccoli, cauliflower, herbs, flowers, sweet corn, apples, berries, and mushrooms.

Delivery/Pickup: Farm pickup and pickup at the Intel Ronler Acres RA1 campus in Hillsboro. Several membership buying clubs around Portland make weekly trips.

Season: April–November.

La Finquita del Buho

📍 7960 NW Dick Rd, Hillsboro 📞 503-647-2595

Grows: Vegetables, herbs, and fruit. Eggs, goat cheese, and flowers are available for an additional fee.

Delivery/Pickup: Farm pickup.

Season: April–October.

Little Frog Farm

www.littlefrogfarmcsa.com

📍 16205 NW Gillihan Rd, Portland 📞 503-280-8044

Grows: Vegetables, herbs, and flowers.

Delivery/Pickup: At Enterbeing on NE 16th Ave and Alberta St.

Season: June–November.

Love Farm Organics

www.lovefarmorganics.com

📍 46125 NW Hillside Rd, Forest Grove 📞 503-515-9939

Grows: Vegetables, salad greens mix, herbs, flowers, berries, and other fruits. Bulk berries available for an additional fee.

Delivery/Pickup: Farm pickup and at pickup sites in Northeast Portland and in Garden Home/Hillsdale.

Season: May–October.

Many Friends Farm

♀ 74999 Lost Creek Rd, Clatskanie ☎ 503-728-2343

Grows: Vegetables, herbs, and fruit.
Delivery/Pickup: Doorstep delivery or to an agreed-upon location.
Season: June–October.

Natural Harvest Farm

🔗 *www.osalt.org/csa_at_natural_harvest_farm.html*
♀ PO Box 1106, Canby ☎ 503-916-9198.

Grows: Vegetables, fruits, herbs, and flowers.
Delivery/Pickup: Farm pickup and pickup at People's Farmers Market.
Season: March–November.

The North Portland Farm

🔗 *www.growinginalldirections.org*
♀ 2124 N Williams Ave, Portland ☎ 503-236-9515, ext 114

Grows: Vegetables, fruit, cut flowers, and artwork.
Delivery/Pickup: Pickup in North Portland.
Season: June–October.

Northwest Organic Farm

🔗 *www.northwestorganicfarm.com*
♀ 17713 NW 61st Ave, Ridgefield, WA ☎ 360-573-4868

Grows: Heirloom vegetables, lettuces, berries, strawberries, raspberries, blueberries, apples, cherries, and pears.
Delivery/Pickup: Farm pickup and pickup in Vancouver, Washington.
Season: Summer share.

Provisions CSA Mushroom Farm

🔗 *www.promushrooms.com*
♀ PO Box 233, Olympia, WA ☎ 360-359-6673

Grows: Oyster, shiitake, pioppini, and lion's mane mushrooms.
Delivery/Pickup: Pickup sites in Northeast and Southeast Portland.
Season: June–October.

Pumpkin Ridge Gardens

www.pumpkinridgegardens.com

31067 NW Pumpkin Ridge Dr, North Plains 503-647-5023

Grows: Vegetables and herbs. Eggs, flowers, and some fruit available for an additional fee.
Delivery/Pickup: Doorstep delivery limited to Multnomah County west of E 82nd Avenue, and to Washington County north of Lake Oswego.
Season: Year-round and seasonal shares.

Purple Rain Vineyard

www.purplerainvineyard.com

21313 NE 147th St, Brush Prairie, WA 360-256-8658

Grows: Vegetables, small fruit, culinary and medicinal herbs, flowers, and eggs.
Delivery/Pickup: Doorstep or office delivery.
Season: May–December.

Queen Bee Flowers

www.queenbeeflowers.com

PO Box 42112, Portland 503-231-2806

Grows: Specialty cut flowers.
Delivery/Pickup: Pickup in Southeast Portland.
Season: May–November.

Rainwater Farm

Cully neighborhood, Portland 503-284-6823

Grows: Vegetables, berries, herbs, fruit, nuts, and occasional eggs.
Delivery/Pickup: Doorstep delivery.
Season: May–October.

Sauvie Island Organics

www.sauvieislandorganics.com

20233 NW Sauvie Island Rd, Portland 503-621-6921

Grows: Vegetables and herbs.
Delivery/Pickup: Farm pickup and pickup sites in St. Johns and Southeast, Northeast, and Northwest Portland.
Season: May–November.

THE FARMER CHEF CONNECTION

A PORTLAND CHEFS' COLLABORATIVE EVENT

The Farmer Chef Connection is an annual all-day event put on by **Portland Chefs Collaborative** in order to bring farmers and chefs together to chew the fat, break bread, share advice, and ... speed date, which is really just another way of saying "make connections." Farmers and producers gather on one side of the conference room and take turns at the microphone introducing their farms and crops. Then restauranteurs, chefs, and others in food service buzz around talking with them about their needs.

For example, at the 2009 Farmer Chef Connection, **Laughing Planet** owner Richard Satnick was trying to source a more reliable supply of poultry for his seven cafés. What he needed: a steady supply of good-quality butchered chicken. He got a couple cards and some scribbled numbers to follow up on. What he found, unexpectedly, was a potential new hot chile connection with **Gales Meadow Farm** in Gales Creek, Oregon. Such is the case with many chefs and owners that attend. In general, a lot of information is exchanged, a lot of hands are shaken, and everyone seems to enjoy themselves.

Lunch at the event is always a big potluck with foods prepared by the farmers and chefs. The 2009 buffet table featured delicious **Picklopolis** pickles from David Barber (super crisp dilly beans, spicy carrots, kraut, and dill chips) a Cattail Creek Lamb roast from **Nostrana**, **New Seasons Market's** spicy Thai lamb ribs, a kale salad from **Organically Grown Company**, **Sweetbriar Farms** pulled pork, **Hotlips** soda (☞ p. 125), and much more.

The benefit of the Farmer Chef Connection is mutual for the farmers hoping to get their produce in local restaurants and for the chefs looking to source nearby. What started as a small gathering in 2001 has grown every year, and will no doubt continue to do so for years to come.

Singer Hill Gardens

www.singerhillgardens.org
701 John Adams St, Oregon City ♪ 503-656-5252

Grows: Vegetables, edible flowers, and herbs.
Delivery/Pickup: Various pickup sites.
Season: Spring share: March–May; summer share: June–October.

Slow Hand Farm

www.slowhandfarm.blogspot.com
Sauvie Island, Portland

Grows: Salad ingredients and vegetables.
Delivery/Pickup: Farm pickup and sites in Northeast and Southeast Portland.
Season: May–December.

Springhill

13340 NW Springville Ln, Portland ♪ 503-292-0410

Grows: Vegetables, herbs, flowers, berries, apples, and eggs.
Delivery/Pickup: Farm pickup.
Season: Year-round shares.

Stockhouse's Farm

www.stockhousesfarm.com
59 W Birnie Slough Rd, Cathlamet, WA ♪ 360-849-4145

Grows: Vegetables, herbs, flowers, chickens, eggs, pumpkins, and vegetable starts.
Delivery/Pickup: Farm pickup and pickup sites in Astoria.
Season: May–October.

Storytree Farm

www.storytreefarm.com
6227 NE 124th St, Vancouver, WA ♪ 360-849-4145

Grows: Vegetables, herbs, greens, gourmet lettuces, flowers, honey, grapes, figs, apples, shiro plums, melons, and heirloom pumpkins.
Delivery/Pickup: Farm pickup.
Season: June–October.

Sunroot Gardens Urban CSA

www.trashfactory.net/sunrootgardens
9 4316 SE 26th Ave, Portland ♪ 503-686-5557

Grows: Vegetables, fruits, and culinary and medicinal herbs.
Delivery/Pickup: Pickup in Southeast Portland.
Season: April–October.

Terra Nova Community Farm at Terra Nova High School

www.tncfarm.org
9 10351 NW Thompson Rd, Portland ♪ 503-577-7612

Grows: Vegetables, herbs, and flowers.
Delivery/Pickup: Pickup at Terra Nova High School.
Season: May–October.

Vicki's Harvest Boxes at Sungold Farm

www.sungoldfarm.com
9 6995 NW Evers Rd, Forest Grove ♪ 503-357-3851

Grows: Vegetables, fruits, herbs, and flowers.
Delivery/Pickup: Farm pickup and pickup sites in Northeast Portland, Aloha, and at Portland, Beaverton, and Hillsdale farmers markets; Intel Campuses (Hawthorne Farm, Jones Farm, and Ronler Acres); Nike World Campus; Columbia Sportswear Headquarters.
Season: June–October.

Winter Green Farm

www.wintergreenfarm.com
9 89762 Poodle Creek Rd, Noti ♪ 341-935-1920, 866-935-1920

Grows: Vegetables, berries, and herbs.
Delivery/Pickup: Pickup sites at various Portland farmers markets.
Season: June–October.

Wobbly Cart Farming Collective

www.wobblycart.com

13136-A 201st Ave SW, Rochester, WA 360-273-7597

Grows: Vegetables, herbs, and fruit.

Delivery/Pickup: Pickup in Northeast Portland.

Season: June–October.

Your Backyard Farmer

www.yourbackyardfarmer.com

7527 SE Ramona St, Portland 503-449-2402

Grows: Vegetables, flowers, and herbs.

Delivery/Pickup: Grown in and delivered from your very own backyard.

Season: March–November.

Salt, Fire & Time Community Supported Kitchen

www.saltfireandtime.com

1630 SE 3rd Ave, Portland 503-208-2758

Tressa Yellig, founder of Portland's first community supported kitchen – Salt, Fire & Time – trained at Manhattan's Natural Gourmet Institute for Health and Culinary Arts, where she met Jessica Prentice, author of *Full Moon Feast*. From Prentice, Yellig learned about and apprenticed for Three Stone Hearth, a community supported kitchen in the San Francisco Bay area. Yellig is now in Portland running a similar business: Salt, Fire & Time – a community supported kitchen and volunteer-based cooking school dedicated to sourcing from local farmers and cottage artisans to produce traditional, nutrient-dense foods.

Anyone can purchase Salt, Fire & Time foods, which are offered on a weekly pickup basis and advertised via e-mail and on the website. Foods for weekly pickup range in price and include everything from cultured vegetables and sauerkrauts to soaked grain and bean dishes to lacto-fermented soda and sprouted-grain, slow-fermented breads. Salt, Fire & Time classes range from DIY cordials, conserves, and syrups to butchering, curing, sourdough bread baking, and eating with food allergies.

Salt, Fire & Time also offers weekly informal community feasts with guest speakers (often farmers, cottage artisans, or health practitioners) and a four-course, all-local meal. Check out the website for more information about these dinners, which usually cost $35 and sell out fast with a limit of thirty-five guests.

THE LIST OF CLASSES in this chapter is just the tip of the iceberg when it comes to Rose City cooking classes. Please keep in mind that in addition to these schools, plenty of restaurants and markets offer cooking classes as well. Check with your favorite market or restaurant for specific cooking class information.

Art Institute of Portland Culinary Arts

www.artinstitutes.edu/portland

Portland's youngest cooking school offers four different culinary programs, including a baking and pastry diploma and a culinary arts associates degree.

Bob's Red Mill

www.bobsredmill.com/cooking-classes.html

The kitchen classroom at Milwaukie's Bob's Red Mill is host to cooking classes such as Italian baking and holiday cookies, all featuring Bob's Red Mill products.

Caprial and John's Kitchen

www.caprialandjohnskitchen.com

John and Caprial Pence of the popular show *Caprial and John's Kitchen* teach evening cooking classes that often work through an entire dinner party menu. Classes top out at fifteen participants.

David's Vegan Kitchen

www.davidspurevegetariankitchen.com

David Gabbe's three-hour vegetarian cooking classes are held regularly in Seattle and Portland. Classes range from vegetarian cooking with greens to beans and grains magic.

The Decorette Shop

www.thedecoretteshop.com

Since 1973 Portland's Decorette Shop has been serving up sweets and sweets-making supplies. Three-hour classes at the shop range from easy candies and chocolate truffles to beginning cake decorating.

Food by Hand Seminars

www.foodbyhandseminars.com

Food by Hand Seminars' motto is "Teach the craft and business of artisan food." These local seminars, which attract national participants, range from how to open a bakery to how to run your own cheese shop. According to Food by Hand founder Heidi Yorkshire, "Classes are short, three days long, so obviously you can't learn everything. But what we hope is that people leave with a road map to starting a successful business."

Food Innovation Center

fic.oregonstate.edu

If you've got a food product you are developing and want to get on market shelves, Oregon State University's Food Innovation Center in Portland offers all kinds of helpful classes. Topics include packaging engineering, shelf life studies, and product marketing.

Hipcooks

www.portland.hipcooks.com

This cooking school got its start in Los Angeles. Hipcooks bans measuring devices, favors fresh and organic ingredients, and encourages tasting while you cook. Classes range from My Big Fat Greek Cooking Class to Thai One On at the North Portland location.

Ivy Manning

www.ivymanning.com

Ivy Manning (author of *The Adaptable Feast, The Farm to Table Cookbook,* and *Crackers & Dips*) teaches private, in-home cooking classes such as sushi rolling, quick and easy suppers, regional Italian menus, and Spanish tapas. Class minimum is four participants, maximum is fifteen.

Heidi Nestler

www.heidinestler.com

Heidi Nestler teaches affordable cooking classes (most classes are $20) at the **Urban Farm Center** in Milwaukie, fifteen minutes south of Portland, on everything from miso soup and Japanese sea vegetables to DIY natto.

Kookoolan Farms Cheese Classes

www.kookoolanfarms.com

If you're up for the drive (one hour southwest of Portland), these year round weekend farm cheese classes are wonderful. Various regional cheesemakers teach classes such as basic soft cheeses, homemade Gouda, mozzarella, and cheddar. The Kookoolan Farms store sells cheesemaking supplies.

Le Cordon Bleu College of Culinary Arts

www.chefs.edu/portland

This downtown Portland culinary school is affiliated with France's Le Cordon Bleu, which has nationwide campus locations. The Portland college offers a patisserie and baking program, a culinary arts program, and a hospitality and restaurant management program.

Lost Arts Kitchen

www.lostartskitchen.com

Chris Musser's wholesome cooking and sustainable home economics classes are hosted at her Northeast Portland home and are limited to six to eight students. Topics include sourcing and cooking natural meat and meal planning for all seasons.

Louisa Neumann

www.louisaneumann.com

Louisa Neumann offers a variety of culinary classes at several locations, including a $75 two-hour knife skills class, a braising and stewing class, and her very popular children's cooking classes. Visit her website for information about private and home cooking classes.

The Merry Kitchen

www.themerrykitchen.com

Julie Merry's Northeast Portland home cooking school hosts classes for children of all ages. Merry's home garden provides much of the fresh seasonal produce prepared in classes such as On Top of Spaghetti (ages 5 to 8), Asian Wraps (ages 6 to 12), and Fondue Party (ages 6 to 10).

Miso Magic School of Japanese and Thai Cooking

⊘ www.misomagic.com

Noriko Hirayama's Miso Magic cooking school specializes in Northern Thai and Japanese cooking. Her six classes include Sushi Maki, Tempura and Noodle Secrets, and authentic Thai courses. Classes are limited to eight students.

Oregon Culinary Institute

⊘ www.oregonculinaryinstitute.com

This Pioneer Pacific College-owned downtown Portland culinary school offers several degrees, including a culinary arts diploma and an associate of applied science degree in baking and pastry.

Portland Community College

⊘ www.pcc.edu

Portland Community College campuses offer a wide array of classes such as Cooking With Kids, Fermentation Science, and A Taste of Africa cooking series.

Preserve

⊘ www.portlandpreserve.com

Harriet Fasenfest runs the show at Preserve, a unique food preservation and householding school in Northeast Portland. Preserve's four-month food preservation series covers everything from making jam and jelly to canning fruits and tomatoes. Classes are limited to eight participants.

Good Keuken

⊘ www.goodkeuken.com

The late chef **Robert Reynolds's Chef Studio** lives on in Blake Van Roekel's Good Keuken cooking school in Northeast's Portland's **Old Salt Marketplace** (☞ *p.* 67) with many Chef Studio alumni, including Van Roekel, on staff. The focus here is on farm-fresh and wild crafted local foods, including butchery and foraging classes and regular farm tours.

Sur La Table

⊘ cookingclasses.surlatable.com

Sur La Table's mostly evening cooking classes in the Pearl District fill up fast and range from Real Risotto and Introduction to Sauces to Easy French Classics and Knife Skills Workshop.

The Cakery

⊘ www.bakerandspicebakery.com/The Cakery

This **Baker & Spice** (☞ *p.* 24)–owned shop hosts all sorts of cooking classes. Classes include The Perfect Bundt, Gingerbread House Workshop, and Make a Pie. The Cakery also hosts the no-cost Pages to Plates cookbook event series featuring cookbook authors.

Whole Foods Market

⊘ www.wholefoodsmarket.com

Whole Foods Market cooking classes, ranging from pasta-making to African cuisine, take place mainly in the evening at the Pearl District Portland and Tigard Whole Foods Markets. Classes at the Pearl District Whole Foods take place in the second floor classroom.

WHEN YOUR KITCHEN NEEDS are specific and your time is precious, head to these Portland spots. I've included small locally owned businesses as well as the big guys, though I'm proud to note that the local independents are in the majority here. As for books on food, more and more Portland chef/restaurant cookbooks are coming out these days, including three big ones in fall 2013: *Toro Bravo: Stories. Recipes. No Bull.* (I co-wrote it!), *Pok Pok: Food and Stories from the Streets, Homes, and Roadside Restaurants of Thailand,* and *Le Pigeon: Cooking at the Dirty Bird.* Go Portland!

Cash & Carry

www.smartfoodservice.com

♀ 731 SE Stephens St, Portland ☎ 503-232-9840 ◷ M–Sa 6am–6pm, Su 8am–5pm
♀ 910 N Hayden Meadows Dr, Portland ☎ 503-289-3120 ◷ M–Sa 6am–6pm, Su 8am–5pm
♀ 1420 NW 14th Ave, Portland ☎ 503-221-8793 ◷ M–Sa 6am–6pm, Su 8am–5pm

Cash & Carry is a great place to find cheap but durable tongs, knifes, strainers, stainless bowls, and other kitchen equipment for the restaurant chef in us all. Most of the kitchen equipment is all about low-cost utility, with large kitchens and commissaries in mind, so don't go looking for pretty gravy boats or colorful mitts. This store is geared toward food service, bulk food, and kitchen equipment, with over fifty locations throughout the West. It's always pretty chilly inside, so wear a coat: the temperature allows for floor storage of sacks of avocados, lemons, limes, potatoes, onions, and other produce.

The long, tall aisles with pallet movers at most ends are stacked and shelved with fifty-pound sacks of masa, flour, and rice as well as five-pound bags of dried shiitakes next to rubber antifatigue mats and chafing dishes. The walk-in freezer and fridge sections are worth checking out even if you don't need big boxes of marionberries, peaches, raspberries, tilapia, crab, goat, or hot wings.

Kitchen Kaboodle

www.kitchenkaboodle.com

♀ 1520 NE Broadway, Portland ☎ 503-288-1500 ◷ M–Sa 10am–7pm, Su 10am–6pm
♀ 404 NW 23rd Ave, Portland ☎ 503-241-4040 ◷ M–Sa 10am–7pm, Su 11am–6pm
♀ 8788 SW Hall Blvd, Portland ☎ 503-643-5491 ◷ M–Sa 10am–7pm, Su 11am–6pm

Locally owned since 1975, Kitchen Kaboodle's three Portland locations (plus the Hillsboro location) are stocked like big-box kitchen stores, so you'll find the same diverse assortment of cookware and dinnerware as at a **Sur La Table** (☞ *p.* 167). Many products – from Le Creuset enamelware and All-Clad pans to kitchen linens and glassware – are displayed throughout the store on tall metal racks. There's a kitchen knife and table cutlery section, a table setting and flatware section, all sorts of gadgets, and even a home furniture section. This store has great selection, friendly service, and competitive prices.

Mirador Community Store

www.miradorcommunitystore.com

📍 2106 SE Division St, Portland 📞 503-231-5175 🕐 M–Sa 10am–6pm, Su 11am–5pm

Every time I visit Mirador Community Store, I come away inspired. Stoneware crocks, canning jars, food dehydrators, juicers, and myriad cookbooks make up the majority of this bright bungalow shop. What began in 1999 as an all-natural baking supply store today carries such items as Harsch German earthenware crocks, grain mills, pizza stones, knife sharpeners, cherry pitters, steam juicers (you can rent one here for $20 a day), Dutch ovens, and all sorts of kitchen doohickeys that you didn't know you needed until you had them.

Mirador also has a cheesemaking section, stocked by Claudia Lucero of **Urban Cheesecraft** (☞ *p.* 36), with cheesemaking kits, as well as individually priced supplies such as vegetarian rennet, cheesecloth, and cheese salt.

Powell's Books for Home and Garden

www.powells.com

📍 3747 SE Hawthorne Blvd, Portland 📞 503-228-4651 🕐 M–Sa 9am–9pm, Su 9am–8pm

Powell's Books for Home and Garden is a foodie paradise, especially with **Pastaworks** (☞ *p.* 93) right next door. You can purchase *The Silver Spoon* – the classic Italian cookbook – and then head over to Pastaworks for some high-quality extravirgin olive oil, canned Italian tomatoes, house-cured pancetta, and house-made pasta, before going home to marry the book to the ingredients.

Some book categories in this amazing store include Food Literature, Wine, Culinary Reference, Northwest, Mexican, Japanese, Indian, Sustainable Eating, Tea, Coffee, Seafood, Sausage and Smoking, Bartending, and more. As with all Powell's Books locations, new and used books are shelved together, so you can often choose between a new, list-price book or its less expensive, used counterpart.

New releases here are always displayed on a tall shelf by the entrance. In addition to food and cooking books, you'll find gifty but useful kitchen supplies such as aprons, tableclothes, cream pitchers, bamboo cookware, and spud scrubbers. The food and drink magazine section toward the front of the store is stocked with all the major publications, as well as some that are lesser known.

Sur La Table

🔗 *www.surlatable.com*
📍 1102 NW Couch St, Portland 📞 503-295-9679
🕐 M–F 10am–9pm, Sa 9am–9pm, Su 10am–6pm
📍 390 N State St, Suite 120, Lake Oswego 📞 503-636-2181 🕐 M–Sa 10am–7pm, Su 11am–6pm

The first Sur La Table got its start in Seattle's Pike Place Market in 1972; since then it has expanded to more than seventy shops nationwide. Portland's Northwest location across from the downtown **Powell's City of Books** is a great place to find a wide assortment of cookware, dinnerware, and houseware. Yes, there are high-end Japanese chef's knives, home movie–style popcorn machines, and enormous paella pans, but you can also pop in for a small, more utilitarian purchase such as oven mitts or pepper mills.

The clearance section is at the back of the store near the children's cooking section. A few steps away is the cutlery section, where you'll often find staff slicing carrots and apples as part of a demonstration. Attached to the Northwest Sur La Table is a demonstration kitchen that hosts cooking classes (👉 *p.* 164) throughout the year.

The Cakery

🔗 *www.bakerandspicebakery.com/The Cakery*
📍 6306 SW Capitol Hwy, Portland 📞 503-546-3737 🕐 Tu–Sa 10am–5pm, Su 10am–3pm

Since opening in late 2008, Hillsdale's sweet little The Cakery has been peddling hard-to-find baking supplies and ingredients. In-house specialties include copper cookie cutters, a wide array of decorating sugars, Viking mixers, cake pans, beautiful glass cake trays, nice vanilla extracts and baking chocolates, rolling pins, meringue powder, and a big selection of baking and sweets books that are sold at 25% off cover prices every day.

For lovers of cold sweets, there are nice gift items such as sets of ice cream spoons and small ice cream/gelato bowls. The Cakery also has a demonstration kitchen at the back with affordable classes that are mostly taught by Julie Richardson of **Baker & Spice** on everything from rustic fruit desserts to how to cook with your child, along with its Pages to Plates no-cost cookbook author event series.

Williams-Sonoma

🔗 *www.williams-sonoma.com*
📍 638 SW 5th Ave, Portland 📞 503-827-8383
🕐 M–F 9:30am–7:30pm, Sa 9:30am–7pm, Su 11am–6pm
📍 338 NW 23rd Ave, Portland 📞 503-946-2300
🕐 M–F 10am–8pm, Sa 10am–7pm, Su 10am–6pm

Williams-Sonoma has more than 250 stores nationwide, and its downtown Portland location fits the boutique kitchen mold. Walking around Williams-Sonoma is a lot like visiting a model home: display tables might be set with French white porcelain, Riedel stemware, and expensive flatware. In addition to tableware, Williams-Sonoma carries top-of-the-line essential and not-so-essential kitchen equipment that you'll pay dearly for, including copper pots and pans, Belgian waffle makers, and remote meat thermometers that let you know when your beast is at the right temperature.

O RGANIC GROWERS, small ex-urban food producers, and farmers markets are the fastest growing sector of the United States food economy, and Portland definitely reflects that. Portland is home to seventeen diverse neighborhood farmers markets, and that number is steadily climbing. And because only 3% of Portland produce is currently purchased at farmers markets, there's a lot of room for growth.

Each market has a unique feel and many different flavors, ranging from the largest and busiest, downtown's **Portland State University Portland Farmers Market**, to the ethnically diverse **Lents International Farmers Market**, to the sit-down-and-stay-a-while **King Farmers Market**.

Most local farmers markets run from spring through fall, but we even have two markets in town – **People's Farmers Market** and **Hillsdale Farmers Market** open year round. Although I have included dates and times for most local markets, please be aware that both are subject to change. Check their respective web sites for up-to-date listings. The Portland Farmers Market has a comprehensive list on its website (*www.portlandfarmersmarket.org*) of all of the current Portland metro markets with all of the vital info.

In the words of the great cultural critic and farmer Wendell Berry, "Eating is an agricultural act." Visit one or more of Portland's local farmers markets regularly and you're sure to make a big difference.

Portland Farmers Market

⚲ *www.portlandfarmersmarket.org*
📍 240 N Broadway, Suite 129 ☎ 503-241-0032

Portland Farmers Market (PFM) is a nonprofit that oversees eight Portland markets: the Portland State University farmers market, the Wednesday Shemanski Park market downtown, the Saturday winter Shemanski Park market, the Pioneer Courthouse Square market, the Buckman market, the Northwest market, and the Kenton and King markets.

Listings and information for each market follow.

Portland Farmers Market (Shemanski Park)

⚲ *www.portlandfarmersmarket.org*
📍 South Park Blocks, SW Park and Salmon St (behind Schnitzer Concert Hall)
🕐 May–Oct W 10am–2pm; Jan–Feb Sa 10am–2pm

This is the only farmers market where you'll see suits on a regular basis. The selection at this downtown market that caters to folks who live and work downtown is a small but decent mix.

OTHER PORTLAND-AREA FARMERS MARKETS

Beaverton Farmers Market
♀ Hall Blvd, between 3rd St & 5th St
🕑 Mid-May–Oct, Sa 8am–1pm,
   mid-June–mid-Aug, W 3pm–6pm
🔗 www.beavertonfarmersmarket.com

Cedar Mill Sunset Farmers' Market
♀ NW Cornell Rd, 1 block West of
   Murray across from Sunset High
   School
🕑 Late May–mid-Oct, Sa 8am–1pm
🔗 www.cmfmarket.org

Clackamas Sunnyside Grange Farmers & Artists Market
♀ 4805 NE 92nd Ave, Portland
🕑 Apr–Oct, Su 11:30am–3:30pm
🔗 www.windancefarmsandart.com

Cully Community Market
♀ 6500 NE 42nd Ave and NE
   Killingsworth St
🕑 June–mid-Sept, Su 10am–2pm
🔗 www.cullycommunitymarket.org

Gresham Farmers Market
♀ Miller St between 2nd and 3rd St
🕑 May–Oct, Sa 8:30am–2pm
🔗 www.greshamfarmersmarket.com

Hillsboro Farmers Market
♀ Courthouse Square
🕑 May–Dec, Sa 8am–1:30pm,
   Mid-June–Aug, Tu 5pm–8:30pm
🔗 www.hillsboromarkets.org

Lake Oswego Farmers Market
♀ Millennium Park, 1st St and
   Evergreen Rd
🕑 Mid-May–mid-Oct,
   Sa 8:30am–1:30pm
🔗 www.ci.oswego.or.us/farmersmarket

Milwaukie Sunday Farmer's Market
♀ SE Main St across from City Hall
🕑 Mid-May–Oct, Su 9:30am–2pm
🔗 www.milwaukiefarmersmarket.com

Woodstock Farmers Market
♀ SE Woodstock Blvd & 46th Ave
🕑 June–Oct, Su 10am–2pm
🔗 www.woodstockmarketpdx.com

Portland Farmers Market (Buckman)
🔗 www.portlandfarmersmarket.org
♀ SE 20th Ave and Salmon St
🕑 May–Sept Th 3pm–7pm

This family-oriented Southeast neighborhood market features a nice diversity of produce, meat, seafood, cheese, and prepared food.

Portland Farmers Market (Kenton)
🔗 www.portlandfarmersmarket.org
♀ N Denver Ave and McClellan St
🕑 June–Sept Fri 1pm–7pm

The tiny but mighty Kenton market kicked off in 2012 with thirty vendors and live music.

Portland Farmers Market (King)
🔗 www.portlandfarmersmarket.org
♀ NE 7th Ave and Wygant St
🕑 May–Oct Su 10am–2pm

The King market is one of the youngest farmers markets in Portland. Visitors often stay awhile, hang out, and eat food.

Portland Farmers Market (Northwest)
🔗 www.portlandfarmersmarket.org
♀ NW 19th Ave and Everett St
🕑 June–Sept Th 3pm–7pm

In 2009 PFM closed its Ecotrust Farmers Market in Northwest Portland and opened this NW 23rd market in a lot donated by Con-way, Inc. Shoppers have their pick of roughly forty carts at this small farmers market.

Portland Farmers Market (Pioneer Courthouse Square)

- *www.portlandfarmersmarket.org*
- SW Broadway and Morrison St
- June–Oct M 10am–2pm

This Monday market in the heart of downtown hosts more than thirty booths. Twenty-six thousand people pass by Pioneer Courthouse Square every Monday, according to PFM, and this vibrant market is a great spot for passers-by to grab lunch or the ingredients for dinner.

Portland Farmers Market (Portland State University)

- *www.portlandfarmersmarket.org*
- South Park Blocks between SW Hall St and Montgomery St
- Mid–Mar–Dec Sa 8:30am–2pm, Nov–Dec Sa 9am–2pm

This downtown Portland Farmers Market is the largest in Portland with 170 stalls. It gets so crowded that in 2009 pets were banned; in 2010 the market expanded by an entire city block to meet demand. There is a little bit of everything at this popular market, including all sorts of produce, meat, seafood, flowers, and prepared food. At the center of the market you'll find seating, live music, and chef demonstrations.

Hillsdale Farmers Market

- *www.hillsdalefarmersmarket.com*
- SW Sunset Blvd and Capital Hwy, Portland
- 503-475-6555
- May–late Nov Su 10am–2pm, Dec–April Su twice monthly

One of Portland's two year round farmers markets, Hillsdale Farmers Market was founded

---

Canby Asparagus Farm fresh

Casa de Tamales
- 10605 SE Main St, Milwaukie
- 503-654-4423
- *www.canbyasparagusfarm.com*

Cooked right in front of you

Evoe
- 3731 SE Hawthorne Blvd, Portland
- 503-232-1010
- *www.pastaworks.com/evoe*

Farm-fresh institution

Higgins
- 1239 SW Broadway, Portland
- 503-222-9070
- *www.higginsportland.com*

From the restaurant's Southwest Hills farm

Meriwether's Restaurant
- 2601 NW Vaughn St, Portland
- 503-228-1250
- *www.meriwethersnw.com*

CSA small plates and nice wine

Navarre
- 10 NE 28th Ave, Portland
- 503-232-3555
- *www.navarreportland.blogspot.com*

Foraged and from-the-farm cuisine

Park Kitchen
- 422 NW 8th Ave, Portland
- 503-223-7275
- *www.parkkitchen.com*

Local farm and ranch Mexican

¿Por Qué No?
- 3524 N Mississippi Ave, Portland
- 503-467-4149
- 4635 SE Hawthorne Blvd, Portland
- 503-954-3138
- *www.porquenotacos.com*

Chef-owner Kevin Gibson

Davenport
- 2215 E Burnside St, Portland
- 503-236-8747

Small plates locally sourced

Aviary
- 1733 NE Alberta St, Portland
- 503-287-2400
- *www.aviarypdx.com*

TRUDY TOLIVER

OF **PORTLAND FARMERS MARKET**

Started working at Portland Farmers Market: January 2011

Position: Executive Director

Work prior to Portland Farmers Market: Executive Director at EarthShare Oregon (workplace fundraising for environmental organizations), Development Director at Friends of Virgin Islands National Park (lived on St. John, USVI in the Caribbean Sea), Executive Director of Human Resources at TriMet and various other positions at TriMet over fourteen years.

Favorite part of the job: Conducting outreach and publicity that promotes the awesomeness of our farmers and food artisans.

Moved to Portland in: When I was about two years old. I was born in Klamath Falls, Oregon.

Why: Because my parents' families were here.

PFM employs: Nine people year-round, fourteen in the warmer seasons.

What you would most like to change about local farmers markets: I'd like to explore a whole new economic model for farmers markets in low-income communities where they have few healthy food choices.

Something additional: I've been known to lick butter right off the knife.

in 2002. This midsize nonprofit market usually works with fifty vendors each year.

Irvington Farmers Market

🔗 *www.irvingtonfarmersmarket.com*
📍 NE 16th Ave and Broadway
🕐 Late May–mid–Oct: Su 10:30am–2pm

Since 2009, the Irvington farmers market has been focused on nutrition and community. From juicers to florists, homemade jams to seasonal produce, there are over twenty-five vendors with live music to boot.

Lents International Farmers Market

📍 Crossroads Plaza, SE 92nd Ave and Foster Rd
🕐 Mid–June–mid–Oct Su 9am–2pm

Lents is Portland's only international farmers market. It offers produce, international prepared foods, kids activities, and live entertainment.

Lloyd Farmers Market

🔗 *www.lloydfarmersmkt.net*
📍 NE Holladay St between 7th and 9th Aves
🕐 June–Sept Tu, Th 10am–2pm

This small covered farmers market usually has eight to twelve vendors and lots of shoppers from nearby offices.

Montavilla Farmers Market

🔗 *www.montavillamarket.org*
📍 SE 76th Ave and Stark St 🕐 Mid–June–Oct Su 10am–2pm

Montavilla Farmers Market is a small outer Portland market with products such as meat and seafood, fruits and vegetables, cheese, flowers, and ready-to-eat foods. There is always some sort of entertainment, including chef demonstrations, live music, and activities for kids.

Moreland Farmers Market

www.morelandfarmersmarket.org
♀ SE 14th Ave and Bybee Blvd ● Mid–May–Sept W 3:30pm–7:30pm

This small parking lot farmers market has a little bit of everything – produce, meat, seafood, cheese, and prepared food.

OHSU Farmers Market

www.ohsu.edu/farmersmarket
♀ Oregon Health and Science University Auditorium Courtyard (near fountain)
● Mid–May–mid–Oct Tu 11:30am–3:30pm

Oregon Health and Science University students, staff, and professors are regular customers at this midsize market. You'll find all the usual suspects as well as a wide selection of prepared food for OHSU folks on lunch.

Parkrose Farmers Market

www.parkrosefarmersmarket.org
♀ West parking lot, Parkrose High School, NE 122nd St and Shaver St
● May–Oct Sa 8am–2pm

This Parkrose High School farmers market draws more than one thousand visitors every Saturday for its variety of food, flowers, drinks, and crafts.

People's Farmers Market

www.peoples.coop/farmers-market
♀ 3029 SE 21st Ave ● year round W 2pm–7pm

This year round farmers market takes place in front of People's Food Cooperative. It's small but very diverse. There are twenty-plus booths in the summer and fewer in the winter.

St. Johns Farmers Market

www.sjfarmersmarket.com
♀ St. Johns Plaza at N Lombard St and Philadelphia Ave ● June–late Sept Sa 9am–1pm

Since 2009 this small North Portland farmers market has been home to twenty-plus vendors.

PORTLAND FOOD AND DRINK EVENTS are constantly changing, but here are some that you can count on. Of course, there are countless other food festivals held throughout the state that celebrate everything from elephant garlic and truffles to cherries and Dungeness crab. Tune into the forums and food blogs in the **Wired** chapter (☞ *p.* 190) to stay up to date.

SPRING

FredFest
⊘ *www.fredfestpdx.com*

Beer fanatics from far and wide convene for this annual **Hair of the Dog Brewing Company** (☞ *p.* 108) celebration of craft brews. Inspired by beer writer Fred Eckhardt, the fest offers a silent auction of rare beers, food and beer pairings, and more than twenty rare craft beers on tap from celebrated regional brewers.

Oregon Cheese Festival
⊘ *www.oregoncheeseguild.org*

This annual farmers market–style cheese festival features sheep, goat, and cow cheeses from Oregon and Northern California cheesemakers with plenty of cheese samples and sales. The festival takes place at Rogue Creamery.

Taste of the Nation
⊘ *www.portlandtaste.org*

This annual Portland feel-good event (proceeds from all Taste of the Nation nationwide events are donated to childhood hunger relief organizations) features food and drink from Oregon's top chefs and producers, along with a silent auction and live music.

SUMMER

Bite of Oregon
⊘ *www.biteoforegon.com*

This huge, time-honored annual outdoor event at Tom McCall Waterfront Park is focused on local food, beer (there's a craft beer garden), wine, and entertainment. The general admission fee does not include food and drink, which are purchased separately.

Bites for Rights
⌘ www.basicrights.org

Restaurants around Portland participate in this annual fundraiser by donating 15% of their sales from the event to the nonprofit Basic Rights Oregon.

Eat Mobile Food Cart Festival
⌘ www.wweek.com

Willamette Week hosts this celebration of Portland street food. Pay the minimal entry fee to sample food from an array of popular Portland food carts plus beer, wine, and spirits from local producers.

Feast Portland
⌘ www.feastportland.com

This big-name four-day food festival that celebrates Oregon food and drink, and is sponsored by *Bon Appetit* magazine, kicked off in fall 2012. Festival pass or individual event tickets cost a pretty penny and include talks, tastings, workshops, and more.

North American Organic Brewers Festival
⌘ www.naobf.org

Overlook Park gets mobbed every year for this admission-free, open-to-the-public celebration of North American and European organic beer. Buy a reusable tasting glass for $6; tastings are $1 each.

Northwest Veg Fest
⌘ www.nwveg.org

Northwest VEG!, a vegetarian lifestyle nonprofit, hosts this vegetarian/vegan festival. Sample all sorts of veggie fare, attend workshops and lectures, watch cooking demonstrations, and listen to live music.

Oregon Brewers Festival
⌘ www.oregonbrewfest.com

One of the nation's longest running beer festivals – twenty-plus years of craft beer sampling and celebration always held the last weekend of July. In 2013 the festival had 80,000 attendees at Tom McCall Waterfront Park.

Polish Festival
www.portlandpolonia.org/festival

The weekend-long North Portland Polish Festival boasts traditional Polish food and drink, including sausage, pierogi, cabbage rolls, and imported beer. Eat while watching traditional Polish dancing.

Portland Fermentation Festival
www.picklopolis.com/PFF2009.html

Sample homemade and professionally made live-culture, homemade fermented foods and drinks, talk with the makers, enjoy food fermentation demos and more at this low-cost stinky fest hosted and sponsored by Ecotrust. I've co-organized the festival with my friends David Barber and George Winborn since 2009.

Raw and Living Spirit Retreat
www.rawandlivingspirit.org

This four-day raw vegan cuisine retreat is held in Molalla every summer. The cost of the retreat includes meals (breakfast and lunch are buffets, dinner is plated), lodging, and all lectures and workshops.

Tour de Coops
www.growing-gardens.org

Growing Gardens hosts this annual one-day tour of Portlanders' home chicken coops. Purchase a booklet with the addresses of all participants and check out their coops, get urban chicken keeping ideas, and ask questions.

FALL

Great American Distillers Festival
www.distillersfestival.com

Small craft distilleries from around the country are the attraction at this weekend-long festival. Attendees enjoy tastings, educational seminars, and food pairings prepared by local restaurants.

Greek Festival
www.goholytrinity.org

Holy Trinity Greek Orthodox Cathedral hosts this festival every summer. Cooking demonstrations, authentic Greek dinners, and plenty of snacks, Greek pastries, beer, and wine are available throughout the weekend.

Northwest Food and Wine Festival
www.nwfoodandwinefestival.com

Although there is food – small plates from local restaurants – at this popular festival, it's more about sampling the hundreds of wines. Cost of admission includes food and drink; a portion of the proceeds go to Oregon Food Bank.

Oregon Mycological Society's Fall Mushroom Show
www.wildmushrooms.org

If you love to geek out about mushrooms, check out this annual event at the Forest Discovery Center. There are more than twenty tables covered in freshly picked and identified wild mushrooms. Other highlights include mushroom cookery, preservation, and books.

Wild About Game Cook-Off
www.nickyusa.com

Competing Pacific Northwest chefs have two hours to complete an original dish using game from Nicky USA's pantry – elk, quail, guinea hen, venison – which is then served up to a panel of judges. In addition to the cook-off, there are game tastings, dinners, and cookbook signings.

WINTER

Holiday Ale Festival
www.holidayale.com

Warm up with more than fifty West Coast winter ales at this five-day tented outdoor beer festival held at Pioneer Courthouse Square. Sample many rare and limited release winter ales.

Portland Seafood and Wine Festival
www.metroproductions.net/seafoodandwine

This large sponsored festival features all sorts of Oregon wine and seafood. Attendees enjoy tastings, cooking demonstrations, live music, and contests.

PORTLAND SHINES when it comes to urban farmsteading and foraging. Where I grew up in the Midwest, you either had a lawn or a farm and there was little in-between. In Portland, most of my friends and neighbors have home or community edible gardens, and I know a lot of folks who keep chickens, pygmy goats, ducks, and bees in their backyards. The days of milk and honey are here, and Portland is tilling the way for the rest of the country.

It can be overwhelming to keep up with all of the organizations and events that are a part of Portland's urban homestead revival. Some standout events include **Growing Gardens' Tour de Coops**, **Portland Fruit Tree Project's** harvesting parties, **Preserve's** canning and food preservation classes, **Urban Farm Store's** chicken keeping classes, **Plate and Pitchfork's** local farm dinners, **Oregon Food Bank's** Plant a Row for the Hungry ... the list goes on and on.

You don't even have to grow a garden to feed yourself in Portland if you have a pair of comfortable all-weather shoes and a means to get out into nature. Inside and outside city limits, wild edibles abound. Here you'll find wild mushrooms, fiddlehead ferns, countless berries, sea vegetables, herbs, lettuces, and much, much more. Sign up for one of John Kallas's **Wild Food Adventures** (available throughout the spring and fall in various locations throughout Oregon and Washington) to learn about wild edibles 101.

Friends of Family Farmers

www.friendsoffamilyfarmers.org
PO Box 1286, Molalla 503-759-3276.

Friends of Family Farmers (FOFF) was founded in 2005 by co-president Kendra Kimbirauskas and received 501(c)3 status in May of 2007. It is a leading voice for Oregon's independent family farmers. FOFF provides organizational resources to help farmers and community members resist and retaliate against factory farms and support socially responsible sustainable farming. Much of the time, FOFF and its small staff are on the road visiting Oregon communities and farmers and assessing what they need.

Friends of Family Farmers now has several programs that tackle local agricultural issues year round, including organizing and drafting the Agricultural Reclamation Act – intended to ensure the survival of socially responsible Oregon farmers. FOFF has hosted a series of community meetings around the state focused on the challenges of family-scale agriculture in Oregon in order to draw up this act.

Every second Tuesday of the month, FOFF holds InFARMation sessions in the events space of **Holocene** (♥ 1001 SE Morrison St, Portland ☎ 503-239-7639). Farmers and community members come together over food and drink to talk about wide-ranging topics such as how to eat locally during the lean months and how to buy directly from farmers. The first InFARMation session I attended was enlightening. That particular evening, Scot Callaway, a Canby resident, spoke about how his community fought and organized against a Foster Farms concentrated animal feeding operation setting up shop in their area. The fight isn't over.

FOFF is always looking for volunteers and donations. Check out its website for more information.

Growing Gardens

🖉 *www.growing-gardens.org*
♥ 2203 NE Oregon St, Portland ☎ 503-284-8420

I have a lot of respect for Growing Gardens – a local green nonprofit that's been around in various incarnations since 1996. Executive director David Greenberg and his staff do important work, organizing organic home edible gardens for low-income Portlanders, leading after-school garden clubs and other youth gardening programs, and hosting all sorts of open-to-the-public beginning gardener workshops throughout the year.

Every summer, Growing Gardens puts on the **Chef in My Garden** series – a popular dinner series featuring food and drink from top Portland chefs served outdoors in various Portland home edible gardens. The $125 tickets sell out fast and benefit Growing Gardens programs.

The annual summer **Tour de Coops** is anoth-

CHICKENS

Plenty of Portlanders enjoy farm-fresh eggs on a daily basis, gathered right from their own backyards. The benefits of raising urban chickens are numerous: farm-fresh eggs, free fertilizer, pest control, unusual pets, and an easy way to dispose of kitchen scraps. Although most feed stores carry chicks year round, the healthiest chicks and the greatest variety of species are available in early spring.

To educate urban chicken owners, the Portland nonprofit **Growing Gardens** (at left) offers regular urban chicken workshops with topics ranging from avian flu education to biosecurity issues. Growing Gardens also hosts the annual Tour de Coops, a tour of Portlanders' home chicken coops.

Portland-based Barbara Kilarski's 2003 book *Keep Chickens!* was the first book to deal with chickens as pets. Providing advice to first-time urban chicken owners is Kilarski's specialty. "Make sure that you have the space and make sure that your neighbors won't mind," she says. "Keeping chickens in the city is still viewed as a somewhat eccentric idea, regardless of

er popular event – a self-guided tour of over twenty backyard Portland chicken coops all within walking distance of one another. Buy the $10 Tour de Coops booklet and you'll get information and addresses for all of the participants, including bike route maps for the event.

Home Orchard Society Arboretum

🔗 *www.homeorchardsociety.org*
📍 Clackamas Community College, 19600 S Molalla Ave, Oregon City 📞 503-338-8479
🕐 Tu and Sa 9am–3pm *(call before visiting)*

The Home Orchard Society (HOS) was founded in 1975 by hobby orchardists as a fruit cultivation education and DIY organization. In 1986 the HOS Arboretum at Clackamas Community College opened, and today the organization has more than seven hundred members worldwide. The 1.6-acre Arboretum is open to the public 9am to 3pm Tuesdays and Saturdays year round, and volunteers are always welcome. It's a great place to learn grafting, pruning, harvesting, and other fruit tree maintenance skills, as well as to check out the amazing variety of HOS's fruit trees, shrubs, and vines.

When you volunteer to help with late summer and fall HOS harvests, you'll head home with a sack of fruit. One third of the harvested fruit goes to the Oregon Food Bank and other relief and hunger agencies. Although the Arboretum needs a lot of hands to harvest fruit in the summer, there are plenty of year round volunteer opportunities. HOS also hosts two major annual events that are well worth checking out: its fall All About Fruit Show and its spring Scion Exchange and Rootstock Sale. To learn more, visit the HOS website.

the fact that your coop will be small and you won't have any strong barnyard smells."

Although Kilarski's two chickens live in what she calls a "palatial estate" – the entire coop space, chicken run, and henhouse measure about one hundred square feet, Kilarski recommends allowing at least four square feet per chicken.

You can find popular purebred spring chicks at feed stores and at **Pistils Nursery** in North Portland. Portland's **Urban Farm Store** (☞ p. 187), **Naomi's Organic Farm Supply**, **Portland Homestead Supply Co.** (both ☞ p. 184), and others carry chicks and chicken supplies.

While chickens produce eggs, most owners grow to consider them pets. The average lifespan of a chicken is eight to ten years, so when considering adding hens to your family, plan your commitment accordingly.

Mercy Corps Northwest New American Agriculture Program

www.mercycorpsnw.org

📍 43 SW Naito Pkwy, Portland 📞 503-896-5076

In the spring of 2006, Suleyman Idrisov, a displaced Meskhetian Turk who sought asylum with his family in Portland in 2005, planted his first American crop of fruits and vegetables on Mercy Corps Northwest's New American Agriculture Program's (NAAP) organic-certified Hayat Farm. NAAP educates and assists refugees and immigrants in the Portland and Vancouver, Washington, areas in establishing small agricultural businesses by leasing local farmland.

These days Idrisov, who speaks very little English, sells his NAAP-supported produce at farmers markets around town. He lets his vegetables speak for themselves, which is why he's been known as the "beet king" and the "turnip king."

The NAAP has grown substantially in recent years. In 2009 NAAP broke ground with a CSA on land donated on a lot just south of Westmoreland Park. The previous blackberry- and weed-infested lot is now a vibrant and productive organic garden cultivated by three Nepalese refugee families. Their Westmoreland Vegetable Box – filled with farm-fresh produce – is available for weekly pickup to those who sign up and pay in advance for nine weeks of summer produce.

Another NAAP development is the Damascus training site established to help train new farmers and launch new farm businesses. Larry Thompson of Thompson Farm in Damascus donates plots on his one hundred–acre farm to NAAP participants who have access to $1,500 start-up grants from Mercy Corps Northwest while they learn to budget for expenses such as land, tillage, water, and seeds. NAAP participants market their organic produce through farmers markets, farm stands, churches, and other diverse channels. Visit the Mercy Corps Northwest website for more information about NAAP.

Oregon Food Bank and Learning Gardens

www.oregonfoodbank.org

📍 Food bank and Eastside Learning Garden, 7900 NE 33rd Dr, Portland 📞 503-282-0555

📍 Westside Learning Garden, 1600 NW 173rd Ave, Beaverton

Oregon Food Bank (OFB) distributes food to twenty regional food banks throughout the state and operates four that together serve Portland, Tillamook, and Southeast Oregon. Those four OFB food banks distribute food to more than 340 food pantries, soup kitchens, shelters, and other programs for low-income individuals in Clackamas, Clark, Multnomah, Washington, Harney, Malheur, and

Tillamook counties. Beyond recovering, repacking, and distributing food to those in need, OFB works to eliminate the root causes of hunger through nutrition education, learning gardens, public education, and more.

Volunteer for Dig In! shifts at OFB's Eastside and Westside Learning Gardens and lend a hand. Both gardens are large and diverse and all of the food harvested is distributed via the OFB. Year-round volunteer tasks include everything from pruning grape vines, harvesting greens, and planting peas to cleaning out the chicken coop and laying down garden paths. OFB provides all of the tools necessary, and tasks are delegated in the morning when volunteers convene.

The spring and summer shifts run from 9am to noon, and there's always a good mix of folks ranging from long-term volunteers to first-timers and kids (youth under 16 must be accompanied by an adult).

Another way to help OFB is by participating in its Plant a Row for the Hungry program. Participants grow certain high-need fruits and vegetables in their own gardens and deliver the harvest to various OFB drop-off locations.

Both Learning Gardens have seasonal and year round Dig In! shifts that you can register for online. Visit the OFB website to find out other ways to volunteer, donate food, and donate funds to the organization.

*Baby goats and chickens, soil amendments,
gardening tools and books*

Naomi's Organic Farm Supply
2615 SE Schiller St, Portland
503.517.8551
www.naomisorganic.blogspot.com

*Sellwood garden and DIY cooking/
canning supplies*

Portland Homestead Supply Co.
8012 SE 13th Ave, Portland
503.233.8691
www.homesteadsupplyco.com

*Chickens and chickenkeeping classes
and supplies*

Urban Farm Store
2100 SE Belmont St, Portland
503.234.7733
www.urbanfarmstore.com

*Hive and beekeeping supplies, classes
and honey*

Bee Thinking
1551 SE Poplar Ave, Portland
877.325.2221
www.beethinking.com

DIY home and kitchen gear

Mirador Community Store
2106 SE Division St, Portland
503.231.5175
www.miradorcommunitystore.com

Portland Fruit Tree Project

↩ *www.portlandfruit.org*
♥ 1912 NE Killingsworth St, Portland
♪ 503-284-6106

The gist of Portland Fruit Tree Project (PFTP) is that there is a lot of good fruit that isn't reaped in Portland – fruit that falls and rots year after year – so PFTP organizes harvest parties to get that fruit from trees, shrubs, and vines to the folks who need it. From January through spring, PFTP also hosts various workshops and classes on fruit tree pruning and maintenance.

Thirty-three-year-old Katy Kolker started PFTP with her friend Sarah Cogan in 2006. Kolker was working as an Americorps volunteer for **Growing Gardens** (☞ *p.* 180) at the time and living in Northeast Portland. Month after month, Kolker would watch fruit trees in and around her neighborhood go unharvested and turn from ripe to rotten. She approached a few households and asked if they would mind if she harvested these fruit trees. Everyone Kolker approached agreed, and so she organized a small group to help out. Since then, that's been the PFTP mode of operation: seasonal harvest parties from summer through fall throughout Portland at registered locations.

PFTP harvest parties take place on weekends and weekdays from July through November and generally begin mid-morning and run for two to three hours. The ten to fifteen reserved harvest party spots fill up fast, and there is usually a long waiting list weeks in advance. Participants meet at a site where PFTP ladders, fruit-picking poles, and milk crates for packing the fruit are provided.

Once the fruit is picked and sorted, the group moves to another nearby site to harvest. For now, fruit is collected in a pickup truck that follows the group from site to site, but eventually Kolker hopes that they can utilize cargo bikes for fruit transport. The best quality fruit goes to the Oregon Food Bank and its hunger and relief agencies, and the rest is distributed among the tree owners and volunteers.

Kolker is quick to add that, "The intention of our program is not to be feeding the food banks. A large part of our programming is to empower people to see their community and the urban ecosystem as a potential food resource and to be an avenue for people to access those resources." For this reason, half of the harvest party spots are reserved for low-income folks.

Preserve

⊗ www.portlandpreserve.com
♀ 4039 NE 14th Ave, Portland ☎ 503-280-9895

I finally met Preserve's Harriet Fasenfest at Portland's inaugural **Portland Fermentation Festival** (☞ *p.* 176) in the summer of 2009. If I had a pickle for every time I've heard her name mentioned, I'd never have to make my own spicy garlic dills again. Fasenfest runs the show at Preserve, a unique food preservation and householding school in Northeast Portland.

If you'd like to learn food preservation basics, sign up for Preserve's private three-hour consultations ($300, $50 hour-long follow-up appointments), which cover everything from your eating style, cooking skills, and personal time in order to create a householding plan for you. Included in the consultation are

DUCKS

When you talk about edible eggs, it is generally assumed that you are referring to chicken eggs. In recent years, however, clucking has made way for quacking. Duck eggs are now stocked in many local stores and food cooperatives, and they are widely available at farmers markets.

As with chickens (and pygmy goats), Portland residents are allowed to raise three or fewer ducks in their yard without a permit. Carol Deppe, plant breeder and author of *Breed Your Own Vegetable Varieties*, says there are some challenges to raising ducks. "I think, in terms of confinement, the egg-laying chicken is a better confinement animal than the duck, which needs a lot more water and is messier in terms of the litter."

Duck eggs are typically larger and more flavorful than chicken eggs, and their yolks and whites have more structure when cooked. Because of these differences, duck eggs should not be cooked the same way as chicken eggs. Although they can be used in any recipe that calls for chicken eggs (great news for those allergic to chicken eggs),

CONTINUES ➡

→ DUCKS, *continued*

duck eggs should be cooked more gently, at a lower temperature, and for less time.

Deppe has raised ducks for more than thirty years. According to her, "When people start talking about a free-range industry – or on a small scale in your backyard – ducks make a lot more sense. Ducks thrive here year round, they eat a bigger variety of the foods we have available, and they're easier to confine with a two-foot-tall fence."

In order to raise residential ducks you need a protected pen to keep them safe from predators at night and a fenced-in area where they can roam and forage by day. Although you can raise ducks without water to bathe, float, and flap in, they will be happier and healthier if they have water access. If space is limited, a kiddie pool can do the trick.

E-mail Deppe (*caroldeppe@ comcast.net*) if you'd like to receive her newsletter, which includes notifications about her regular duck workshops, or if you'd like to purchase some of her spring Ancona ducklings.

copies of Fasenfest's book, *A Householder's Guide to the Universe,* and her DVD, *Preserving with Friends.*

According to Fasenfest, "Being able to create your own stores at home from, and with, the generous bounty and hard work of the universe and farmers is as much a spiritual practice as it is an opportunity for environmental and economic change."

Slow Food Portland

www.slowfoodportland.com

Slow Food Portland is not only the oldest of the over two hundred Slow Food chapters in America, it actually predates the New York–based Slow Food USA by nine years. Since Slow Food Portland was founded in 1991, the chapter has become a diverse, volunteer-run organization that hosts all sorts of regular food and drink events, political and otherwise, throughout Portland.

Slow Food Portland's annual dues-paying members are invited to monthly low-dough or no-dough events, including urban farmstead bike tours, cooking demonstrations, farm visits, and popular happy hours at which various speakers talk about local and national food issues such as child nutrition and the ethics of genetically modified food.

The Portland Slow Food chapter is volunteer-run and hosts various fundraising events throughout the year. The largest ones drum up funds for Slow Food International's **Terra Madre** – Slow Food International's biannual conference in Italy for nominated delegates from around the world. Those chosen to represent their country at Terra Madre attend discussions, events, and tastings focused on gastronomy, globalization, and economics. Slow Food Portland usually covers the airfare of many of its Terra Madre representatives, particularly farmers. Check out Slow Food Portland's website for an up-to-date listing of events.

Urban Farm Store

🔗 *www.urbanfarmstore.com*
📍 2100 SE Belmont St, Portland 📞 503-234-7733
🕐 M–F 10am–6pm, Sa 9am–6pm, Su 11am–5pm

Since early 2009 Robert and Hannah Litt's edible gardening, urban chicken, and pet supply store has stocked everything from affordable chicken coop kits and organic and regional seeds and seed-starting supplies to chicks, pullets (six to eight-week-old chickens), and rabbits, as well as high-quality dog and cat food.

The goal of Urban Farm Store is to carry everything Portland urban homesteaders might need, including canning and preserving books and supplies, animal feed, and fruit trees, vines, and shrubs. Urban Farm Store also offers free seminars and workshops to the tune of worm composting, chicken butchery, and chicken keeping.

Wild Food Adventures

🔗 *www.wildfoodadventures.com*
📍 4125 N Colonial Ave, Portland 📞 503-775-3828

As a child, John Kallas was very interested in wilderness survival and the hunting and gathering ways of Native Americans. This interest carried over into Kallas's adult years as he obtained a doctorate in nutrition, a masters in education, and degrees in zoology and biology.

WILD MUSHROOMS
AND THE OREGON MYCOLOGICAL SOCIETY

The Oregon Mycological Society, now 600 members strong, formed in 1949 to study local fungi and determine how they function in Oregon's environment. Judy Roger, active member and contact for the Oregon Mycological Society, says, "Scientific study was the major focus, then it migrated to the 'is it edible?' focus, but now it is swinging back the other way."

The society hosts a wide range of events in and around Portland, including informative monthly meetings, educational field trips, and beginning to advanced level classes for fungal identification, microscopy, cultivation and dyeing techniques, and culinary uses.

The Pacific Northwest is a wonderland of wild mushrooms, and plenty of the varieties found here are edible and delicious. The most popular edible mushrooms in the Pacific Northwest include chanterelles, king boletes, morels, and matsutake; hedgehog, lobster, oyster, and candy cap mushrooms are also well loved. Many Orego-

CONTINUES ▶

······→ **WILD MUSHROOMS**, *continued*

nians believe that the highly prized white and black truffles of Oregon are as good as – if not better than their European counterparts.

Getting a recreational mushroom permit isn't difficult and is usually free. More than likely you'll need to visit the ranger station in the area where you'd like to collect, or sometimes Forest Service permits can be issued online. If you're interested in foraging edible mushrooms but don't know where to start, contact the Oregon Mycological Society (*www.wildmushrooms.org*).

Monthly meetings
Every fourth Monday except in July and December, at the Forest Discovery Center (formerly called the World Forestry Center), Cheatham Hall, 4033 SW Canyon Rd, Portland. Classes start at 6:30pm; a lecture follows at 7:30pm.

After teaching wild edible courses at Michigan State University for seven years, he moved to Portland. In 1993 he founded Wild Food Adventures, and since then he's hosted wild edible workshops every year from spring through fall in which participants learn how to identify, harvest, and prepare local wild edibles.

I've participated in a number of John Kallas's Wild Food Adventures, and I've loved them all. From Kallas I've learned that barnacles and the leaves and flowers of big leaf maples are edible. I've also tried all kinds of tasty wild edibles such as sea cabbage, kombu, stinging nettles, juicy red huckleberry shoots, sheep sorrel, and more as a result of his workshops. Most Wild Food Adventure workshops top out at twenty-five people or fewer (make your reservations online well in advance; most workshops sell out) and participants are diverse – young and old, families and friends, from Portland and beyond.

In addition to daytime workshops (usually $25–$50 per person) in the Portland area and along the Oregon Coast from March through October, Kallas also organizes numerous extended overnight wild food gatherings and adventures detailed on his website. Also keep an eye out for Kallas's wild edible book series *Edible Wild Plants*.

||||||||||||||||||||||||||||||||||||||||||||||||||||||||||||||||||||||||||||

CLAM-HAPPY

Although geoduck doesn't lurk beneath the beaches of the Oregon Coast – you'll have to head north for that twenty-pound mollusk – we do have plenty of tasty, sizable gaper clams and other briny edibles for the taking.

Pick up an Oregon Department of Fish and Wildlife (ODFW) shellfish license, pack a bucket, cooler, and garden shovel, and you can harvest everything from razor, cockle, and littleneck clams to crabs, mussels, barnacles (yes, you can eat them), and more. Mussels and clams can be found in most Oregon estuaries, but popular spots to harvest them, thanks to diversity and abundance, include Tillamook, Netarts, Yaquina, and Coos bays.

The best time to dig for clams is usually an hour before or an hour after low tide. No matter what type you're after, you want to locate the "show" (the hole revealed by a clam on the surface of the sand as the tide recedes) and then dig around it, not straight into it, with a shovel, clam rake, clam gun, or your hands, depending on the type of clam you're after. Once you've gotten close to the clam's depth, finish digging with your hands so that you don't damage the neck or break the shell. Remember to always refill those holes so that remaining clams have access to the surface.

John Kallas of **Wild Food Adventures** has advice for Oregon shellfish gatherers: "Carry your license with you at all times, and don't take over your limit. They've got Parks people out there, and they'll fine you."

Determine how you'll prepare your catch before you start hunting, harvest only what you know you'll eat – clams don't keep long – and store your haul in a cool place where they can breathe. In other words, honor thy shellfish.

Tainted shellfish can kill you if it contains high concentrations of biotoxins such as saxitoxin or domoic acid, which are responsible for paralytic and amnesic shellfish poisoning, respectively. Before heading out with a shovel and bucket, visit the Oregon Department of Agriculture shellfish website, or call its shellfish safety hotline for up-to-the-minute alerts on when it's safe to harvest. And never take clams that are chipped, broken, or open. You want to eat only those that are alive and healthy.

Licences
Shellfish licenses ($7 for Oregon residents, $20.50 for nonresidents) can be purchased at most stores that sell fishing equipment in Oregon, including Fred Meyer, Andy and Bax Surplus, or at any ODFW office.

Shellfish status
Call 503-986-4728 or 800-448-2474. Visit the website (www.oregon.gov/ODA/FSD/shellfish_status.shtml) for shellfish advisories.

What to bring
Shellfish license, shoes that can get wet and drain well, change of clothes, towel, backpack, sack lunch, five-gallon bucket, durable trash bag or large cooler, garden shovel (preferably square-bladed), clam or steel garden rake, mesh bag.

THESE INFORMATIVE Portland food and drink websites will keep you up to date on everything from local food politics, restaurant and bar openings, and industry gossip to seasonal food and drink events and grower profiles.

Barfly

www.portlandbarfly.com

This site covers Portland-area bars and lounges and includes reviews written by patrons, current happy hour specials, and a music calendar.

Chowhound

www.chowhound.com

Chowhound's Pacific Northwest board is a good online forum with Portland food and drink information, but you will have to sift through a lot of Washington posts as well.

Cooking up a Story

www.cookingupastory.com

Rebecca and Fred Gerendasy's Portland-based short-documentary site – most posts feature a short embedded video – focuses on local food, family farmers, sustainability, food history, and food culture.

Culinate

www.culinate.com

Culinate is a great resource for articles, news briefs, and user blogs about food sources, food ethics, and food culture. Deborah Madison contributes a monthly column, plus you'll find a variety of tasty recipes.

Edible Portland

www.edibleportland.com

This magazine contains a wealth of information about local food. On the website you'll find interviews with local growers and producers, seasonal recipes, and profiles of food businesses and organizations.

eGullet

www.forums.egullet.com

The Pacific Northwest and Alaska forums about dining, cooking, and baking on this national food and drink site have a lot of good Portland information. You must be a member to participate in eGullet forum discussions; membership is free but donations are encouraged.

An Exploration of Portland Food and Drink

www.portlandfoodanddrink.com

This dynamic website run by the Food Dude (an anonymous critic) has everything from Portland restaurant reviews and news to copies of local menus and food forums.

ExtraMSG

www.extramsg.com

Intrepid eater Nick Zukin (who wrote the Latino/Mexican market section of this book) is the keeper of this food blog, which chronicles his eating adventures – mostly in Portland. It's a great place for food roundups on everything from local ethnic markets to taco trucks.

Food Carts Portland

www.foodcartsportland.com

This site features detailed profiles of Portland food carts by Brett Burmeister (who wrote the food cart chapter of this book) and site founder Lizzy Caston. Food Carts Portland is constantly growing, and most cart profiles include tasting notes and sample menus.

Pacific Northwest Cheese Project

www.pnwcheese.typepad.com

Tami Parr's (author of *Artisan Cheese of the Pacific Northwest*) blog chronicles local cheese and cheesemakers. It's a fantastic resource for cheesemaking news, profiles, recipes, and events.

PortlandFood

www.portlandfood.org

This popular Portland food forum run by Nick Zukin offers a wealth of information on Portland restaurants, food carts, bars and wine bars, food markets, food media, and more. Forum members regularly post and comment so you can get up-to-the-minute information on all things Portland food and drink.

Taplister

www.taplister.com

Founded in 2009 by several tech and beer geeks, Taplister is an online community resource that details which craft beers are on tap at any given moment in Portland. And "any given moment" is quite literal in this case since Taplister has installed pubcams at **EastBurn** and **Saraveza** to display live feed of the establishments' tap boards.

Urban Edibles

www.urbanedibles.org

Michael Bunsen and Bobby Smith's open-source website Urban Edibles contains a wealth of information about natural food foraging in Portland. The site has publicly edited wiki pages and features an interactive map of Portland with flags designating where to find everything from park fruit trees, vacant lot fig trees, abandoned-parking-strip herbs, and other unclaimed urban edibles on both private and public terrain.

INDEX